THE CORPORATIONS AND THE STATE

Tan Philipon

*the text of this book is printed
on 100% recycled paper*

STATE AND REVOLUTION

THE CORPORATIONS AND THE STATE
Essays in the Theory of Capitalism and Imperialism
James O'Connor

THE MAFIA OF A SICILIAN VILLAGE, 1860–1960:
A Study of Violent Peasant Entrepreneurs
Anton Blok

IN PREPARATION:

ALIENATION AND INEQUALITY:
The Political Economy of Education
in Capitalist Society
Samuel Bowles and Herbert Gintis

THE
CORPORATIONS
AND
THE STATE

Essays in the Theory of Capitalism and
Imperialism

James O'Connor

HARPER COLOPHON BOOKS
Harper & Row, Publishers
New York, Evanston, San Francisco, London

These essays first appeared as follows: Chapter One in *Intermountain Economic Review* 1, no. 1 (Fall 1970), as "Social Production, Social Needs, and Social Organization"; Chapter Three in *New Left Review*, no. 40 (November–December 1966), as *"Monopoly Capital"*; Chapter Four in *Socialist Revolution* 2, no. 1 (January–February 1971), as "Who Rules the Corporations? The Ruling Class"; Chapter Five in *Science & Society* 33, no. 4 (Fall–Winter 1969); Chapter Six in *Socialist Revolution* 1, nos. 1 and 2 (January–April 1970); Chapter Seven as a Radical Education Project pamphlet (1968); and Chapter Eight in *Science & Society* 34, no. 1 (Spring 1970). Chapter Two is published here for the first time. Copyright 1966, 1968, 1969, 1970, 1971, 1974 by James O'Connor.

A hardcover edition of this book is published by Harper & Row, Publishers, Inc.

CONTENTS

Preface   ix

PART I—CAPITALISM

One   The Need for Production and the Production of Needs   1

Two   The Theory of Surplus Value   16

PART II—THE CORPORATIONS

Three   Baran and Sweezy's *Monopoly Capital*   43

Four   Fitch and Oppenheimer's Theory of Finance Capital   55

PART III—THE STATE

Five   Scientific and Ideological Elements in the Economic Theory of Government Policy   79

Six   The Fiscal Crisis of the State   104

PART IV—ECONOMIC IMPERIALISM

Seven   The Meaning of Economic Imperialism   153

Eight   International Corporations and Economic Underdevelopment   197

1.

When you answer "economics" to people who ask what you write about, nine times out of ten the next question is "What do you write about economics?" Right away you have to make clear that there are two kinds of economics and economists, "Marxist" and "bourgeois" (variously called "academic," "official," "establishment," and so on). Marxists sometimes write bourgeois economics without knowing it and, less frequently, bourgeois economists inadvertently write Marxist economics, but normally there is considerable overlap between the professed aims of economists and the actual result of their work. The chief aim of bourgeois economists is to keep capitalism going indefinitely by concocting various recipes for economic planning and reform. As it has turned out, much of the work of the post-World War II economists has been of practical value to corporate and government planners. On the other hand, the aim of Marxist economists is to tear down capitalism and replace it with a more rational and humane system —socialism. Although it is much harder to measure the practical result of Marxist economic studies in recent years, I think that on balance this work has made a positive contribution to the development of revolutionary or socialist consciousness.

As for our second question, if you are a bourgeois economist who has been molded into a narrow specialist as the price of getting and keeping your job at a university, you will say almost mechanically that you write about "money and banking," "international trade," "statistics," or some other particular subject that most people at least vaguely recognize as a field of study. If you are a Marxist and are trying to answer the question for the first time, you may stumble around for a few moments, finally replying "world capitalism," "imperialism," "class struggle," "revolution," or something else that sounds unsatisfyingly vague. So you try to elaborate and explain that you think that society has certain "laws of motion" (Marx's phrase, meaning tendencies of economic and social change) based on how the economy works and on the connections between economic, social, and political life.

My thanks and appreciation to Rod Aya, who originally suggested this collection, and who helped greatly in setting out its purpose and organization.

You say that you think social change is mainly the result of social conflict—workers against capitalists, socialist countries versus capitalist countries, advanced countries versus the Third World, women against men, blacks versus whites, and other "contradictions of the system." And you add that you think that by trying to see world economy and capitalist society as a totality made up of "contradictory parts," you can discover with a fair amount of accuracy the scope and limits of these social conflicts and their influence on social change in general.

Any Marxist economist will say something like the above, no matter what his or her special interest. Speaking personally, I would add that I have been writing about the same subject over and over again, going at it from different angles using different methods and even different writing styles. "Going over and over the same subject" does not mean only or even mainly keeping up with statistics of employment, prices, interest rates, and so on, or staying close to new trends in government economic policy or corporate planning. Hundreds of bourgeois economists are paid to do this kind of work, and in fact do it well. By "going over the same subject" I mean trying to formulate more and more clearly the "laws of motion" of capitalism at successively higher levels of generalization. A good example of what I mean is the work on imperialism by Paul Baran and his followers (in particular André Gunder Frank). The main importance of Baran's and Frank's work does not lie in their detailed investigations of the specific mechanisms of imperialism (although both have made such investigations). What makes their work stand out is the *general theory* of capitalism that emerges from the pages of Baran's *The Political Economy of Growth* and Frank's *Capitalism and Underdevelopment in Latin America*. This is the theory that economic development in the advanced capitalist countries (or poles) of the world economy has actually *caused* economic underdevelopment in the Third World *and vice versa*. Thanks to the work of Baran and company, we can see more clearly the development and underdevelopment of the world economy as a single process, as a whole.

2.

The essays in this book discuss modern U.S. capitalism and imperialism. Each chapter tries to delineate the relationship between "economic" and "political" processes, or at least recognizes the unity between them. More precisely, the unifying theme of this volume is the role of the large corporations in American society and world economy, and the relationships between these corporations and the capitalist state.

Chapter One provides a general introduction to the relationship between the growth of production and the development of new kinds of social organization, including political organization in the form of the state. This essay also shows some ways in which society produces its own economic needs, as well as the means of satisfying them (or frustrating them, as the case may be). In Chapter Two, I lay out some categories of Marxist analysis as an interdependent economic, social, and political whole. Most important, I introduce the principle of surplus value (*the* basic Marxist theoretical category), and suggest how surplus value theory can be applied to modern state capitalism. I also try to show that capitalist production is not governed by prevailing wants and needs, but rather by the capitalist's need to organize the production of surplus value. Chapter Three consists of a summary and critical review of the most influential modern Marxist account of the giant corporation, Paul A. Baran and Paul M. Sweezy's *Monopoly Capital.* Chapter Four summarizes and criticizes the best-known attempt by younger American Marxists to revive and modernize an older theory of monopoly capital, specifically, the development of finance capital, or bank control of industry.

In Chapter Five, I present a critique of the efforts of bourgeois economists to develop a theory of the economic role of the state in advanced capitalist societies. This chapter provides an introduction to the problems explored in Chapter Six, "The Fiscal Crisis of the State." This is an analysis of state capitalism, showing that the state is a kind of Atlas holding up the corporate economy and passing on private and social costs of private enterprise to the taxpayers. It also suggests that the increased fiscal drain of the state (including and especially military expenditures) has created a permanent crisis in which the state is increasingly unable to generate enough revenue to finance growing demands for higher state spending.

In Chapters Seven and Eight, the emphasis shifts from the relationship between the corporations and the state at home to imperialism and world economy. "The Meaning of Economic Imperialism" is a critical review of the major theories of imperialism and an outline of the structure of contemporary imperialism, with special attention paid to the functioning of the state in the world economy. "International Corporations and Economic Underdevelopment" tries to show how international companies backed by parent states perpetuate the underdevelopment of the Third World through monopoly controls over the utilization of its resources.

In some of these essays I have made a number of minor changes, additions, and deletions.

3.

I should caution the reader that each of these studies is partly experimental, two of them being preliminary versions of longer works. Parts of "The Theory of Surplus Value" will be part of a book on political economy that I am now working on, and "The Fiscal Crisis of the State" is an abbreviated version of an article that provided one starting point for a book that came out in 1973 under the same title. It is probably important to try to explain why the need for the experiments, why some false starts, why the sometimes erratic shift back and forth between method and theory, theory and application.

The reason is twofold. On the one hand, bourgeois social theory in general and economics in particular have little to offer anyone who is trying to grasp the "laws of motion" of capitalism. Bourgeois social scientists do not often stray from their specialized fields, and when they do what they have to say seems incomprehensible (Talcott Parsons' theory of "structural functionalism" is a good example). Moreover, official economics has little to say to the average person precisely because its main purpose is to help to control and regulate the system— or, more accurately, to help the businessmen, bureaucrats, and politicians who have the power to control and regulate the system. Furthermore, official economics seems unreal because economists *qua* economists have a highly distorted view of human nature (failing totally to see people as the products of history and in certain well-defined ways the shapers of history). In fact, most economists probably know little or nothing about daily life outside the narrow world of economics departments and economic research organizations. For example, there are "experts" in industrial organization and labor who have never visited a factory or talked with a trade union official (much less a rank-and-file worker). There are "specialists" in economic development who have never seen much less felt the incredible poverty of the Third World, and "researchers" in the field of monetary economics who have never had a drink with a banker. There is at least one mathematical economist known to me who believes that he has the whole process of the transition from feudal to capitalist economy compressed into a few mathematical expressions (which needless to say no one but himself can grasp). I have learned a little about bits and pieces of economics from some of these people and quite a lot from a handful of them. What I failed to learn because it was not taught was a way to think about society that permits you to grasp the whole of it, the totality of the dominant social relationships that make it up.

On the other hand, Marxism also has its officialdom in economics (and every other subject). Unlike the academics, official or party-line Marxists do have the equivalent of a "unified field theory," but I believe that this theory is, on the whole, very weak. It is weak partly because it does not sufficiently recognize that the modern worker is culturally, socially, politically, and in nearly every other way very different from the nineteenth-century proletarian who was the central figure in Marx and Engels' original theories. The same can be said about the modern banker, landlord, corporation head, farmer, politician, and bureaucrat, not to speak of the relationships between economic classes and strata. A related reason is that although the working class has taken up the "problem of class struggle" in contemporary capitalism as a practical matter, Marxist intellectuals by and large have failed to take up the problem as a theoretical matter—the theory of national liberation struggles standing as the major exception. These are probably the main reasons why I have learned so little from official Marxist economists. I hasten to add that I have learned a great deal from the histories of capitalism and socialism and the critiques of economic thought written by Marxists such as Maurice Dobb and Ernest Mandel. Of course, I have learned a vocabulary from official Marxism, but this vocabulary is sometimes more of a hindrance to communication than a help, although it is the best that they or anyone else has been able to do. The underlying historical reasons why official Western Marxism went stale are too well known to go into here. Suffice it to say that official Marxist writings—the party-line literature—have inspired little new and creative work in the field of political economy.

The same cannot be said about the "unofficial" Marxist economists. The people from whom I've learned most are independent Marxists— scholars, journalists, activists, and others who have kept an open mind about the nature of advanced capitalism and revolution and have tried to think through the issues for themselves. I will not even try to name these people or mention their work outside of economics, but in my field the two outstanding names in this country are Paul Baran and Paul Sweezy. For all its failings, Baran and Sweezy's book, *Monopoly Capital,* is a fresh attempt to grasp the nature of competition in the modern period. Whether you like it or not, the book is a seminal work, and nearly all subsequent studies of "corporate capital" by independent Marxist economists can be defined in relation to it (positive or negative). Even more important, Paul Baran's *The Political Economy of Growth,* which was written in the early and mid 1950s, has been important to me (as well as many others), not for any particular analytic contribution, but rather (as noted above) for Baran's ability to absorb huge amounts of knowledge, sort it all out, and use what is needed to totalize or grasp the nature of world economy as a whole.

Next, let me turn to the more general subject of politics itself, again with the aim of trying to explain why this volume should be seen as an experiment, rather than as a polished and final work. I was too young in the 1930s and 1940s to be involved in politics at all. I therefore had no need to define myself in terms of the official parties that were hegemonic on the left at the time. In fact, I became interested in left-wing thought and politics in the mid and late 1950s, while involved in the "ban the bomb" movement. By 1955 or 1956 I thought of myself as holding some kind of socialist opinions or other, but even in 1960 I was doing bourgeois economics! Needless to say, this situation was highly unstable, and it finally became a question of studying Baran and other modern Marxists and reading some of the classics before I could unlearn the economics that I learned in the university and begin to learn a new economics. The disadvantage of this situation is obvious —I have been a kind of amateur Marxist with the benefit of absolutely no systematic training in Marxism. The advantage of not coming out of the official Marxist tradition is also obvious—I could and can develop my own economic thinking, at my own speed and in my own way.

On the other hand, I was too old to get totally immersed in all of the currents of the New Left of the 1960s (although I was too young not to participate in many movement activities directly). The advantage and disadvantage of this situation are also clear. Closer to the movement than the average radical my own age, I have had the benefit of direct involvement in struggle of various kinds. And, closer to the academic world than the average movement activist, I have had the benefit of leisure time and an atmosphere that at best can be conducive to serious intellectual work. Balancing these facts is another: I have never developed the outlook or temperament of either a full-time militant (who plays a crucial role and whom I admire) or a full-time Marxist scholar (whom I also admire). The significance of these facts for this book is that the essays herein are not as scholarly or careful or scientific as they might have been were my concerns wholly intellectual. Nor are they as full of life and feeling as most of the writings of people who have been (or remain) full-time radical activists. For myself, for good or bad, one meaning of the old Marxist slogan "combining theory and practice" is that I have had one foot in one world and one foot in another, and about the only important time they really came together was during the San Francisco State student and professors' strikes in the late 1960s. Yet I would say that being partly in one world and partly in another has at least one advantage—namely, the development of a certain skepticism about both worlds, at least for people temperamentally capable of moving back and forth between them.

THE CORPORATIONS AND THE STATE

PART I
CAPITALISM

CHAPTER ONE
The Need for Production and the Production of Needs

Production thus produces consumption: first, by furnishing the latter with materials; second, by determining the manner of consumption; third, by creating in consumers a want for its products as objects of consumption. It thus provides the object, the manner, and the moving spring of consumption.—Karl Marx, The Grundrisse

1. MANKIND'S NEED FOR PRODUCTION

Men and women have always been compelled to satisfy their material needs through production: the day-to-day labor required to transform natural objects and nonhuman life into useful things—food, clothing, shelter, tools, and other extensions of man's own physical powers. The production of the means of subsistence is never wholly repetitive or habitual; it is always partly creative because of mankind's capacity for reflective thought and conscious activity. The processes and aims of production are ordinarily in a state of flux, at times advancing slowly, at times rapidly, and sometimes unvarying and stationary. More or less periodically, new tools are invented, new ways to organize work are discovered, and new objects are produced.

In the course of developing new production techniques, reorganizing production, and producing new objects, men and women relate to each other in new ways and acquire and develop new abilities and skills. Through these channels production constantly evokes or awakens new expectations and new needs. Marx hit upon the truth that production not only provides the objects that satisfy human needs, but also creates the needs that the objects satisfy.[1] He meant that production is a dual process: mankind's abilities, needs, and expectations both determine and are determined by the number and kind of objects that are available and the ways in which they have been produced. Today, for example, there is a correspondence between the production of a large variety of man-made objects serving a large number of specific purposes and the development of an abundance of complex human needs regularly expressed in new and original forms.

Natural objects and plant/animal life are scarce in the absolute sense that they exist in finite quantities. Of more significance, these "natural resources" are scarce in relation to mankind's needs, precisely because the growth of the means of satisfying needs and of the needs themselves is in reality the same process. Further, the meaning of "scarcity" constantly changes because the means of satisfying needs are regularly redefined. Natural resources are scarce only in relation to specific needs expressed in definite ways. Water on an arid plain is not scarce until human beings begin to cultivate the plain and discover the need for irrigation. Salt in the ocean became scarce when mankind learned to salt foods in order to preserve them; then salt ceased to be scarce when the modern process of desalinization was discovered.

More specifically, the availability of new technologies multiplies and diversifies material possibilities. First, the creation of new objects to satisfy old needs invariably creates some new needs that the new objects are not able to satisfy. The spinning jenny and flying shuttle

---

1. . . . consumption produces production by creating the necessity for new production. . . . Consumption furnishes the impulse for production as well as its object. . . . It is clear that while production furnishes the material object of consumption, consumption provides the ideal object of production. . . . No needs, no production. But consumption reproduces the need. In its turn, production:

1. Furnishes consumption with its material, its object. Consumption without an object is no consumption, hence from this point of view production creates and produces consumption.

2. But it is not only the object that production provides for consumption. It gives consumption its definite outline, its character, its finish. Just as consumption gives the product its finishing touch as a product, production puts the finishing touch on consumption. For the object is not simply an object in general, but a definite object, which is consumed in a certain definite manner prescribed in its turn by production. Hunger is hunger; but the hunger that is satisfied with cooked meat eaten with fork and knife is a different kind of hunger from the one that devours raw meat with the aids of hands, nails and teeth. Not only the object of consumption, but also the manner of consumption is produced by production; that is to say, consumption is created by production not only objectively but also subjectively. Production thus creates the consumers.

3. Production not only supplies the want with material, but supplies the material with a want.

[Karl Marx, *The Grundrisse*, ed. and trans. David McLellan (New York, 1971), p. 25]

were at one time revolutionary technical advances that consigned the spinning wheel to the junkpile of mankind's technology in the economically developed countries. These and related technological advances helped to make cheap cotton products available to the majority of the population. From 1770 to the end of the Napoleonic wars the English people substituted cottons for woolens and found uses for cottons previously unimaginable, developing the need for easily maintained fabrics useful for a large variety of purposes. Partly in this way, the development of the cotton textile industry laid the foundation for today's seemingly unlimited demand for the products of synthetic fibers.

Second, the creation of new techniques to produce old objects that satisfy old needs also creates the need for still newer techniques. Harnessing the first crude steam engine to the jennies and later on to the looms in the "dark, satanic mills" of England's Industrial Revolution revealed with dramatic power the engine's basic inefficiencies. Factory owners and mechanics set to work to improve the new source of power in order to run their machines more efficiently. Today the development of the modern petrochemical industry not only substitutes synthetic for natural fibers but also creates possibilities for the production of new objects and the awakening of new needs, both on the part of workers and others who want to acquire final products for immediate consumption and capitalists who want more and better means of production.

Clearly, human beings may not satisfy all the needs that they themselves have created in production. This is the basic reason why production remains the prime requisite of human life. Production continues to be humankind's most important need because the satisfaction of other needs depends on production. Of course, men and women may consciously decide to reject the needs formed and shaped by production, and deliberately alter production with the aim of eliminating or redefining certain needs. For example, today's "back to the earth" movement eliminates the need for many household appliances and redefines the need for transportation and communication. A combination of traditional and modern production techniques substitutes for conventional technologies and modes of work organization, and the reintegration of work, living, and recreation on the modern "commune" does away with many needs for rapid ground transportation. But the rejection of the general run of conventional needs requires a total revolution in the day-to-day activities and relationships that human beings establish with one another.

2. CAPITALISM AND SOCIAL PRODUCTION

Both production and the needs awakened and satisfied (or frustrated) by production are social in character. "Needs are satisfied socially," Ernest Mandel writes, "not by a purely physiological activity, by single combat between the individual and the forces of nature, but by activity which results from mutual relations established between the members of a human group."[2] Mankind has always satisfied its material needs cooperatively; one individual cannot work successfully unless other individuals complete their work successfully. Men and women work with each other, and also for each other in the sense that what they produce is used by others.

As with production, so with distribution. It is possible to imagine one person satisfying his needs in "single combat" with nature, an activity combining the process of production and distribution. It is not possible to imagine two persons working cooperatively in production without establishing some channel of distribution or exchange, some customary arrangement through which the fruits of production are shared. In Oscar Lange's words, "the social character of distribution is obvious; distribution by its very nature is a social act."[3]

Modern anthropology has demonstrated beyond any doubt that even primitive man gathered, hunted, and fished cooperatively. In ancient Egypt men and women were trained in specific skills and crafts and the division of labor was accepted in a matter-of-fact way. In the feudal epoch in Europe lord and peasant often shared grazing privileges on the "common." The tradition of village cooperation in production and distribution in China dates back a thousand years. Examples of the formal and informal organization of production through the division of labor, the specialization of work functions, and the social organization of distribution could be cited endlessly.

The development of capitalist production in Europe from the fifteenth century onward—and the spread of capitalism to the New World, Asia, and Africa, particularly after the Industrial Revolution of the eighteenth century—magnified a million times the social nature of production. Modern capitalism finds its historical roots in a number of underlying social changes that revolutionized Europe five hundred

2. Ernest Mandel, *Marxist Economic Theory,* 2 vols. (New York, 1968), 1:24.
3. Oscar Lange, "The Subject Matter of Political Economy: Elementary Concepts," reprinted from *Political Economy,* vol. 1 (Warsaw, 1963), in David Mermelstein, ed., *Economics: Mainstream Readings and Radical Critiques* (New York, 1970), p. 9.

years ago. Under the impact of the great discoveries and the subsequent widening of international trade there developed a social division of labor when European towns and cities began to specialize in the production of particular lines of goods. Land seizures and enclosures and an increase in agricultural productivity provided a potential source of industrial and urban labor, the potential to feed a vastly increased urban population and to supply factory industry with raw materials, and a potential market for the products of factory industry. The accumulation of money in the hands of a relatively few large merchants and bankers owing to the rape of India, Africa, and the New World, and the expansion of trade, offered possibilities for large-scale investments in factory production. And technological advances, such as the development of an efficient steam engine, made factory industry more feasible from an engineering standpoint.

These changes combined to produce a particular system of social production and a particular society—capitalism. This system had definite historical beginnings and followed a definite course of development. Independent of the decades of its birth, its national origins, the ethnic or racial composition of the people who made it up, the new system began to display two basic, related characteristics. The first characteristic was that precapitalist forms of wealth such as land, water, farm animals, and precious metals began to be replaced at an accelerated rate by another form—commodities, or objects that are produced for sale on the market rather than for direct use by the producers. In every region of the world penetrated by capitalist production, traditional restrictions on the use of land were relaxed or eliminated in order to facilitate its purchase and sale in the open market. Conventional barriers to the acquisition of mining, manufacturing, and other productive facilities by the "highest bidder" were overthrown. Historical restrictions on the "right" to trade and exchange, such as state monopolies and tariff walls, were reduced or eliminated. And traditional practices by artisans, craftsmen, and peasants that were originally designed to preserve the exclusiveness of particular occupations and trades were also eliminated. Accompanying the growth of markets for tangible and intangible goods there developed a market for human labor power, which began to be bought and sold in the marketplace like land, minerals, and other physical goods.

The second universal feature of capitalism—which accelerated the growth of commodity production—was the divorce of artisans, craftsmen, and peasants from the means of production. The sale or appropriation of land, tools, materials, and other productive resources was the precondition not only for the emergence of a market for labor power and a class of wage laborers, but also for the growth of a capitalist class. Private property and private control over the production mechanism by only a fraction of the population were the result of the development of a propertyless working class. The growth of capitalist production divided society into two classes—those who own the means of production and those who do not, those who buy labor power on the market and those who sell labor power, those who control the production apparatus and those who are controlled by it.

In a fully developed capitalist society (ignoring for the moment the growth of the service sector and the state economy), all objects are commodities and the employer and employee classes claim every individual. Both production for direct use by producers and an independent artisan-craftsman class are nonexistent. Totally divorced from the means of production, employees do not have any juridical rights to their own product. At the end of a day's work, the entire day's product is appropriated by employers. Employees receive a claim to a certain amount of goods that they themselves produce: this claim is wages in the form of money.

Money is the most important link between people in capitalist society. Money ties together individuals, who otherwise would be isolated, into exchange relations, the typical form of capitalist social relations. Exchange relations consist of the "contract" that buyers and sellers make in the marketplace, not only in the labor market and the market for consumer goods where contracts are made between employers and employees, but also in the market for means of production where employers contract with each other to buy and sell productive equipment, raw materials, fuel, and other production inputs.

The number and variety of exchange relations in any particular capitalist society depend on the size of the market, which in turn depends ultimately on the degree of capital accumulation and capitalist development. With improvements in the techniques of production, the growth of capital, and the development of markets, more and more people become increasingly integrated into the same production network. They do not join the production system directly as freely associated producers, but indirectly as sellers of labor power and buyers of consumer goods. Thus, workers are not necessarily conscious of their place in production, their dependency on others, and the interrelatedness of the production mechanism as a whole. On the contrary, because individuals enter the system as sellers of labor power, they seem to have every reason to believe that they are competing rather than cooperating with other human beings.

Technological change and capital accumulation have led ultimately to mass production techniques, strict quality control of production, and other features of developed capitalist society that permit the manufacture of uniform products. Uniformity of production in turn widens the market and integrates more people into the network of capitalist exchange relations. Technological advances in packaging, canning, freezing, and other forms of processing make tangible goods more storable and permit the extension of local markets to national and international markets. More efficient transportation and communication also advance social production by widening markets. In the market for labor power itself, the breaking down of caste, ethnic, race, sex, and other "nonmarket" distinctions, the elimination of traditional relations of status, and the growth of foreign trade and investment integrate millions upon millions of people into the same worldwide capitalist production and distribution system.

The expansion of capitalist production and distribution breaks down local autonomous economies—communal, tribal, semifeudal economies that escaped the first waves of capitalist expansion—and more or less rapidly replaces subsistence farm production, craft and artisan production, and production in the home in all geographical and social spheres subject to capitalist investment and trade. As time goes on, the number of commodities, markets, and capitalist producers, and the frequency of market contacts, multiply. The individual small producer—Egyptian craftsman, Peruvian artisan, Georgia sharecropper, and Kansas housewife—enjoys less and less independence. The world division of labor and specialization of production functions deepen, and, ultimately, all social relations tend to be transformed into exchange relations.

Finally, there emerges one single world capitalist system—whose laws of development are modified only slightly by the survival of independent tariff, fiscal, monetary, and other nationalist economic policies —a single world labor force, and a single world social product. Today "gross national product" measures that part of world social product that is appropriated by the people of a particular country, and is not a measure of production, but rather of distribution. By contrast, two centuries ago the vast majority of humankind lived in comparative economic isolation, and it was possible to calculate with a relatively high degree of accuracy a village's, and even an individual's, contribution to production. At present, few men and women live in societies that are not at least partially integrated into the world market (putting aside for the moment individuals in the socialist countries). The objects that humankind uses are made of materials drawn from dozens of different countries and embody labor from all of the continents of the world. And no man or woman would be "worth" the equivalent of even a few dollars yearly were his or her labor not "mixed" or combined with the labor of millions of other producers.

3. CAPITALISM AND SOCIAL NEEDS

The discovery and application of new production techniques and ways of organizing work and the design and development of new objects are creative activities that help humankind to develop not only its physical and cognitive abilities but also its effective and aesthetic powers. As human society acquires more abilities and skills and creates more advanced technologies and products, humankind's needs become more complex and original. It is difficult to imagine eighteenth-century man acquiring the cognitive abilities to create twentieth-century technology or undergoing the emotional traumas that give rise to twentieth-century art. It is impossible to imagine twentieth-century man being content with either eighteenth-century technology or art. Even the dropouts from "modern life" who are reorganizing production and distribution in small communes draw heavily on twentieth-century techniques and visions, as a glance at (for example) the *Whole Earth Catalog* quickly reveals.

The expressions "complexity of needs and expectations" and "abundance of needs" do not mean that each individual in advanced captalist society has unique needs that set him or her apart from other individuals. These words mean that society as a whole has more and different needs (as well as skills and abilities) than previous generations. In fact, individual needs today are very much alike—much more so than in earlier centuries when humankind lived in isolated, self-contained communities and drew upon local raw materials, employed limited production techniques, and developed provincial patterns of consumption. This can be illustrated by contrasting today's International Style in painting with the three or four hundred distinct styles of African tribal art, or by comparing the contemporary worldwide use of the internal combustion engine and prefabricated concrete housing with the abundance of so-called primitive modes of power and dwelling materials in use five hundred years ago.

Put another way, modern capitalism breaks down provincial differences in production and distribution, social organization, and even personality types. Two hundred years ago in Europe, work was organized in many different ways: the traveling artisan, family cottage industry, and state trading monopolies coexisted with peasant farming, guild craft production, and remnants of the feudal manorial system. Today the tendency is for all production to be organized bureaucratically within the capitalist or state enterprise in the interests of economic "efficiency." Adam Smith, "the father of economic science," was struck by the sharp differences between the needs and aspirations of English, European, and Chinese laborers. A century and a half later, Lenin could speak of a "world proletariat." Contemporary society even tends to break down and unify descriptive categories useful in the analysis of human personality and behavior. To take an extreme example, many psychiatrists believe that the concept of an "obsessive-paranoid personality structure" is not in fact a diagnostic category but rather describes *the* personality of "modern man."

"Modern man" is quintessentially social in character. He has complex and variegated needs, but they are social needs—needs that he shares in common with others. These social needs are not only physical, but also psychological, aesthetic, and even spiritual (as suggested by the almost universal tendency toward monotheism).

As indicated above, the development of social needs accompanies the growth of social production. Common experiences arising from the integration of millions of producers into the same production networks, and the ensuing breakup of age-old patterns of thought, habits, and traditions, have meant that abilities, skills, and needs have become less particular, less parochial, and more universal, more social. The spread of capitalist production techniques and organization tends to establish uniform consumption patterns not only throughout the developed capitalist world but also in the underdeveloped capitalist countries. Today the use of certain basic commodities—such as cottons, drugs, beer, and other consumer goods, and concrete, steel, and other capital goods— is nearly universal.

It is not only that day laborers in Houston and London expend roughly the same amount of physical energy and require food of a certain bulk, protein content, and so on. Nor that nearly all workers in developed capitalist countries require fast ground transportation owing to the increased geographic separation of places of work, residence, and recreation. Nor even that women employed as secretaries in San Francisco, Brussels, and Tokyo—and increasingly in Tehran, Buenos Aires, and Bombay, as well—need certain styles and personal accessories to get and keep their jobs. Nor even that the socialization process experienced by students in French technical institutes and North American engineering colleges is increasingly similar.

It is also that both men and women tend to develop a universal need for certain kinds of affective experiences and interpersonal relations. At the turn of the century in the United States, the immigrant factory worker needed a wife who could run a boardinghouse for single male workers with diligence and dispatch; the prairie farmer needed a pioneer woman; and the rising executive needed a showpiece. In turn, the immigrant wife needed a man of great physical strength who accepted uncomplainingly the discipline of the factory for twelve or fourteen hours a day; the prairie woman needed a "good provider" who was obsessed with the idea of economic independence; and the executive's showpiece needed a bold and ruthless entrepreneur with few loyalties to any particular organization. Today's skilled Detroit factory worker, commercial garden farmer, and steel executive need women with the psychological abilities to relieve their husbands' tension and play other, similar roles required to maintain the nuclear family intact and to preserve the "sanctity" of hearth and home. In turn, their wives require good union men, good farmer association men, and good corporation men—that is, good organization men—respectively.

In short, the satisfaction of definite social needs that tend to become universal—needs that develop out of, and in turn help to advance, further social production—is necessary for capitalist society to reproduce itself in its given material and social condition. In this sense, it is literally true that the more things change, the more they become the same. To be sure, individual producers—in their role as consumers —continue to decide what commodities to purchase, and in what quantities, but their decisions originate in their socially determined needs, by their relation to the means of production, and by their place in society as a whole. Their "individuality" is shaped and formed by society, and it is a commonplace among both casual and serious observers of the social scene that "individualism" is a thing of the past. Yet producers continue to discover their individuality in society, not outside of it. Thus, they act only within the framework defined by their role in society, and, in the last analysis, their particular individuality differs little from that of other producers in a similar life station.

4. SOCIAL ORGANIZATION

The growth of social production—the world division of labor, specialization of work functions, and network of exchange relations—depends on the development of more advanced forms of social organization. Historically, every step human beings have taken toward economic integration has brought them closer to social integration. Economic integration and interdependence, social coordination and control—these words refer to historical processes so intimately connected as to be in the long run virtually the same.

History clearly records that feudal social organization proved to be incompatible with economic expansion in Europe from the eleventh century onward. The manorial system that was held together by the acceptance of mutual rights and obligations by lord and peasant, and which was based on the exploitation of serf labor, could not adjust to the new economic system of generalized commodity production and exchange. Nor could the prevailing forms of political organization. The international division of labor and growth of markets were made possible only by the gradual elimination of local tariff and other trade barriers, the development of customs unions, and, finally, by the unification of Europe into the modern nation-state system. (Today, contemporary trade expansion and economic development are partly indebted to expanded political integration in the form of the European Economic Community.)

History also records that social organization in capitalist societies has been revolutionized under the impact of expanded social production and distribution. In the developed capitalist countries, the small family firm typical of "entrepreneurial capitalism" in the nineteenth century gave way to the large, publicly owned corporation. Production units specializing in one or two products at one particular stage of manufacture were largely replaced by the vertically integrated corporation that controls sources of raw materials, processing and fabricating facilities, transportation networks, and wholesale and retail outlets. Today, the business firm producing for a handful of related markets is declining in favor of the conglomerate corporation, which organizes production in dozens of unrelated industries and in many different countries. One reason is that man-made materials made possible by the social production of technical-scientific knowledge (vast government subsidies to business for research and development, mass technical higher education, and so on) tend to dissolve older, more traditional industry lines. For example, Phillips Petroleum and General Mills (a food-processing company) have formed Provesta Corporation to develop synthetic high-protein foods; and a tire-petroleum combine (Goodrich-Gulf) is presently producing a wide range of synthetic rubber products. In this way, technical knowledge—a productive force that is far more social than the traditional means of production (land, buildings, machinery, and so on) because it is impossible for any individual, interest group, or nation to monopolize permanently—becomes a major form of capital. Modern technical knowledge multiplies and diversifies material possibilities, holding out new material opportunities that in turn require new forms of organization to exploit. Partly for this reason, the regional and national corporation that dominated the economic scene two or three decades ago is giving way to the giant international corporation that disposes of economic resources on a worldwide scale. And within the giant corporation, the development of cooperative decision making by a vast "technostructure" is partly replacing production decisions by individual owners and boards of directors with a kind of social decision making.[4]

A simple illustration of the relationship between social production and social organization is provided by the development of the electrical power industry. Two general kinds of systems are technologically possible: on-site generation of power and interconnected systems. On-site power generation traditionally has been owned and controlled by local corporations, cooperatives, and governments. Interconnected systems require the cooperation of many corporations or governments in different regions of the country. The displacement of on-site power generation by interconnected systems has thus required more coordination of decision making, production and investment plans, and load planning. Advanced forms of social integration are necessary because integrated systems are technically more efficient than a multiplicity of independent local systems. The latter are burdened with higher fixed or overhead costs of production, compelled to maintain larger power reserves, and cannot use large generating units efficiently. Interconnected systems enjoy more diversity and a greater utilization factor, and are more reliable and afford the opportunity for closer frequency control.

A similar trend toward more social integration is visible at the level of public organization and government. At the level of local government, the municipal reform movement that ousted the entrenched "machine" in dozens of cities early in the twentieth century was motivated primarily by the need to control and coordinate city-wide decisions, and therefore by the necessity to abolish the ward system of government. Today, corporate planners in the major metropolitan areas face similar problems: social production and distribution is manifest in the form of area-wide pollution and traffic congestion, regional drainage and sewerage breakdowns, and various other metropolitan area-wide development and planning problems. Economic integration tends to make traditional government anachronistic, forcing policy makers to try to broaden the unit of economic and social control; for

4. John Kenneth Galbraith, *The New Industrial State* (Boston, 1967), chap. 4.

example, there is presently a strong tendency for suburbs to unify school, water, sewer, and other special districts.

The federal government also plays a larger and larger role in local economic and social life. Federal agencies assume more power and responsibility for "local" transportation, communications, education, health, and welfare problems, and exercise more control over social production generally. One of many examples of federal government coordination of the economy as a whole is provided by the shift from metallic to inconvertible paper currency, which requires day-to-day control of the monetary system by the Federal Reserve System and the Treasury Department.

Increased interdependence of economic life and social relations in general under capitalism also necessitates the consolidation of government agencies at all levels, and the coordination of the activities of private and public institutions. In the words of Emmanuel Mesthene, "It used to be that industry, government and universities operated independently of one another. They no longer do, because technical knowledge is increasingly necessary to the successful operation of industry and government, and because universities, as the principal sources and repositories of knowledge, find that they are adding a dimension of social service to their traditional roles of research and teaching."[5] All of these trends are part of a larger trend toward expanded social integration, a trend toward new, more general forms of social organization required to "contain" the social productive forces that constantly threaten to "spill over" established boundaries of economic, social, and political control.

5. SOCIAL ORGANIZATION AND PRIVATE PROPERTY

The oldest established boundary of economic control in capitalist society is the institution of the monopoly of private property in the means of production. It is also the most inviolable boundary. Business and government policy makers have subverted or overthrown other long-standing institutions when the institutions have ceased to "work" —the ward system in municipal government, home rule, university autonomy, and the gold standard are some examples cited above. Business and government leaders also have been compelled to modify the "rights" of private property in times of social emergency—for example,

5. Emmanuel G. Mesthene, "How Technology Will Shape the Future," *Science* 12 (July 1968): 139.

the federal government in the United States imposed strict controls over prices, production, and investment during World War II. Moreover, zoning statutes, safety, health, and antipollution laws, government protection of labor unions, and similar restrictions on "property rights" and "managerial prerogatives" are illustrations of the growing number and scope of laws and administrative decrees encumbering private property with more and more "social responsibility."

Nevertheless, the institution of private ownership of the means of production remains the pillar of capitalist society. Production, investment, price, and other economic decisions are still made privately by property owners, or by those charged by the owners with managing the instruments of production. These decisions are still made largely in the self-interests of the owners and managers. Large corporations do not locate new branch plants in accordance with a general plan for the development of a particular region or metropolitan area, but rather on the basis of profitability. Businessmen do not expand employment opportunities because men and women are out of work, but rather only when it is profitable to do so. Manufacturers do not produce goods for poor people simply because they are poor, but rather on the assumption that production will bring in a profit. Owners and managers do not deploy technology on the basis of the need to raise productivity in low-productivity regions, but rather with an eye to profit. The impulse behind investment and technological change is not a collectively worked-out plan designed to maintain humankind in harmony with the forces of nature, but is rather the stimulus of fresh profits. And at the level of private property in the means of consumption, well-to-do suburbanites resist any movement toward metropolitan-area-wide government and planning owing to their fear that the inner-city poor would benefit at their expense.

In the context of highly integrated production and distribution networks where private economic decision making has many and varied ramifications, business decisions made on the basis of private gain tend to be increasingly inconsistent with the general welfare. Further, as social control over social production becomes more and more needed, it becomes more and more difficult to penetrate into the network of private property and privilege. For these general reasons, private ownership and the system of rights and privileges that evolved with private ownership are, in the last analysis (and only in the last analysis), inconsistent with the further development of social production.

Unquestionably, as we have indicated, social organization in the developed capitalist countries has proven to be quite flexible. The private organization of production has broadened, and now assumes the form of the international, conglomerate corporation. Political organization also has expanded and become more centralized: in the United States there is more area-wide planning; the federal government coordinates more area-wide decisions; within the federal government, the representative branch that speaks mostly for local, parochial interests is less powerful, and the executive branch that is relatively more responsible for acting on the "general interests" is more powerful. Overall fiscal and monetary policy is commonplace throughout the developed capitalist world, although (especially in the United States) overall production and investment planning is still very undeveloped.

It is clear from this brief survey that the advance of social production has made many forms of economic and political organization redundant, and that the twentieth century has ushered in a tremendous concentration and centralization of economic and political power. It is also clear that "to the extent that technological change . . . multiplies the choices that society will have to make . . . these choices will increasingly have to be deliberate social choices . . . and will therefore have to be made by political means."[6] Whether these "deliberate social choices" will be made by an elite corps of experts or by the people themselves, whether these "political means" will be authoritarian or democratic, how long social production can continue to be contained by the system of private property, in what ways capitalist society tends to plant the seeds of its own destruction, and in what sense socialism "necessarily" replaces capitalism—these questions have top priority on the agenda of the study of political economy.

6. Ibid., p. 192.

CHAPTER TWO

The Theory of Surplus Value

1. WHAT IS CAPITALISM?

"Is it history that shapes men? Or do men shape history? The answer, it seems to me, lies somewhere in between. Both history and human nature have their immutable laws. But somewhere they must intersect, and somehow we must eventually locate their interface."[1] So propounds Christopher Lehmann-Haupt. The question has been asked over and over again; Lehmann-Haupt's very words have a depressingly familiar ring about them. Eventually, the question bores us, and in our personal lives we give up trying to answer it. The reason is not that the answer is wrong but rather that it is too abstract. "Intersect" is a geometrical term. The "interface" of human beings and history means simply that at times men and women learn to face up to their past. History does not have "immutable laws" running parallel to, but independent of, the "laws" of human nature. And "human nature" is nothing if it is not historical.

As the radical feminists have taught us, history means "his story" —the story of the male of the species. As we learned in school, his story consists to a large degree of theft, plunder, land seizures, murder, warfare, slavery, and endless other large and petty cruelties visited on human beings by each other. It would seem that his story is a very dark chapter in the tale of the species. But what we are sometimes not told is that, usually, material things have to be produced before they are stolen, land has to be improved before it is worth seizing, a civilization has to be built up before there is anything to plunder, some people have to grow food and make clothes for others before men have enough free time to make war and rape women, and society has to be able to produce surplus foods and other articles before it can afford to stop the practice of murdering captives of war on the spot, and, instead, enslave them.

In other words, both his story and her story are primarily tales of *material production,* and only secondarily of *material distribution,* or of

1. Christopher Lehmann-Haupt, "Between History and People," *New York Times,* 12 April 1971.

theft, plunder, war, and more benign forms of distribution. What is not produced can be neither sold, given away, nor stolen. The "intersection" of men and history is not found in the first instance in the cruelties and heroics of war and conquest, still less in the tensions, conflicts, and indignities of daily life in the home, community, and politics. If victory in war were that significant, the Japanese and German economies would not be running away with the prizes today. If what happens in parliaments and ministerial chambers were so important, politicians would be able to straighten out some of society's messes, instead of making the messes worse, which ordinarily is the case. And life in the community and home, far from being an engine of history, is where we try to withdraw from and escape history.

In fact, people and history meet in the course of production, the process of transforming natural materials into objects that satisfy human needs. We are social animals, and production is a social process: people have always worked with each other and for each other in the course of producing things to meet their needs. However, and this is carefully screened from view in the typical American school, *the social relations that people have had with each other in production normally have been exploitive.* In other words, if his story and her story are primarily sagas of production, and if the story of production is a tale of exploitation (not random or occasional exploitation such as occurs in wars, plagues, famines, and other unusual natural and man-made disasters, but the normal exploitation of daily life), then it follows that his and her stories relate a narrative of exploitation, and its converse, the struggle against exploitation.

We are concerned with *capitalist production,* the system of production in which we work, and the only one which most of us have firsthand knowledge of. This means that we know almost everything and almost nothing about the system: we know almost everything about capitalism because we move through its interstices and live in its pores. Our birth, childhood, schooling, coming of age, marriage, divorce, parenthood, sickness, old age, and death are all in whole or in part activities organized along capitalist principles. For most of us, a gift of money is more welcome than a gift of love (even though we may not admit it), the accumulation of things takes precedence over the accumulation of good human relationships, and the business of America remains business.

But at the same time we know almost nothing about the system. The reason is that we know very little about its opposite, socialism. We have had little or no direct experience with any form of socialism, whether it be the bureaucratic socialism of the Soviet Union, the socialism of

China based on a centuries-old tradition of cooperative production at the level of the village, Cuban socialism, where an extremely individualistic people have to learn to cooperate in production as the price of survival, Yugoslav socialism, in which factory workers actually take considerable responsibility for what they produce, and how they produce it, or Vietnamese socialism, a permanent peoples' war communism. Nor do most of us have any firsthand experience in mini-socialist societies such as living communes, production cooperatives, work collectives, monasteries, or other institutions organized along noncapitalist or anticapitalist lines. For most of us, the closest we have come to socialism is the occasional decision made collectively by our families, the joint work project for a volunteer social club, or the help extended to a neighbor studying for an exam or moving a refrigerator.

In other words, we tend to take the capitalist system for granted and accept its premises and daily operations in a matter-of-fact way because we are only dimly aware that there could be any real alternative to it. This is the reason why any study of capitalism must begin with a description of the system's basic premises and social relationships. It is ironic but true that we have to be reminded of the most elementary facts about our lives, about the simplest features of capitalist daily life.

The first important fact is that capitalism is a system in which people produce things not for their own use, or for barter, or to give away to their neighbors, but rather for sale on the market, for *exchange.* Things that are produced with the aim of selling them on the market are called *commodities,* to distinguish them from things that are produced and used directly by the people who produce them. "A rose is a rose is a rose," but a rose that you grow in your garden has a different social meaning than does the rose that you buy at the store. You grow the garden rose for yourself under conditions of your own choosing: you tend your flowers and plants when and how you want to, and you do what you want to with the final product. The rose that is bought in a store is produced by wage labor, by farm workers who are employed by a farmer under conditions of the farmer's choosing. Thus, the commodity *form* of an object hides a *social* relationship. This is the second important fact about capitalism. One group of people "hires" the labor power of another group. One group (workers) sells its creative physical, mental, and other powers for a specified period of time to another group (capitalists) in return for a specified payment (wages).

Capitalism is unique in this regard, even though superficially it appears that wage labor also exists in socialist societies such as the Soviet Union or Cuba. The difference is that in the socialist world work is considered to be everyone's responsibility (even though in practice this is sometimes ignored). Work is seen to be a duty to society as a whole, and the hardest and most creative worker is highly honored, whether he or she be Cuban, Chinese, Russian, or Bulgarian. People who do not work are considered to be parasites, and those who manage to discover and live in a corner of society in which they do not have to work spend a good deal of their time pretending to work, or making it seem that they are doing something useful to society as a whole.

In capitalist societies, by way of contrast, the most honored people are often the people who do no work whatsoever, but rather rule. The hardest and most creative workers are paid well by their immediate bosses, but are normally put down by co-workers for raising the standard output, surpassing the standard work performance. The way to be really admired by co-workers and capitalists is to figure out a way to stop being a worker and to become a capitalist. If one had to choose between being Cash McCall and Joe, who could resist being the sexy tycoon, and who would want to be the bigoted worker? The point is that in capitalist society work is necessarily *alienated work;* people do not work for themselves but for someone else because relatively few people own society's tools or means of production. Further, capitalists buy the labor power of workers not for any personal services which the latter render the former, but rather for what workers can produce in the way of value in the market. Thus, however friendly and intimate the relationship between capitalists and workers becomes, there is an insurmountable barrier to true friendship because capitalists do not want workers for *what* they can produce *(use value),* or how well they can produce it, but for how much what they produce will bring on the market *(exchange value).* A falling market will spoil the best of friendships between capitalist and worker. But the rich family's gardener, maid, butler, and chauffeur stand in a more or less permanently friendly (although in the last analysis dependent and oppressive) relationship with their employer, precisely because they are hired for what they can do and how they do it rather than for the exchange value of their products. Striking examples of this difference were common in Cuba in the first few years of the Cuban revolution. At the same time the factory and office employees of the Cuban capitalist class were seizing buildings and taking over management of businesses and firms, the many retainers of the wealthy classes who were hired to perform personal services remained loyal to "their" families, even after there was little or no money left to pay them.

Work is alien in capitalist society because it is forced work. The ordinary person is forced to work for someone else, because he or she does not own or control the means by which objects are produced—

factories, tools, land, warehouses, power systems. A common objection to the Marxist position that capitalist work is forced labor is the view that most people would rather work for someone else anyway, that most people do not want the responsibility that goes along with planning and controlling one's own work, or other people's work. This may very well be true in a static sense, but the point still remains that in capitalist society there is no way for most people to really choose between working for someone else and working for oneself, precisely because most of the means of production are already owned and controlled by the capitalist class. And the average worker is very aware of this fact, even if given a choice he or she would just as soon work for someone else. The point is that if an individual *wanted* to take responsibility for production, there is no way to do so (short of revolution, which requires that the working class as a whole take responsibility for production).

No wonder then that in capitalist societies people who manage to free themselves from the daily grind are considered lucky. Of course, there are individuals who work for corporations or other profit-making enterprises, but who are engaged in tasks that are intrinsically interesting to them (such as a scientist working on a problem that personally interests him or her), and whose labor is to that degree not "forced labor." And there are hippies and others who do little or no work at all. And there are professional and small businessmen who work for themselves. Finally, there are many people who work for the government and other "nonprofit" employers. But none of these individuals has truly freed himself or herself from work.

In point of fact, *the only way in capitalist society to accumulate time that is absolutely free, the only way to free yourself from the need to do work that you do not really choose to do, is to get someone else to work for you.* In socialist societies, this is not only impractical, but illegal. But in capitalist societies, it seems natural for someone to strive to become a capitalist—a status that nearly everyone would strive for if he or she were able, if he or she had the money, connections, foresight, and intelligence to do so. There is no collective way (except through the activity of trade unionism, and this is a highly imperfect avenue) for individuals to decide how much they need to work, and to what degree they will free themselves from this necessity. As a result, the only way to become free is to acquire by hook or crook some of the society's surplus. By contrast, the principle of socialism is that people do not use surplus production to free themselves as individuals from work, but rather put the surplus into a common pool, and free everyone to a small degree from necessary work. Needless to say, this procedure requires either a high degree of social consciousness (which exists here and there in the socialist world) or an authoritarian government with near absolute control of the productive mechanism (which is much more frequent). But in either case, although workers receive wages and thus seem to be condemned to the same status as workers in the capitalist world, in fact it is impractical or impossible for workers to become capitalists (that is, free themselves from the need to work by getting others to work for them), and hence the whole problem of freedom must be solved cooperatively or collectively, by either democratic or authoritarian means.

2. SURPLUS VALUE

As we have seen, the essence of capitalism is the appropriation of the product of one person's labor by another person. This surplus labor time, or the labor time that workers do not need to put in to keep themselves together body and soul, is called *surplus value.* The idea that capitalists live off workers in this crude sense of stealing some of their workday (or, to be more precise, stealing the product of part of their workday) is offensive to most Americans, even most American workers. For nonworkers who are not capitalists, it is offensive because it suggests that their society is at bottom basically an exploitive one. And it is hard to believe that your society is exploitive and at the same time go about your daily life with little or no public life or concern for other people. The idea is offensive to the capitalists for an obvious reason: these days no one likes to think of himself or herself as exploiting someone else, nor does he or she want other people in society believing this. And workers often find the idea offensive because they like to think of themselves as the equals of anyone in society (our political and cultural heritage is overwhelmingly egalitarian, at least among white men). As a result, few people think very deeply or very long about the nature of the relationship between capital and labor. And fewer people really believe that the capitalists "live off" the workers in the sense that slave owners lived off their slaves in the antebellum South and lords lived off their serfs in feudal times. No respectable social scientist (especially no economist) would deny that slave and feudal societies were exploitive in the obvious sense that slaves worked for slave owners and serfs were forced to spend so many days every year working for their lords, and that slave owners did nothing for slaves except to keep them in the slave state and the lords did little for the serfs except to recruit them to fight in wars that ostensibly were organized to defend the serfs but in fact were initiated by the lords themselves for reasons of power, wealth, honor, religious principle, and so on. But no respectable social scientist would concede that capitalists exploit workers in the same sense. In fact, the hallmark of respectability in American social science is the belief that both capitalists and laborers contribute something valuable to production, and that the rewards that accrue to both (profits and wages) are more or less equivalent to their respective contributions to production. Since few people in America believe that workers produce "surplus value" for capitalists, and since an understanding of the nature of this exploitive relation is absolutely indispensable for an understanding of how and why society as a whole ticks, it is incumbent on us to provide the closest thing to an airtight proof of the principle of surplus value.

It is easy enough to state the formal proof discovered by Karl Marx, which many think was Marx's greatest discovery. It goes like this: As we know, capitalists do not hire workers for the utility of whatever it is workers produce for the capitalists; capitalists themselves do not use the objects produced by their workers. Rather they hire workers with the aim of acquiring money in the marketplace for these objects. Now suppose that these products exchange at their value and bring $100 in the market (this is called the *exchange value of the product of labor*). Next, recall that labor power is a commodity in capitalist society, in the sense that it is bought and sold in the market and thus has a price, which is called the wage rate. Now, it is absolutely clear that no capitalist in his right mind would buy some labor power at a price of, say, $150 weekly, if the weekly product of this labor power brought only $100. Even if the capitalist was a friend of the worker, every week he would be losing $50 (plus the cost of raw materials and other expenses), and sooner or later he would go broke, and be forced to fire his friend. It is obvious therefore that, normally, capitalists will not hire workers unless the exchange value of the product of labor (price) exceeds the exchange value of the labor power itself (wage rate). This calculation of course assumes a given *productivity* of labor. To return to the example used above, if originally the worker were producing ten toasters per week, each of which brought $10 on the market, and if the prevailing wage were $150, then the capitalist would not hire the worker (except perhaps temporarily, if the worker were a needy cousin or niece). But if the worker labored harder or longer, or if he or she were equipped with more or better tools or both, or if the worker learned more of the skills used in the production of toasters, or if all of these things happened at the same time, then the worker would be able to produce more than ten toasters every week—let's say, twenty toasters. Assuming that the price of toasters remains the same ($10 each), the exchange value of the product of labor has jumped to $200. If the exchange value (wage) of labor power remains the same, it is clear that now it *will* pay the capitalist to allow the worker access to his factory, machinery, know-how, and so on, and put the worker to work. Similarly, if the wage could be cut to, say, $50 weekly, it will pay the capitalist to hire the worker, even though the exchange value (price) of his or her product remains unchanged.

These hypothetical examples are useful in the sense that they illustrate that the principle of surplus value is reasonable, and not simply wild propaganda. Nevertheless, even though this principle is elucidated in any number of books, relatively few people actually believe that the theory of surplus value is true. As we know, part of the reason is that people have an emotional or material stake or both in *not* believing it.

For another thing, people ask, if there is such a thing as surplus value, and if workers freely enter into contractual arrangements with capitalists (that is, if the capitalists don't force workers to work for them by using the police or army), then why don't the workers insist that they be paid the full value of the product of their labor? This is a question that lies beneath much popular skepticism about the idea of surplus value. The answer to this question comes in two parts: First, capitalist production is *social* in character, the division of labor and specialization of work functions are highly developed, and producers are extremely interdependent. Thus, one group of workers cannot demand and expect to get the full value of its product, precisely because its product has no exchange value in and of itself. Spark plugs are useless without cars, which require roads, which cannot be built without construction equipment, including cars, and so on. It follows from the interdependency of modern production that we cannot speak of the surplus value of a particular worker or group of workers, but only of the surplus value of the working class as a whole. The idea of surplus value does not make sense in any other light. And it follows from this that if the working class as a whole demanded and received the full value of the product of its labor, capitalist production would become impossible, and the workers would have to be prepared to manage production themselves. Moreover, it is a fact that when workers in a particular company or industry do demand significantly more than the exchange value of their labor power (enough more to threaten to reduce sharply the share of income going to profits), there frequently occurs a strike or lockout, and sometimes back-to-work orders by the government (backed by force), the importation of strikebreakers under police protection, and other moves on the part of capital which involve physical violence or the threat of violence. So it is not true that the exchange of labor power is always free of obvious and blatant physical force.

Nevertheless, people continue to reject the principle of surplus value, because while they may agree that it is logical, they think that a logical argument can be made for practically anything. What they want is proof that the principle *works*. This is particularly true in America, the most pragmatic of pragmatic societies.

Let us see whether or not the idea does work. The only way to tell whether or not any principle will work is to work out its implications, and test these implications in practice. One of the implications of the surplus value principle is that capitalists live off workers—or, to put it another way, that capitalists appropriate some unpaid labor time from workers. If this is true, it is clear that when workers stop working, capitalists stop living (at least in the style to which they are accustomed). Now let us consider two different kinds of historical events, labor strikes and revolutions. In labor strikes workers temporarily withhold their labor power from companies owned by capitalists. In revolutions workers permanently refuse to work for the capitalists. In the first event, production comes to a halt, and after the capitalist has sold goods in inventory, sales fall to nothing. The product of labor is zero, and so is its exchange value. The exchange value of labor power is not realized because labor power is no longer being bought and sold. Surplus value is thus zero. The practical consequences of this are twofold: In the first place, if the strike lasts long enough, the company will go bankrupt, in the sense that it won't be able to pay its creditors. Or perhaps the company will lose so many of its customers that it will take a long time for it to get on its feet again after the strike is over. These possibilities are examples of the *economic* consequences of strikes. Secondly, in the simple case of a capitalist having all his capital tied up in one company, if the company goes bankrupt, the capitalist ceases to be a capitalist and is forced to become a wage laborer. This is a daily happening in the ranks of small business, although it rates very little attention in the news media. And although few people think of the happening in this way, it is an example of *workers forcing capitalists to become workers. The ultimate power of the working class is the power to compel capitalists to become workers;* this is the obverse of the power of capital, whose ownership of the means of production has forced people to become workers in the first place. This observable fact constitutes an indisputable practical proof of the idea of surplus value.

This idea is so important that we must take the time to look at it in a slightly different way. In the example above, it is important to note that although the workers forced capitalists to become workers, the workers were not able to accomplish this *so long as they continued to work.* Put another way, so long as they worked, they produced surplus value, which is the material basis for the existence of the capitalist. When they refused to work, they were able to compel capitalists to become workers. In other words, it is only when workers become nonworkers that capitalists cease to be capitalists.

The actual relationship between capital and labor is revealed fully in a socialist revolution in which the means of production are taken away from the capitalists. Two things occur: First, the capitalists are deprived of the material basis for their wealth and power (surplus value), and thus are forced to seek work like anyone else. Second, in contrast to the situation in which a group of workers forces a company into bankruptcy and its owner into the army of the working class, the workers cannot afford to allow the entire productive apparatus to become "bankrupt" (in the sense of becoming idle). In the event that the working class failed to take *responsibility* for production (responsibility that formerly was the property of the capitalist class), the society would not be able to feed, clothe, and house itself. In short, the difference between a ruinous strike and revolution is that in the former the workers are not forced to take responsibility for organizing the production of things that satisfy their needs, while in a revolution they are forced to do so. The principle of surplus value helps one understand why. In a ruinous strike, one or a few capitalists are eliminated from the capitalist class, but capitalism as a system remains intact, and thus other capitalists, state functionaries, and so on continue to bear the responsibility for maintaining production. In a revolution, all capitalists are eliminated, thus abolishing the capitalist class itself and all shreds of capitalist responsibility.

As these examples suggest, the principle of surplus value is the indispensable link between an understanding of economic structures, on the one hand, and social structures, on the other. Surplus value theory is the passport between the sciences of economics and sociology, properly understood. In view of this, it is not too much to say that both his story and her story are incomprehensible without a working knowledge of surplus value theory. The ultimate proof of surplus value theory is in fact historical. It is an observable fact that there has never been a capitalist class in the absence of a working class (putting aside the class of mercantile "capitalists" who got rich in the course of trade, not in production). Everywhere a group of people *created* a working class (by freeing others from feudal bondage and the restrictions of the guilds, then depriving them of the means of production in one way or another), and subsequently became dependent on this class, in much the same general way slave owners are dependent on their slaves. Everywhere it has been true that the more productive the working class, the richer and more powerful the capitalist class. In America the working class is more productive than in any other country, and the capitalist class has greater wealth and power; by contrast, in the typical underdeveloped country, the working class is small and unproductive, and the capitalist class is weak and its rule tenuous. And it is also empirically verifiable that just as the growth of the wealth and power of the capitalist class has depended on the growth of the productivity of the working class, its willingness and ability to produce surplus value for the capitalist class, the demise of the capitalist class in revolutionary countries is explicable only in terms of the workers' unwillingness or inability to produce a surplus for the capitalists. The principle of surplus value is thus essential in understanding not only the general relationship between economic development and social classes, but also specific changes and upheavals within the social class structure throughout historical time.

3. MODES OF SURPLUS VALUE PRODUCTION

The production of surplus value and its appropriation by capitalists are characteristic of *all* capitalist societies. This is therefore significant for the study and understanding of no *particular* capitalist society. Left propagandists often make this mistake: they present a general theory of capitalist economy and social classes based on the analysis of surplus value, and then proceed to try to understand some particular society on the basis of the general idea. This is impossible, just as it is impossible to understand a particular slave society, for example, the antebellum South, on the basis of the obvious assertion and general notion that slave owners need slaves to work for them, and hence stand in a certain dependent relation to the slaves. But how deep the dependence runs, how foreign it is to the slave owners to "get their hands dirty," and what the slave owners actually do with the surplus labor they steal from their slaves depends on the *particular* nature of the *particular* society under investigation.

To drive the point home, the monopoly of control by one class over the means of production, wage labor, and commodity production is essential to the existence of surplus value in general, and the existence of two general socioeconomic classes. But these general facts do not tell us how big or powerful either class will be, what aims the two classes will have, what the relations between the classes in the spheres of circulation or exchange, production, and politics will be, what specific forms the conflicts between and within these classes will take, or the nature of economic and social life (including crises) at particular stages of capitalist development. Without going beyond a general formulation of surplus value theory, we have no basis for a theory of economy or history. For example, although we know that life and labor, economy and politics, and society and culture were very different in the nineteenth century than in the twentieth century, we have no theoretical basis for understanding the difference between the two. Or, from the standpoint of differences between economic sectors at one particular point in time, although we know that the character of the working class and capitalist class (together with the character of the production relations, and many other phenomena) are very different in sweatshop industries such as runaway garment firms, automated industries such as oil refining, and government industries such as aerospace production, the general theory of surplus value throws no light on the origins, development, and general significance of these differences. So with Marx we are concerned with the "organic connection [between economic and sociopolitical relations] within modern bourgeois society."[2] But more than a century later we must look at the different historical phases "bourgeois society" has passed through and the different economic sectors that today characterize it, before we can grasp this "organic connection" with precision.

What we need to know to begin to understand this "organic connection" in this or any other capitalist society is threefold: *first, how surplus value is produced; second, who appropriates the surplus value that is produced; and, third, what is done with the surplus value that is appropriated.* As we will see, these questions are highly interrelated. To answer them fully would require a rigorous political economic analysis. Our aim at present is merely to introduce some ways of thinking about surplus value, with some factual and historical material used for illustrative purposes only.

Let us start with the first, and most important, question: How is surplus value produced? There are only two ways, both of them discovered by Marx, and developed at length in the first volume of *Capital.* The first is called *absolute surplus value,* and the second *relative surplus value.*

The production of absolute surplus value consists of the expansion

2. Karl Marx, *A Contribution to the Critique of Political Economy,* trans. N. I. Stone (Chicago, 1904), p. 304; the quotation is from the General Introduction to *The Grundrisse.*

of surplus value and productivity by making workers labor longer hours for the same pay, or by making them work harder or more intensively in a given workday (the stretch-out and the speedup).[3]

The production of relative surplus value consists in raising productivity in other ways. One is the reorganization of the work process, which historically was the first way that relative surplus value was produced. Credit for full awareness of the significance of reorganizing work belongs to Adam Smith, the father of (bourgeois) economics, who pointed to the separation of occupations, the division of labor, and the specialization of work functions as the main secrets of the growth of productivity and production. In the era before the introduction of modern mass production, Smith was absolutely right. Compared with precapitalist production, the reorganization of work with the aim of increasing the division of labor and specialization of tasks was a revolutionary advance. The reason is that the growth of capitalist production meant that the work process was reorganized with great stress on saving time. Originally, the "discipline of the factory system" had little or nothing to do with mechanization, but rather was necessary for the capitalist to squeeze the last drop of labor from his workers. Put another way, the rigid separation of work and play that we take for granted is rooted in capitalist social relations, not mechanization. But in comparison with the second way to raise efficiency, Smith's source of the "wealth of nations" is relatively minor. The second path is to give workers more or better tools to work with (this is analytically separate from the first, although normally equipping workers with machinery goes hand in hand with the reorganization of work and division of labor). Historically, the development of special metals, electrical power, the internal combustion engine, the assembly line, and other familiar technological advances of the past century have led to an unprecedented growth of productivity, a truly amazing increase in the amount of commodities that the working class is able to produce with the expenditure of a given amount of energy. Nevertheless, the triumph of machine production fades into insignificance when contrasted with the third way to increase productivity; namely, by educating workers in such a way as to release their inventiveness and creative powers, and by applying these to production. The expansion of surplus value

3. Capitalists can also reduce the wage rate below the exchange value of labor power, thus acquiring a larger part of the social product. Moreover, in the monopoly stage of capitalism, when large corporations have considerable control over prices, capitalists can reduce the real purchasing power of the workers' wages (lower the wage rate in relation to the exchange value of labor power) by raising prices. The government also can alter the share of the social product going to capital and labor by incomes policy.

increasingly has been put on this basis in the developed capitalist countries, as the growth of higher education and research and development activities has led not only to better training for workers in the performance of specific tasks but, of much more importance, to the creation of a working class that is able to invent and develop the precise kinds of machinery and work processes that in turn will maximize productivity consistent with maximum profits.[4]

Next, let us consider the various ways that surplus value can be *appropriated*. In the first place, it can be appropriated *directly*, either by the capitalist who has organized the production of surplus value (i.e., the old-fashioned entrepreneur of ideological fame), or by other capitalists who have not organized the production of surplus value but who own *financial claims* on surplus value. For example, absentee owners who own stock in a corporation and bankers who own bonds issued by the corporation appropriate surplus value directly because they own financial claims on profits (which is one of the forms that surplus value takes when it is realized in the market). Secondly, surplus value can be appropriated *indirectly*, specifically by the government extracting taxes from the stream of income flowing through the corporation (these taxes can take the form of either individual income taxes withheld from the worker's paycheck or corporate income taxes). Historically, indirect surplus value appropriation is becoming increasingly important, as the government's role in the economy becomes more central.

Finally, we review the various ways that surplus value can be *disposed of*. First, it can be spent on capitalist consumption or consumer items that add little or nothing to society's productive forces because they are utilized by nonworkers. Second, it can be converted into capital in the form of a new plant and equipment, raw materials, and the purchase of additional labor power. Third, it can be spent in the selling and communications sectors of the economy with the aim of selling goods, that is, to raise the demand for goods over and above the level of demand in the absence of such sales expenditures. Surplus value used in this last way is said to be spent to *realize surplus value* produced in the past (but is as yet unrealized). Finally, surplus value can be used by the government (or state) for various purposes, including all of the above purposes, but also for system maintenance expenditures—in par-

4. In the "classical" epoch of machine production, inventiveness was the monopoly of the capitalists and their immediate managers and engineers, who constituted an economic and social elite. Today, with the growth of free higher education (especially since the recent introduction of open admissions policies won through the political struggles of the black movement), creativity and inventiveness are more and more properties of the entire working class.

ticular, for military, police, and other repressive agencies, on the one hand; and welfare and other social expenses of production, on the other (see Chapters Five and Six).

These are the general ways that surplus value can be produced, appropriated, and utilized. A simple example will help us understand these differences, and illuminate some of the consequences of different modes of surplus value production, appropriation, and utilization.

Suppose that I become a capitalist and organize the production of marijuana cigarettes, or joints. I hire someone to roll joints with materials that I have bought surreptitiously outside of the local head shop. I lay out, say, $10 for an ounce of grass, and employ a worker who is able to roll twenty joints an hour by hand from the grass in the lid I have supplied the worker with. I sell each joint on the street for, say, $1. The exchange value of the product of one hour's labor is thus $20. The "constant capital" I had to start with amounted to $10, and when I recover this amount I have $10 left. Clearly, if I pay my worker $10 per hour, or the full value of the product of his labor (less raw material outlays), I do not make any profit, and for this reason will not be able to survive in business. Unless I try some other branch of production, I will be forced to work for someone else, rather than having others work for me. On the other hand, suppose that it costs my worker only $5 hourly to "reproduce himself" (that is, to keep himself alive at the conventional standard of life). If I pay the worker only $5, he has produced a surplus of $5 for me. I appropriate the surplus value directly, not in the form of unpaid labor itself, but rather in the form of the product of unpaid labor, specifically the product of one half of my worker's working day. This is an important point: by contrast, the feudal lord acquired unpaid labor directly in the form of labor, so many days or weeks per year during which the serf worked for the lord in his grist mill, repairing his roads, or producing crops for the lord's table. On the other hand, I acquire surplus value in the form of ten joints, but in order to realize surplus value (to be able to buy more lids, have more joints made for me, and set the whole process in motion again), I must *sell* these joints. Clearly, if I am to survive as a capitalist, I have to organize not only the *production* of surplus value but also the *realization* of surplus value.

Next, suppose that competition in my line of business increases. We do not have to look very far for the reason: it is very easy for someone to get into the business of manufacturing joints because capital requirements are limited to wage payments and raw material outlays. In good weather, workers can roll joints out-of-doors, and in bad weather they can use their own homes (exactly as the first cigar makers did). So capitalists do not really need to lay out funds on plant or equipment. As other capitalists spring up, the supply of joints will rise, and there will be a tendency for the price of joints to fall. Some of the workers I hired may very well seek to become capitalists, as they have acquired all the skills necessary in the labor process. I, too, might choose to expand my business if I have been making a good profit in the past, and this action, together with expansion elsewhere, will also tend to drive the price down and increase sales.[5] Suppose the price falls from one dollar to half a dollar per joint as a result of the pressure of competition. What options or responses do I have? Sad to say, I must pursue a single course of action. The price of staying in business is to squeeze more unpaid labor power out of my workers *absolutely*. I lengthen the work day or force my workers to roll more joints per hour on pain of dismissal. Or I cut wages below the exchange value of labor power.

Whatever the method chosen, and I may experiment with all three methods, it is easy to see that other capitalists will be forced to do the same thing to survive. Throughout the whole industry, prices fall, profit margins become narrower, and money wages are squeezed. If the spiral of increased work loads and declining prices and wages continues long enough, both capitalists and laborers will be hopelessly impoverished. Fortunately for the members of this spaced-out economy, supplies will not expand (and work conditions and prices and wages will not decline) indefinitely. The reason is that when profit margins are zero, or near zero, it will not pay anyone to become a capitalist, nor will it pay any existing capitalist to expand supplies still further. Moreover, from the standpoint of the standard of living of the workers, the wage decline may not necessarily augur bad times. In our simple (and simpleminded) economy there is only one commodity, and workers buy what they produce (presumably they need to get stoned in order to lighten the burden of work—and if this seems to be absurd, consider the fact that both tin miners in Bolivia and auto workers in Fremont, California, use dope to reduce the physical and mental suffering of work). Although wages decline, prices also decline, and it may be that workers will be able to buy as much dope with their smaller wage packet as they did before the wage cut.

5. The logic of this process is simple. It is assumed that people will buy more joints if the price is lowered, first, because their income is now "worth more" because the price of one of the things they buy is less than it was, and being in this sense "richer" they will buy more of everything, including joints; second, because joints are cheaper in comparison with LSD, mescaline, and other close and distant substitutes for marijuana there will be a tendency for heads to substitute the latter for the former. The first process is called the *income effect* of a decline in price; the second process is called *substitution effect*.

As we know, when surplus value is produced *absolutely,* the basis of economic expansion is sweating the work force. Further, the mode of surplus value production described above is called *direct* surplus value, because unpaid labor time is appropriated directly by the capitalist from the worker. It is called *absolute* surplus value for two reasons: first, competition forces capitalists to try to appropriate absolutely more surplus value from workers as the price of survival—to put it another way, there is a tendency for the absolute amount of the total product going to the workers to decline (although this tendency may be partially or wholly offset by the decline in prices under the pressure of competition); and second, there is a tendency for precapitalist producers of joints—people who roll their own for themselves, and sell the rest in the market (say, the foreign market, in which they can buy other commodities)—to be put out of business by capitalist producers. In comparison with precapitalist production, I have organized the work process more "efficiently"—that is, my workers are working harder. Moreover, I might take advantage of the benefits of specialization of work function and division of labor: some workers might be taking papers out of the box, others rolling joints, others packaging the final product. To the degree that precapitalist producers cannot meet the competition of capitalist producers, they are driven out of business and into the ranks of the working class. In the event that all or most of them are unable to find jobs in the capitalist sector, even during a boom, there will arise *absolute* unemployment of labor, or an *absolute surplus population.*

The production of absolute surplus value has many important implications for the nature of work, the kind of relations capitalists have with their workers, the course of economic development, the nature of the government, and so on. For example, it is almost impossible for workers and capitalists to live with each other on good terms if capitalists are always under pressure to reduce wages, lengthen hours, or employ the speedup or stretch-out. To follow the argument through somewhat, under these conditions the development of labor unions would be ruinous for capitalists, who will use whatever influence or power they have in government to fight unions in every way they know how.

But let us focus on an extremely important *methodological* point—that is, underline an important *way of thinking* about economy and society based on the idea of surplus value. To begin with, note that surplus value theory first and foremost is a theory of social classes. As we know, the simultaneous existence of two classes, capitalists and workers, is inexplicable except by way of reference to the production of surplus value by workers and its appropriation by capitalists. More specifically, when the production of surplus value is on an *absolute* basis (as in our example above), there is always a tendency for wages to fall, or at least a tendency for wages to be rigid in an upward direction. *This is not attributable to some mechanical "law" of economics, but to the social fact that the material survival of the capitalist class depends on cutting wages and keeping them low.* To put the point another way, we do not know the course of wages in an economy in which surplus value is produced absolutely until we have analyzed the nature of the so-called production relationships between capitalist and worker. *We need to have a theory of social classes before we can hope to have a theory of wages.* Pushing this argument one step forward, since we need a theory of wages in order to have a theory of economic development and crisis, it follows that an analysis of social classes and social structure is indispensable to a theory of economic development and crisis. In a system in which all surplus value is produced absolutely, a simplified theory might go as follows: The only sure basis for the survival of individual capitalists under intense competitive pressures is to reduce wages (especially when increasing the intensity of work *lowers* worker output by raising the level of physical or mental exhaustion). Further, competition, because it entails the risk of losing markets, forces capitalists to expand their operations. Thus, an economy organized on this basis tends to generate *underconsumption of consumer goods* (owing to the fall in wages, and presumably the wage share of total income), and *overproduction of capital goods* such as work sheds, raw materials, and so forth (owing to the intensity of competition among the capitalists). Put another way, there is not enough consumer purchasing power to buy the potential output of the (enlarged) capital goods sector of the economy. There occurs a redistribution of income in favor of capitalists and against workers, which manifests itself in an expansion of the production of commodities that capitalists buy (capital goods) and a contraction in the production of commodities that workers buy (wage goods or consumer goods). This combination of events is a recipe for a serious economic crisis, that is, a generalized reduction in the production of all commodities, a rise in unemployment, decline in workers' income, more poverty. Again, it must be stressed that although this simplistic model of economic crisis is not very useful in practical work, it is impossible to build *any* meaningful model of economic growth and crisis without *first* working out the implications for social class structures and relationships of the particular mode of surplus value production (and utilization).

At the risk of driving the reader up the wall, this point will be stressed one final time. We insist on the fact that what is important in the development of capitalist society in general, and capitalist economies in specific, is the *interaction* between capitalists and workers. The character of this interaction is determined by the way that surplus value is produced, appropriated, and utilized, or by the way that the elites get unpaid labor time from the masses and by what the elites do with the unpaid labor time they appropriate; and, finally, by how much unpaid labor time is appropriated in comparison with the needs of the masses. Further, we insist that the nature of this interaction is of crucial importance for phenomena which *appear* to be strictly economic phenomena; that is, that the theory of surplus value is not very useful as a theory of economic development and crisis in any direct sense, but that it is indispensable for a theory of social classes and social structure, which in turn determine the course of economic events.

Let us now return to our hypothetical economy based on the production of dope. It will be recalled that I have increased my output of joints in response to competition from other capitalists. Most if not all other capitalists follow suit. It will also be recalled that in an economy in which surplus value is produced absolutely, the *only* way to expand the production of commodities is to hire more workers to produce them (and build more work sheds, acquire more raw materials, and so on). In the language of formal economics, the volume of production is determined by the amount of labor time used in production. As a result, I am compelled to hire more workers. Where will I find them? In the surplus population, in the ranks of the ex-independent producers who have been put out of business by superior capitalist production. *So long as the surplus population exists, I am able to hire all of the workers I want to employ at the going wage rate.* Put another way, I do not have to compete with other employers for a limited supply of workers; rather I can hire unemployed workers without offering wages higher than the going rates. But sooner or later, the surplus population will disappear, and I will no longer be able to recruit fresh "peasant" labor at the current wage. The supply of labor power becomes relatively inelastic; that is, to expand my work force, I will have to pay higher wages to attract employed workers away from their present jobs. Clearly, the inelasticity of labor tends to put a floor on wages, results in a tendency toward an upward drift in wages during times of strong labor demand, and strengthens the incipient labor organizations that the workers have been trying to organize since the introduction of capitalist production. Historically, exactly when this happens depends on many factors that are unique to particular regions and countries of the world. In the classical case of European capitalism, the ability of capitalist producers to recruit labor extensively from the countryside ended around the third quarter of the nineteenth century, and subsequently technological and other changes that caused reductions in the amount of labor time per unit of output were introduced as a response to increasing shortages of labor power, as well as to competition from other capitalists.

At this stage in the development of the production of joints, we capitalists find ourselves in a double bind. On the one hand, it becomes increasingly difficult to keep ourselves going by cutting wages and increasing the intensity of work. On the other hand, there is more and more competition forcing down prices. In the last analysis, capitalist production based on absolute surplus value becomes impossible (as a matter of fact, it is possible only when there is a surplus population, although it is possible temporarily when there exists "technological unemployment"). Finding myself being squeezed from above and below, under pressure from both my competitors and my workers, I follow the only course available to me. I desperately try to find ways to produce the *same* volume of joints with *fewer* workers (or work hours).

Thus, I invent or acquire some hand-operated cigarette rolling machines, equip my workers with them, and watch labor productivity turn sharply up. *Now our mini-economy increasingly becomes based on the production of relative surplus value.*[6] There is a double meaning to this statement: first, production is more efficient because the work force has more (or better) tools to work with; second, production requires *relatively* fewer workers precisely because it is more efficient. In other words, there is a sociological fact that corresponds to the economic fact

6. Most bourgeois historians, economists, and others, identify the development of capitalism with mechanization and industrialization. The truth of the matter is that capitalism is in essence a particular *social relationship*. The essential historic change was the shift from petty commodity production to surplus value production, which involves the buying and selling of *hours of work* or *time*, rather than the buying and selling of *products*. Clearly, the concept (and practice) of *buying time* must precede historically the concept (and practice) of *saving time*, which is of course the main purpose of mechanization.

I should add that I have departed from Marx's analysis of the historical "stages" of capitalism in order to spotlight "pure" absolute surplus value production. In terms of the actual labor process (in Marxian language, "concrete labor"), Marx began with the stage of *manufacture*, in which the workers used tools that were essentially the same tools that precapitalist independent commodity producers used. The next stage, the transition to "modern industry" or mechanization, has the double function of specializing labor tasks even more and also specializing tools in the form of machinery. This permitted capitalists to employ relatively unskilled laborers and simultaneously prevented the workers from escaping wage labor by reverting to independent commodity production, which becomes a practical impossibility with machine production. Thus, "modern industry" permits closer control of labor and the laborers. In the model of capitalist development presented in the first volume of *Capital*, the introduction of machine production increases relative surplus value by expanding productivity, and because machine production permits closer control of the workers by the boss, it also permits an increase in absolute surplus value.

of expanding productivity—namely, that capitalists lay off some of their workers, increasing unemployment (unless there is a surge upward in the demand for labor elsewhere in the economy) and expanding the *relative surplus population.* This means simply that there is a surplus population relative to the normal demand for labor in the capitalist sector of the economy. In other words, there is unemployment relative to the means of employing workers in the capitalist sector; labor-saving technological and other changes reduce the relative number of workers needed in production.

The important thing to note about the production of relative surplus value is that production expands primarily on the basis of mechanization, rather than the intensity of work and the number of workers employed. The significance of this is twofold: First, far from having to lengthen hours, increase the intensity of work, and cut wages to the bare minimum, I can now afford to *raise* wages, *reduce* work hours, and *improve* conditions of work. In fact, it may be true not only that I can afford to make these changes, but that it will pay me to make these changes, precisely because if I pay my workers more, they will be able to buy more of the products which they produce but which I own and offer for sale in the market. Suffice it to mention that Henry Ford said that he established the "five-dollar day" partly to enable his workers to buy Ford cars.

Second, although the expansion of an economy based on relative surplus value may have the effect of redistributing income from workers to capitalists, it is impossible (or highly unlikely) for the *absolute* amount of income going to the working class to fall. The significance of this for the capitalists is that they are better able to establish a live-and-let-live relationship with the workers. To be sure, the capitalist class is still living off the unpaid labor of the working class, but the workers are more productive, and their standard of life can rise, thus tending to reduce the sharp antagonisms between capital and labor that characterized the production of absolute surplus value. As a capitalist, I therefore feel more secure, more in charge of my destiny, more powerful because I am much wealthier as my workers are more productive and because the danger of revolt and revolution by the working class is for the time being minimized. In the long run there are definite limits to the production of absolute surplus value, limits that are rooted in the physical capacities of workers, their willingness to accept speedups without complaint after experiencing periods of relatively good work conditions, popular standards regarding the standard workday (standards that are often codified in hours laws), the power of trade unions to prevent wage cuts, minimum wage laws, and so on.

Sooner or later, other capitalists producing for the same market will also introduce machinery (the price of failing to do so is economic ruin). Once again competition will tend to turn reductions in costs per unit of output into reductions in prices. Once again fresh capital will enter the industry, and capital already in the industry will expand. Every possible way to increase labor productivity will be attempted (consistent with maintaining the volume of surplus value), including speedup and stretch-out. Steam power, fossil fuels, electrical power, and, finally, atomic power will be harnessed to expand productivity. Productivity will rise to previously undreamed of heights, and the basis for the material existence of both the capitalist and working class will rapidly expand.

However, an economy based on the production of relative surplus value is not without its economic problems. Again we wish to suggest the connection between the production of surplus value, the nature of social classes and class relationships, and economic development and crisis. As we know, an economy based on relative surplus is able to grow and develop very rapidly; in the course of development, workers and capitalists share in increases in income that result from expanding productivity. Using trade associations, labor unions, government agencies, and community organizations as instruments of class collaboration (instruments that insure that productivity gains are in fact shared between the two classes), capital and labor normally are able to establish a harmonious relationship. *It is this harmonious relationship that is the basis for further development.*[7] More specifically, assuming that unions and other organizations of workers are indifferent to the plight of the relative surplus population, workers who do keep their jobs are able to get higher wages and more income by collaborating with capitalists when the latter introduce labor-saving, more productive machinery, plant, and production methods generally. From this we can deduce that the real basis for the ongoing development of capitalist production in this stage is the creation of a bifurcation, or split, within the working class, the establishment of essentially two classes, the preoccupation of the employed sector of the working class with expanding productivity and winning higher wages, and the neglect of the relative surplus population by the established labor unions.

Thus, it is a particular social structure and system of social relations that is the real secret of capitalist development and wealth. The reader's

7. In the last analysis, "capital" is a social relationship in which one class appropriates the leisure time (or potential leisure time) of another class, and uses this time to expand the material basis for increased exploitation in the future. In the absence of this particular social relationship, there is no material expansion, no accumulation.

appreciation of this point will be keener if he or she considers the course of capitalist development when employed workers are unwilling to allow technologically unemployed workers to sink into the relative surplus population. In brief, technological change and economic growth come to a halt. If this seems too fanciful, consider the situation in one industry today in which workers have resisted technological unemployment by insisting on "make-work" practices, "featherbedding," and so on—namely, the railroad industry. In this industry, technological change and expanded productivity have slowed down, and at times have come to a halt, *in part precisely because the railroad workers have attempted to resist the bifurcation of the work force into one group of privileged employed workers and another group of impoverished unemployed workers.* Without attempting to establish a formal proof of this idea, we believe it can be shown that the development of *entire capitalist economies* can be slowed or thwarted by the unwillingness of labor organizations to serve as the instrument of the creation of a relative surplus population. The present author has argued that this was one of the main factors inhibiting the growth of the prerevolutionary Cuban economy,[8] and it also has been argued convincingly that the present-day British economy is stagnating partly for the same reason. This *class* consciousness (as opposed to special-interest consciousness) of the working class establishes production relations between capital and labor that thwart or slow down the development of the productive forces (or the growth of production itself) and *simultaneously* establishes the precondition for the take-over of the productive mechanism by the working class and the *further* development of the productive forces. In other words, class consciousness is needed to foul up capitalist production, on the one hand, and establish socialist production, on the other.

Returning to our dope economy, sooner or later the production of joints will be placed on a large-scale basis, which results in the growth of output and surplus value by permitting closer control over both production and the producer. Assembly lines, automated equipment, scientific production planning and control, and other features of modern production will characterize the joint industry (just as they are features of the modern cigarette industry). Now each capitalist needs a bigger market to justify the introduction of mass production equipment; no capitalist can acquire a bigger market without mass production equipment which keeps unit costs to a minimum. Survival thus increasingly depends on realizing economies of large-scale production (lower average costs with greater volume of production). Survival also

8. James O'Connor, *The Origins of Socialism in Cuba* (Ithaca, N.Y., 1970).

depends on getting economies of scale in distribution, that is, the lower costs of marketing joints in the context of large-scale, far-flung distribution networks, a sales army, national advertising and branding. And survival depends on customer loyalty, which requires brand names and trade marks. In short, after a certain period of development, the joint industry closely resembles the modern cigarette industry, perhaps with the difference that Mellow Yellow, Wow, Far Out, and Out of Sight replace Camels, Winstons, and Kents.

In this industry, there is a strong tendency to end destructive competition (competition that is destructive of profits). For everyone without massive wealth, it is difficult or impossible to set up business and become a capitalist. Like the modern tobacco industry, a handful of giant corporations dominate the industry. Prices are administered, or set in accordance with specific profit criteria, by the corporations themselves; profits therefore do not reflect relative surplus value alone but also contain a monopoly element, or an "extra" that capital obtains by keeping prices high and noncompetitive. The system is for the time being prevented from collapsing in an embarrassment of riches; monopoly control and monopoly pricing inhibit the development of excessive production capacity, overproduction, price depression, and a fatal squeeze on profits.

This does not mean that the basic contradictions of capitalism are in any important respect resolved. For example, the elimination of price depressions creates the conditions for *permanent inflation,* which ushers in new problems.

4. INDIRECT SURPLUS VALUE

Up to this point, we have neglected to deal with the economic role of the state.[9]

When I first began to organize the production of surplus value, I needed workers who were skilled at rolling joints by hand; when my operation became mechanized, I needed men and women willing and able to work at the unskilled or semiskilled and repetitive tasks of tending machinery or working on an assembly line. As production

9. Over thirty years ago, one of America's most insightful students of the history of ideas wrote that "the main task of those who wish to employ the Marxian theory in concrete economic analysis is to adapt it to the requirements of an economic process which involves a vast amount of government regulation and participation" (Leo Rogin, "The Significance of Marxian Economics for Current Trends of Government Policy," *American Economic Review Supplement* 28, no. 1 [May 1938]: 10).

processes became more complex, in particular when I decided to introduce continuous process production techniques (automation) in order to lower costs and meet the competition, I began to need different kinds of workers: system engineers, computer programmers, material handling engineers, instrument monitors, and other scientists, engineers, and technicians. Immediately, I am faced with a serious problem. These kinds of "modern proletarians" perform highly skilled and specialized functions, and require years of formal and on-the-job training. If I decide to bear the expense of training my own work force, I have absolutely no guarantee that my workers will not quit and decide to take jobs with my rivals, or in other industries. Other capitalists organizing the production of relative surplus value with modern techniques are faced with a similar dilemma. Moreover, as time goes on, research and development expenses, outlays for overhead investments such as plant, transportation and communications facilities, pensions, and similar costs begin to get out of hand. My solution is a model of simplicity: I decide (along with other capitalists) to shift these costs to the state in order to *socialize the costs* of retirement pensions, health plans, manpower training, research and development, and other outlays which I cannot profitably absorb.

In turn, the expansion of state agencies requires the growth of state employment (engaged in military as well as civilian tasks). Men and women employed and supported by the state need to be clothed, housed, and fed. Thus, whether or not I actually anticipated the growth of a new market, sooner or later the state begins to place orders with me for joints needed in hospitals, mental institutions, prisons, and the army (my product had proven to be a powerful pain reliever and a successful solvent for social tension). In other words, I have become dependent on the state not only on the supply side but also on the demand side. At the limit, I may specialize in the production of joints for the state, and, *as a result, cease to produce commodities (objects produced for sale on the market) altogether.*

The significance of this transformation for the nature of social classes and class relationships and economic development is far-reaching. In the first place, if my workers no longer produce commodities, then they no longer produce surplus value. Quite the contrary, the new basis for my wealth and power becomes tax monies, together with control of state expenditures. Means of production, markets, and profits come to depend more and more on control of the state administration and the state budget. In the happy event that my capitalist friends and myself monopolize the state budget (having monopolized political power) and that other people accept the budgetary priorities that we

establish, we begin to appropriate surplus value *indirectly*. This means
that we have to get our hands on surplus value in a roundabout way,
by controlling the state administration, taxing mechanism, and expenditures policy. In these circumstances, the expansion of indirect surplus
value is theoretically unlimited, or more exactly, it is limited solely by
the extent of the market and the level of productivity prevailing in the
economy as a whole.[10] In sum, chances are that my main concerns will
be establishing budgetary priorities in my favor, avoiding taxes on my
business and personal income, and keeping up demand and productivity (and hence the tax base) in the economy as a whole. In fact, to the
degree that I am producing on one form of "cost-plus" contract or
another, I may actually neglect productivity in my own business.

In the second place, the workers whom I employ also depend on
tax monies (directly in the case of employees of the government, indirectly in the case of workers employed by state contractors). Increases
in wages come out of taxes, not profits. Thus, my workers and myself
(i.e., my management) do not have to engage in that permanent quarrel
over the distribution of the surplus value that they produce for me for
the simple reason that they do not produce surplus value. I am pleased
to learn that I can expect much more cooperation and goodwill from
my work force (and can afford to give goodwill in return) than I was
able to in the old days when I was appropriating surplus value directly.
Decisions not only to invest in such and such field and produce such
and such good or service but also to establish certain wages and hours
of work are determined less and less at the actual point of production,
and more and more by the political mechanism. This is very important.
In the absolute and relative surplus value "stages" of capitalism, the
volume and distribution of surplus value are determined by the laws of
the market. By contrast, in the indirect surplus value "stage" the
amount of surplus value produced and its distribution between and
among capitalists and workers are determined politically. In this sense
(admittedly a limited one), "state capitalism" is another name for class
collaboration, at least as far as struggles at the point of production over
the distribution of the social product are concerned.

In the last analysis, not only is it objectively possible to bring my
employees around to my way of thinking (at least concerning government contracts and the distribution of the tax burden), but it is essential

10. Perhaps an argument can be made that because capitalists now are relatively more
concerned with the generalized production of relative surplus value by increases in
productivity economy-wide, for the first time they are compelled to develop *class* interests
(in contrast to industry or interest group interests)—interests that can't be defended and
enlarged without the cooperation of the power elite (state bureaucracy).

for me to do so. The reason is that the state bureaucracy and the politicians mediate between the total pool of surplus value available for distribution and myself. In a very basic sense I have become dependent on these politicians and bureaucrats whom in an earlier epoch I despised. And to influence or control them I need all the allies that I can get, including and especially my workers, who in their own way have as much to gain or lose from my success or failure as I do.

At this point, we bring our simple analysis of the anatomy of capitalist economy to an end with one word of caution. Enough has been said to indicate the profound significance for social life in general of the different modes of surplus value production, appropriation, and utilization. But no capitalist economy is or ever was based on one particular mode of surplus value production or distribution. To use Lenin's phrase, society is the end product of the "combined and uneven development" of past and present modes of production and is obviously much more complex than we have described. Although the "theory of surplus value" is essential as a *way of thinking* about capitalist society as a whole, it cannot substitute for political economic analysis of any specific society. All it is is a method for carrying out such analyses.[11]

11. Two applications of the method are possible. One is to use surplus value theory to analyze the different phases capitalism has passed through (as I did in my example of joint production). The other is to use the theory as a way to analyze the various sectors of an economy at any particular point in time. I have used the latter approach in *The Fiscal Crisis of the State* (New York, 1973), chaps. 1 and 2.

PART II

THE CORPORATIONS

CHAPTER THREE

Baran and Sweezy's Monopoly Capital

1. BARAN AND SWEEZY'S THESIS

In the first volume of *Capital*, Marx demonstrated how and why the concentration and centralization of capital inevitably accompany the accumulation of capital. Capital concentration means that individual capital units (firms or corporations) grow larger in absolute size—that is, each firm uses more labor power, owns more machinery, and so on. Capital centralization means that fewer and fewer firms hire more and more of the total work force and organize the production of more and more of the total surplus value and social product. Marx showed that two factors were responsible for both capital concentration and centralization: competition and credit. He argued that large-scale production and large-scale production alone is consistent with survival in the competitive marketplace. Further, the expansion of the credit system affords the opportunity for individual firms to grow even larger in both absolute and relative terms. Reduced to a formula, Marx claimed that competition plus credit equals monopoly.

Although Marx developed the outlines of a theory of the transition from competitive capitalism to monopoly capital, he did not take up the problem of how a monopolistic economy actually worked, nor did he give more than passing reference to the problem of why competition actually survives in some branches of the economy. In the course of the twentieth century, a number of economists and social theorists, using different methods and techniques, have tried to describe the anatomy of monopoly capitalism and the "laws of motion" of modern capitalism as a whole. Some theorists have emphasized the relationship between the growth of monopoly and imperialism (see Chapters Seven and

Eight), while others have focused on the growing interpenetration of monopolistic corporations and the capitalist state (see Chapters Five and Six).

Perhaps the most influential work on monopoly capitalism published in this country during the past two decades is Paul A. Baran and Paul M. Sweezy's book, *Monopoly Capital,* which examines the role of the giant corporation in contemporary United States industry.[1] In particular, Baran and Sweezy are concerned with the problem of "absorbing economic surplus" (or realizing surplus value, in classical Marxist terms) in modern capitalism, and play down or ignore altogether the process of surplus value production and appropriation. Similarly, the roles of imperialism and the state are explored mainly insofar as overseas investment and government spending "absorb surplus." Bearing these limitations in mind, we can proceed to summarize Baran and Sweezy's main theses, and then conclude with a brief critique of them.

As suggested above, the authors depart sharply from orthodox practice by placing monopoly at the very center of their analysis. "Today," they write, "the typical unit in the capitalist world is not the small firm producing a negligible fraction of a homogeneous output for an anonymous market but a large-scale enterprise producing a significant share of the output of an industry, or even several industries, and able to control its prices, the volume of its production, and the types and amounts of its investments." Large-scale business is organized along corporate lines and is typical in the sense that a relatively small number of industrial giants own a large share of industrial assets. Controlled by a group of self-perpetuating professional managers, allied with a handful of the wealthy owners, the big corporations retain the lion's share of their earnings and enjoy a great measure of financial independence. The older interest group theory (which Sweezy himself pioneered) is replaced by a model of an economy dominated by independent corporations selling in oligopolistic industries. The dissolution of the old Rockefeller group into competitive Standard Oil companies is cited as supporting evidence.

The analysis of big business' main impulses rests substantially on James Earley's empirical studies of "excellently managed" corporations. According to Earley's findings, the corporations systematically "focus on cost reductions, expansion of revenue, and the increase of profits." The corporations are not *more* profit oriented than the individual entrepreneur of textbook fame, but the giants do strive for the

1. Paul A. Baran and Paul M. Sweezy, *Monopoly Capital: An Essay on the American Economic and Social Order* (New York, 1966).

greatest *increase* in profits possible in any concrete situation. Armed with the new managerial techniques, including market analysis and the science of stimulation, the corporations are well equipped to seek out maximum incremental profits. The managers' drive for profits is rooted in the specific socioeconomic situation in which they operate and in no sense depends on orthodox economics' fragile individual psychological explanations of the profit motive.

The managers normally ally themselves with the corporations' largest stockholders, who prefer to realize their income in the form of capital gains rather than dividends. Both groups seek to augment corporate size and growth and promote integration and diversification of product lines. Profits are the key to all three major standards of success. Enterprising, but hardly combative, the corporate giants have a relatively long-time horizon and recognize each other's retaliatory power, finally evolving a live-and-let-live attitude.

On the basis of a brief but lucid description of the role of big business in the U.S. economy, the authors define monopoly capitalism as a "system made up of giant corporations," asserting that "overall, monopoly capitalism is as unplanned as its competitive predecessor." How does this unplanned system work? It will be convenient to follow the authors' example by first examining the price and cost policies of the corporation and then working out the implications for the volume of investment and aggregate demand.

On the basis of the description of corporate behavior outlined above, Baran and Sweezy accept the theory of monopoly price as a relevant description of pricing under monopoly capitalism. Price cutting as a mode of competition has long since been banished from big business' arsenal, and price wars are left to the small fry. The characteristic form of monopoly control is price leadership and normally the price leader will establish a price which will maximize incremental profits for the industry as a whole. This is perhaps the most striking result of the corporate live-and-let-live attitude. The economy as a whole, however, does not function as if it were composed of pure monopolists because the industrial giants are locked in a struggle for market shares. The need to maintain and if possible expand its share of the market compels the corporation to lower production costs and improve efficiency. Higher profits, arising from lower costs and fixed prices, are necessary to support the research and development, advertising, and other expenditures which are the chief weapons in the battle for market shares. For their part, firms producing capital goods fail to maintain *their* markets unless they offer for sale cost-reducing equipment. It follows from this line of reasoning that if we provisionally define the economic surplus as corporate profits and selling expenditures there will be a "tendency for the surplus to rise" over time. To put it another way, the lion's share of the benefits accruing from lower costs is appropriated by corporations rather than passed on to consumers.

The authors then advance the crucial question whether or not the economy generates sufficient investment outlets to absorb the rising surplus. Grafting the Keynesian concept of aggregate demand onto their theory of oligopolistic market behavior, they submit that surplus which is not utilized (in more orthodox terms, savings which are not spent) will be surplus which is not produced; and surplus which is not produced means productive capacity which is not utilized and unemployment.

After disposing of the notion that endogenous investment (investment spending generated from within the system) might be expected to provide sufficient outlets, the authors examine in detail the role of exogenous investment opportunities. First, the idea that an increasing population will offer sufficient outlets is summarily disposed of; quite the contrary, the causal arrows run in the opposite direction as a high volume of investment generates a rapid growth of per capita income and thus early marriages and bigger families. Second, because the United States is a net importer of capital on private account, it is asserted that foreign investment cannot be considered a significant outlet. Unhappily and surprisingly, Baran and Sweezy's brief discussion of foreign investment must be considered inadequate even granting their own limited intentions. There is no attempt to separate short-term from long-term capital movements, and there is no mention of "foreign aid" (actually, public foreign loans mainly raised in the private capital market) as a mode of utilizing the surplus by borrowing from future demand. Nor do the authors refer to the possibilities of disposing of surplus abroad without a *quid pro quo* (for example, lavish postwar gifts toward European reconstruction).

Finally, the relationship between technological change and investment spending is analyzed in one of the most important and lucid sections of the book. The authors make a convincing case that under a regime of monopoly capitalism the rate at which new techniques will supplant older technologies will be significantly slower than in a competitive economy. Innovators producing and selling in competitive markets have every reason to introduce new cost-reducing, output-increasing techniques because they expect to be able to sell the expanded output at the going market price. What is more, the competitive system disciplines the technologically laggard producer, while under

monopoly capitalism firms do not have to hurry to replace old equipment with new because there is no real or potential pressure on prices.
Put simply, the monopolist or oligopolist, unlike the competitive enterprise, can guard the value of existing capital from the onslaught of new
technologies. In the authors' words, "under monopoly capitalism there
is no necessary correlation, as there is in a competitive economy, between the rate of technological progress and the volume of investment
outlets. Technological progress tends to determine the *form* which
investment takes at any given time rather than its amount." My only
quarrel with this analysis is that changes in technology induced by
changes in relative input prices receive no mention (in fact, there is
nowhere in the book a satisfactory discussion of pricing in input markets). Apparently the authors fail to consider this special type of *endogenous* investment important, although I do not think it can safely be
neglected in an epoch in which many of the giants are in a position to
order their inventions in much the same way that firms have always
been able to order new plant layouts and other organizational changes.

2. OFFSETS TO THE SURPLUS

In the world of Marx's *Capital,* the fundamental economic problem
is the falling rate of profit and hence the lack of capital to sustain
economic growth. In Baran and Sweezy's *Monopoly Capital,* the problem is a surplus of capital (savings) without profitable outlets. A clear
recognition of this proposition sets the stage for a discussion of possible
offsets to the surplus. Second only to military expenditures as a means
of utilizing the surplus, the "sales effort" includes ". . . advertising,
variation of the products' appearance and packaging, planned obsolescence, model changes, credit schemes, and the like."

For some time the mainstream of economic orthodoxy has acknowledged that the chief purpose of advertising is to manipulate consumer
demand, rather than convey objective product information. Baran and
Sweezy contend, however, that the influence of advertising extends
well beyond merely changing the pattern of demand. Its real impact is
on the level of demand. First, advertising expenditures are "self-
absorbing" in the sense that they provide their own outlets. A convenient way to analyze the expansionary, self-absorbing character of advertising is to interpret advertising as a tax placed on the consumer in
the form of higher product prices. The tax lowers consumer income,
but spending is not reduced proportionally since some of the tax is

financed out of savings. Thus advertising outlays reduce spending by an amount less than the outlays themselves. Second, by synthesizing new wants, advertising creates new industries and hence investment opportunities. Third, the increasing importance of the sales effort has created a new social stratum which controls a large volume of "discretionary spending." The authors miss the chance to bring out the automanipulative character of this group, whose members are at one and the same time the fashion leaders and style setters, and the account executives and copywriters. For the sales effort to succeed requires first and foremost that this stratum wage an "unrelenting war" on their *own* savings.

Probably the most significant, and least understood, aspect of the sales effort is the interpenetration of selling expenses and production costs. The authors consider this to be one of the most important phenomena of monopoly capitalism—a phenomenon which is either ignored or misunderstood by orthodox economics, but which is given great importance by the corporations themselves. We are shown evidence, for example, that General Electric views itself more as a marketing enterprise than a production company. Products are constantly redesigned yet serve the same function as the products which are replaced, hence the sales effort, which was previously a mere adjunct of production, increasingly "invades factory and shop." The significance of the fact that product design is determined by marketing strategies based on regular or frequent style changes lies in the "planned obsolescence" of commodities. In this way, the sales effort generates a high level of replacement demand, raising the level of aggregate demand still higher. It is too bad that the authors failed to state explicitly that product life must be constantly reduced if replacement demand is to be expected to absorb an increasing portion of the surplus. One fundamental limit on the ability of the sales effort to expand demand lies in the physical impossibility of reducing the useful life of most commodities below certain fixed levels.

A far more significant limit on the expansionary effects of sales outlays has escaped the authors altogether. Although they show conclusively that advertising expenditures have the *effect* of raising aggregate demand, they fail to make clear that the *intentions* of most advertisers are confined to increasing their share of the market. Once a certain level of advertising expenditures has been reached (which will vary from firm to firm and industry to industry), the extra cost of advertising will exceed the marginal returns. The advertising budget is then frozen, or actually cut back (Anheuser-Busch, for example, in 1966 reduced outlays for advertising by 25 percent and is presently contemplating another 25 percent cut), thus *indirectly* lowering the level of aggregate demand.

In two subsequent chapters, "Civilian Government" and "Militarism and Imperialism," the authors next analyze the process of surplus creation and absorption by the government. Like the sales effort, state spending, it is contended, does not redistribute the surplus (with the exception of those rare periods of full employment) but rather creates surplus. By raising the level of aggregate demand, government policies increase the private and public surplus simultaneously. Below we discuss in what sense state spending can be considered as surplus and in what sense it cannot. It will suffice to say for the present that the authors rest their case mainly on the undisputed fact that corporate profits after taxes normally reach their greatest level during periods of high and growing government spending. They fail to mention, however, the possibility that sales expenditures and government spending ordinarily move in opposite directions; that war-induced government spending and conditions of high demand may reduce the burden on the sales industry. As a general point, the reader will search in vain for an analysis of the interrelationships between the different modes of surplus utilization. This shortcoming obviously weakens the authors' conclusions regarding the limits on the various ways of absorbing surplus.

A standard Marxist analysis is applied to civilian government expenditures. Dominant ideological and material private interests effectively bar the way to massive state programs designed to meet pressing human needs. Government expenditures in relation to Gross National Product show a strong secular rise, but this trend is basically due to a rise in military expenditures and transfer payments. Even a large part of the latter represents debt interest arising from deficit financing of past wars. At the close of a good, commonsense discussion of why capitalists and workers alike support (or at least do not oppose) arms spending, the authors contend that the future expansionary impact of military expenditures is likely to be small. The basic reasons are the labor-saving nature of modern military technology and the self-limitation of the nuclear arms race. The authors recognize that it would be foolish to make any hard-and-fast predictions in this area, but it would seem that they underestimate U.S. military needs, and hence possible offsets, in the struggle against national liberation movements. Furthermore, there is hardly a word about space expenditures as a mode of surplus utilization.

3. *CRITIQUE OF* MONOPOLY CAPITAL

Our critique of the theoretical aspects of *Monopoly Capital* can be conveniently organized around three subjects: the meaning of "economic surplus"; the meaning of the concepts of "firm" and "industry"; and the relation between base and superstructure in a regime of monopoly capitalism.

The first question which we raise is the sense (or senses) in which the authors' concept of "economic surplus" can be considered a surplus. It is obviously of prime importance to have a clear notion of what the surplus is since one central thesis of *Monopoly Capital* is that it tends to rise over time.

The economic surplus is defined as "the difference between what a society produces and the costs of producing it." Nowhere is there an attempt to explicitly develop a theory of costs; the use of the modifier, "socially necessary costs," merely begs the question. According to the authors, the world of monopoly capitalism, and hence stagnation and unemployment, invalidates the labor theory of value since surplus can be created by the expenditure of surplus. What, then, is the relationship between "costs" and "surplus"?

First, consider the surplus as something that can be appropriated under capitalism without affecting total output. Clearly, in this sense nothing is surplus since "surplus that is not utilized is not produced." Second, consider surplus as expenditures which can be reallocated for alternative bundles of goods and services without affecting total output. In this sense of the word, the surplus is pure surplus and in no way a cost. The authors imply that under capitalism (as well as socialism) total product and the mode of surplus utilization are independent, but some of the expenditures which they include in the surplus clearly cannot be legitimately treated as such. To take an extreme hypothetical example, if all government expenditures were redistributed to capitalist consumption, not only would the composition of the surplus change, but also its volume. Capitalists would have to lay out certain essential expenditures (police services, for example) from their own pockets, thus raising the level of total demand and the surplus itself.

More realistically, the authors assert that the surplus absorbed by government spending would not have been produced had the government not absorbed it. The contention that all government spending is a pure offset obviously strengthens the authors' law of rising surplus and tendency toward stagnation. The contention rests on the implied assumption that public expenditures do not complement private spending—an unusual assumption for Marxists to make, and one which is contradicted by the authors' own description of civilian and military government spending. If the main seats of state power are occupied by the corporate oligarchy, then state spending must serve ruling class interests. Thus, in the absence of government financial programs, the corporations themselves would be compelled to maintain utilities, transportation facilities, the health of the work force, and so on. The authors are correct to argue that state spending does not reduce the private surplus, but it is wrong to conclude from this that a large-scale decline in public spending would lead to a comparable decline in *total* spending, employment, and capacity utilization.

There is another important sense in which the total product and the modes of surplus utilization are not independent of one another. Marx himself stressed the subjective and historical nature of the "subsistence wage" and hence socially necessary costs. It may not be stretching the point too much to argue that some outlays on style and model changes are needed to maintain what can be conveniently called the "psychological minimum" of the work force and thus should be figured into "socially necessary costs." More concretely, in the absence of frequent changes in the appearance of commodities, workers would probably choose to take out a larger share of their real income in the form of leisure. If this line of analysis is at all correct, there is another reason for believing the law of rising surplus to be somewhat weaker than the authors suppose.

4. "FIRM" AND "INDUSTRY"

The second set of theoretical problems in *Monopoly Capital* arises from Baran and Sweezy's use of the concepts of "firm" and "industry." It will be recalled that the authors deduce the law of rising surplus from the specific relations between large corporate firms *within* a given industry. The absence of a satisfactory analysis of *inter*industry relations raises a number of problems which we can do no more than mention here.

First, we are told that the policy of maximizing industry profits is the logical result of the live-and-let-live attitude of the corporate giants. The authors, however, define "industry" quite narrowly. There is an implicit assumption that the cross-elasticity of demand between, say, steel and aluminum is low, although in many industrial and final uses these commodities are competitive. Since harmonious price policies *between* the steel and aluminium "industries" are still in an incipient stage, the law of rising surplus is correspondingly weakened.

There is a second sense in which Baran and Sweezy's definition of "industry" bears importantly on the law of rising surplus. Taking the extreme case (thus borrowing a leaf from the authors' book), General Motors has utilized much of its surplus to snap up small and medium-sized firms and presently operates in nearly 150 different "industries." Small businessmen are often paid in General Motors stock, and in this way corporate generated investment-seeking surplus is channeled into capitalist consumption. It would seem reasonable to believe that the increasing concentration and centralization of capital will indirectly provide some outlets for the surplus for an indefinite period.

Finally, we believe the authors' separation of price and quality changes to be somewhat artificial. From a strictly analytical point of view, an improvement in product quality may serve as a substitute for a reduction in price, and thus represent a hidden form of price competition. To be sure, in many consumer durable industries quality tends to progressively deteriorate under the impact of the sales effort, although in consumer nondurable sectors (tobacco products, for example) there is some reason to believe that quality has improved. Thus, costs are increased and both the total surplus and the investment-seeking part of the surplus are correspondingly reduced.

5. BASE AND SUPERSTRUCTURE

These problems fade into insignificance compared with the difficulty arising from the authors' conception of base and superstructure (more specifically, the corporation-state relationship) in a regime of monopoly capitalism. The law of rising surplus and the tendency toward stagnation are based on the contention that "overall, monopoly capitalism is as unplanned as its competitive predecessor." In turn, this contention is rooted in the observation that even the largest of the corporate giants accounts for only a small share of the economy's total output.

It will be recalled that in their discussion of intraindustry relations Baran and Sweezy demonstrate that the degree of concentration (as measured, say, by the proportion of total value added accounted for by the three or four largest firms) is a poor measure of the degree of monopoly control and industry-wide planning. Few industries are more concentrated today than at the turn of the century, but in the great majority of key industries there is a good deal more monopoly control. We believe that similar reasoning can be applied to *inter*industry relations. From a strictly quantitative point of view, each corporate activity within any given industry is merely a tiny speck on the economic landscape. But increasing integration and diversification extend the power of the corporate center to a wide range of industries. What is more, there is more interindustry planning between independent corporations than in the past. We believe that this is a highly significant tendency which deserves careful and intensive future study, even though it does not as yet include cost and price planning.

We offer the following reasons for raising the possibility that the "laws of motion" of monopoly capitalism (the law of rising surplus and the tendency toward stagnation) may soon undergo considerable modification. First, General Motors (admittedly the extreme case) is big and diversified enough at present to consider the effects of its investment and other decisions on the economy as a whole. According to Mr. Sloan, one of the motivations of GM's billion-dollar expansion program in the 1950s was precisely to raise the level of aggregate demand. The giants continue to buy up small and medium-sized firms at a very rapid rate, and it is likely that the biggest corporations will account for an increasing share of total output. Even in the event that productive assets remain in the hands of nominally independent owners (automobile dealerships, for example), the giant corporations indirectly control their investment policies.

For another thing, independent corporations located in different industries presently formulate common investment policies at the municipal and regional levels. Sometimes municipal and regional planning is initiated by the corporations themselves (as in the case of many aspects of "urban renewal"), but often the initiative springs from the local, state, and regional development agencies and the giant independent public authorities. Admittedly, interindustry planning does not directly penetrate the process of commodity production itself, but in the case of automobiles and other transport equipment, cultural and recreational services, and other commodities, there is a very thin line between investment planning for commodity production and investment planning for complementary infrastructure.

There is, after all, some reason to believe that the corporations are becoming increasingly aware of the "surplus disposal problem" and objectively are in a position to do something about it. If local real estate interests are opposed to large-scale public housing programs, it is because they are not politically powerful enough to compel the state to make such a program profitable. When and if the corporate oligarchy (specifically, the large-scale banking sector) comes to dominate the local real estate interests, then this will no longer be true. It seems to us that if the corporate oligarchy and its political allies can dictate the political and social content of fiscal policy and lay down the main lines of foreign policy, if the corporate ideology finds increasing expression in the mass media, and if the small business interests which dominate the Congress are increasingly undermined by the growth of the corporate-dominated executive branch, then it is difficult to understand why big business will refrain indefinitely from creating an economy-wide investment planning machinery.

These considerations perhaps do not weaken the thesis of the *tendency* toward stagnation so much as the notion that the tendency will increasingly become *fact*. Perhaps the United States—as the authors admit may be true for some "second-echelon" capitalist countries—will soon arrive at a "stage of neocapitalism" characterized by the adoption of national planning. Certainly the authors somewhat uncritically equate the economic size and strength of a country and the advanced character of its monopolistic institutions. The question still to be resolved is, Does the United States show Gaullist France the future, or is it the other way around? Or will the future hold a synthesis of both?

CHAPTER FOUR
Fitch and Oppenheimer's Theory of Finance Capital

1. INTRODUCTION

"The larger corporations [have] gradually won more and more independence from both bankers and dominant stockholders," Baran and Sweezy write in *Monopoly Capital,* "and their policies accordingly [have been] geared to an ever greater extent each to its own interests rather than being subordinated to the interests of a group." The authors of *Monopoly Capital* do not go so far as to claim that interest groups have disappeared. But they "do hold that they are of rapidly diminishing importance and that an appropriate model of the economy no longer needs to take account of them." In brief, Baran and Sweezy are the main protagonists of the thesis that corporate capital has replaced finance capital as the dominant form of capital, to the degree that "finance capital" means bank control of industry, or the dependence of industry on bank capital.

Some Marxist economists in the United States and Great Britain, most notably Victor Perlo *(The Empire of High Finance)* and Sam Aarnovich *(The Ruling Class),* continue to argue the classic "Leninist" position. There is a good deal of evidence in support of their view that industrial corporations are not that financially independent from the banks, especially in recent years. Surveying available data on the external obligations of nonfinancial corporations, Lintner "is impressed by the rather extraordinary stability in the broad patterns of financing used."[1] During the first decade following World War II, nonfinancial corporate debt in relation to total assets grew more or less steadily from 29 percent in 1945 to 41 percent in 1955. Of greater potential significance, institutional investors hold an increasing proportion of corporate stocks and bonds. Mutual funds, pension funds, and insurance companies (all with some degree of commercial bank involvement) together account for over one-third of the value of all listed stocks on the New

1. John Lintner, "The Financing of Corporations," in Edward S. Mason, ed., *The Corporation in Modern Society* (New York, 1966), p. 177.

York Stock Exchange. In 1970 pension funds held $40 billion in corporate stocks and another $25 billion in bonds. Mutual funds controlled about $53 billion in stock. But the largest block of corporate stock, more than $600 billion in equities, was controlled by bank-managed trust departments.[2]

The problem is that these trends do not tell us very much about the actual locus and, more important, function of *control* of the large corporations. As Baran and Sweezy argue, the behavior of the top managers of the giant manufacturing companies is structurally determined and depends on the specific market position of the oligopolistic firm. An extension of this argument is that even if "outsiders" succeeded in establishing control, production, pricing, investment, and other major decisions would not change radically. Yet there have been few empirical studies of corporate decision making and no systematic theoretical investigations of the behavior of "corporate capitalists"—men who are neither bankers, merchants, nor industrialists alone, but who must combine and synthesize the roles of all three. As one bourgeois economist has recently written, "Quite clearly, the financial policies of the industrial enterprises should be meshed with their industrial behavior, but exactly how remains an open question."[3]

One Marxist approach to this question has been suggested by Maurice Dobb. "Is not the essence of Lenin's notion," he writes, "the increasing dominance of financial *influences and motivation* over industry; which may, surely, come about by large industrial combines converting themselves, or spawning off, virtual financial companies as much as by the 'classic' German method of investment bankers financing industry and holding a controlling interest in it?"[4] Dobb apparently refers to the tendency of some large industrial corporations, alone or in combination, to set up financial companies which specialize in consumer credit, home mortgages, overseas loans and investments, and so on. The increasing number of interlocks (and in some cases the outright control of commercial banks by industrial corporations) also testifies to the growing interpenetration of industry and finance.

It does not necessarily follow, however, that industrial companies

2. Richard Barber, *The American Corporation: Its Power, Its Money, and Its Politics* (London, 1970), p. 56. Barber claims that the 49 largest banks, as primary lenders and trustees, have enough stock to "control" 150 of the largest 500 nonfinancial corporations. He also asserts that these banks have representatives on the boards of directors of 300 of these corporations.

3. Edwin Kuh, *Capital Stock Growth: A Micro-Econometric Approach* (Amsterdam, 1971), p. 16.

4. Maurice Dobb, "Some Problems Under Discussion," *Marxism Today,* March 1967, p. 88, emphasis added.

are increasingly dominated by "financial influences and motivations." In the late nineteenth and early twentieth centuries, the major activity of bank capital was the promotion of new industry and the merger of existing industry with the aim of inflating the value of new and outstanding stock in order to reap huge, quick profits. Bank capital was largely speculative in character, and depended heavily on "insider information" to maximize the turnover of money capital. Today, however, "the picture of a few finance capitalists manipulating stock, acquiring huge, overnight profits, and frantically putting together and taking apart industrial empires with an eye to immediate financial gain is simply not consistent with what is known about managerial decision-making in the vast majority of large corporations."[5]

The latest attempt by American authors to argue the finance capital thesis is "Who Rules the Corporations?" by Robert Fitch and Mary Oppenheimer.[6] This account of the relationship between financial and nonfinancial institutions in modern America is useful for two reasons: first, because it makes available a great deal of information previously accessible only to those willing and able to plow through recent staff reports of various congressional committees; second, the authors raise a number of questions about the economic significance of the relationship between banks and other financial institutions and industrial corporations—questions that are slighted or ignored in most recent Marxist economic works. I will not try to review their entire account or take up every problem that they raise, but rather consider the following three general issues that might be of some importance for the American left: Who controls the major American industrial and other nonfinancial corporations? What are the goals of those who control the corporations? What is the significance of control for investment, production, prices, and so on in any particular industry?

2. WHO CONTROLS THE CORPORATIONS?

The materials that the authors have assembled show that there exists an enormously complex set of interlocks within and between financial institutions and nonfinancial corporations. Their findings that financial

5. James O'Connor, "Finance Capital or Corporate Capital?" *Monthly Review* 20, no. 7 (December 1968): 32.

6. Robert Fitch and Mary Oppenheimer, "Who Rules the Corporations?" *Socialist Revolution* 1, nos. 4, 1 6 (July–August, September–October, November–December 1970). There are three parts to this article, references to which appear in the text hereafter in the form, for example, I:75, meaning part one, page 75.

institutions control an increasing share of the national wealth and that nonfinancial corporations increasingly rely on external sources of credit are indisputable. And their conclusion that "financial institutions control stock in non-financial corporations, sit on their boards, finance their activity, and take an active part in corporate affairs" (II:97) is convincing. But what their account fails to make clear is the actual locus of control of the great industrial corporations.

A good place to begin is to discuss the ways that Fitch and Oppenheimer use traditional Marxist theoretical categories. On the one hand, the authors refer to "bank control of corporations" and "bank influence over corporations" (I:76, 100). In the Marxist literature, bank capital is defined as "capital invested in establishments which engage mainly in giving loans in the money form."[7] Thus, when the authors write that "banks control the corporations" it is reasonable to assume that they mean that the owners of bank capital control the corporations.

On the other hand, Fitch and Oppenheimer make a number of references to "finance capital" and "controlling financial groups." We are told that the "giant corporations [are] dominated by finance capital" and that the "social surplus . . . is controlled by the great financial institutions" (I:80; III:44; II:114, 77). The problem immediately arises that bank capital and finance capital have very different meanings: bank capital is owned by moneylenders who are *rentiers* pure and simple, while finance capital is owned by individuals who "are not merely rentier [s] but the head[s] of gigantic industrial-banking complexes."[8] Let us get around this problem by assuming that the authors mean "finance capital control" when they say "bank control": certainly, this assumption is consistent with their empirical studies which show the complex and interdependent nature of the relationships between financial and nonfinancial institutions.

Elsewhere in their work, Fitch and Oppenheimer write that "the very large corporation is almost always dominated by outsiders" (I:83). Presumably, these "outsiders" are the owners of finance capital, or at least their representatives. In still another place, we read that "the banks . . . represent—in relation to industry—the real owners of capital" (II:94). In this passage, unless "represent" is used to mean "own," the authors seem to be saying that the banks are merely the representatives of the "real owners"—that is, that the banks do not stand in an independent relation to industry. On the other hand, nowhere in their

---

7. S. Menshikov, *Millionaires and Managers* (Moscow, 1969), p. 140. This book is an excellent empirical study of the financial and economic network of the American ruling class.

8. Ibid. p. 15.

article do Fitch and Oppenheimer concede that the banks are also dominated by "outsiders." Nevertheless, they do acknowledge that the "great capitalist families" have "merged industrial into financial capital through the trust department mechanism" and that "finance capital involves a merger of industrial and financial capital" (I:95; II:97). Putting all of these passages together, it would seem reasonable to conclude that Fitch and Oppenheimer believe that "great capitalist families" are the "real owners" of *both* banks and industrial corporations. Put another way, the authors seem to believe that the American ruling class is composed primarily of finance or monopoly capitalists ("the heads of gigantic industrial-banking complexes"), not industrial capitalists on the one hand and bank capitalists ("merely rentiers") on the other. I am in full accord with this view.

I want to cite one or two final examples of the authors' confusing economic vocabulary. In a discussion of the rapid increase in external corporate debt during the past few years, Fitch and Oppenheimer write that "the suppliers of external finance—especially commercial and investment bankers—see the opportunity to create and profit from a speculative boom by financing takeovers" (II:82). To be consistent with the thesis that the "great capitalist families" have "merged industrial and financial capital," we would have to rewrite this passage and substitute "commercial and investment banks" for "commercial and investment bankers" because finance capitalists cannot be described as "bankers" any more than they can be called "industrialists."[9]

9. If Fitch and Oppenheimer fail to supply a clear answer to the question, Who rules the corporations? (as we have seen, at times they seem to say that bankers control industrial capital and at other times that finance capitalists control industry), they do succeed in explaining who *doesn't* control industrial corporations. In fact, they go to great lengths to dispute the managerial revolution thesis. Despite the fact that I am inaccurately described as a "Marxist managerialist," I wish to make only one or two comments on this subject (the *Monthly Review* article that Fitch and Oppenheimer cite was speculative in nature and designed more to raise questions than provide hard answers—but far from accepting the managerial revolution thesis, I refer to the " 'corporate capitalist' who necessarily combines and synthesizes the motives of the merchant, industrialist and banker"). The reason is that I believe that Fitch and Oppenheimer are attacking a straw man. To my knowledge, there are no Marxist economists who seriously believe that managers of industry have wrested control from the large owners and exercise that control (for more than a short time, anyway) in their own special interests. Although Paul Sweezy can defend *Monopoly Capital* far better than I can, I cannot help remarking that I think it is a pity that in their rush to "prove" some new "thesis" Fitch and Oppenheimer have to lump Baran and Sweezy's seminal work with the stupid and apologetic doctrines of the bourgeois managerial revolution theorists. The heart of *Monopoly Capital* is the theory of the generation and absorption of the "economic surplus." Nowhere do Fitch and Oppenheimer even begin to come to grips with this theory. Moreover, the authors claim that Baran and Sweezy "accept the factual premises of simplistic managerialism" (I:86)—by which they mean the idea that there is a separation of ownership from management arising from the wide dispersion of stock ownership, and hence an indepen-

At this point, let us leave off our examination of Fitch and Oppenheimer's economics vocabulary and reconsider the precise meaning of the word "capitalist." A capitalist is an individual who owns money capital (money over and above consumption needs) in sufficient quantities to buy labor power plus the requisite raw materials, equipment, fuels, and so on. Labor power is not purchased for any services rendered directly to the capitalist, but in order to produce tangible or intangible objects for sale in the market. The capitalist makes a profit if the exchange value of labor power (wages) is less than the exchange value of the product of labor power (commodity prices). In terms of the labor time expended in production in relation to the labor time that the capitalist can command as a result of the sale of the commodity, this is called surplus value. In terms of money itself, it is called profit. Capitalists thus depend for their material survival on their ability *(a)* to organize production in such a way that surplus value can be *produced* and *realized,* and *(b)* to organize the financing of production in such a way that they can *appropriate* the surplus value for themselves. For example, if an industrial capitalist organizes the production and realization of surplus value in some particular branch of the economy, but if all of the surplus value (in its money form, profits) is owed to a bank capitalist, then it is the banker who appropriates the surplus value, not the industrialist. In the event that the industrial capitalist is unable to win financial freedom from the banker, sooner or later he will be reduced to the status of hired manager. In this process, the bank capitalist is at first exclusively preoccupied with the problem of appropriating surplus value (that is, the problem of finance). At a certain point, however, the industry's loan/asset ratio reaches a high level and the bank capitalist must concern himself more and more with the problem of producing and realizing surplus value (that is, the problem of production and sales). At this point, the owner of the bank ceases to be a bank capitalist ("merely a rentier") and transforms himself into a finance capitalist ("head of an industrial-banking complex").

Workers produce surplus value in two ways: Marx called these absolute surplus value and relative surplus value. Surplus value that is produced by forcing workers to work harder or longer at the same wage rate is called absolute surplus value. It is obvious that a capitalist

dent managerial class that functions more or less autonomously. Without going into the pros and cons of Baran and Sweezy's own thesis, I would like to recall that these authors write of "the *combined* power of management and the *very rich:* the *two* are in fact *integrated* into a harmonious *interest group* at the top of the economic pyramid" (*Monopoly Capital* [New York, 1966], p. 37, emphasis added). This is hardly the "factual premise of simplistic managerialism."

cannot accumulate great wealth by appropriating absolute surplus alone. A speedup or stretch-out enriches a capitalist only to the degree that the capitalist can sweat a few extra minutes of labor power out of the workers. Surplus value that is produced by equipping workers with more and better tools or by exploiting their scientific, technical, and administrative know-how in production is called relative surplus value. The great capitalist wealth today (and the great wealth of advanced capitalist societies as a whole) has its roots in relative surplus value.[10]

Let us consider next the ways in which surplus value is *appropriated*. As Fitch and Oppenheimer write, the ruling class draws its income not from industrial profits per se, but rather from the financial claims on industrial profits (III:43). The major financial instruments are bonds and stocks—these represent the chief claims on surplus value in the money form. Owners of stocks and bonds appropriate surplus value *directly*—that is, they acquire unpaid labor power directly from the workers in the form of profits. The question arises, Who owns the stocks and bonds? In the family-owned, family-managed company the answer to this question is in principle simple. The individuals who organize the production and realization of surplus value are precisely the same individuals who own the financial claims on surplus value. Today, however, as Fitch and Oppenheimer demonstrate, financial claims on surplus value are owned not only by wealthy capitalists in their own name. These claims are also owned and/or controlled by owners of commercial banks holding corporate bonds and stocks (the latter in their trust departments), investment banks, insurance companies, mutual and pension funds, and other financial institutions.

Finally, the question arises, If the financial claims on surplus value

10. Although this formulation is sufficient for our immediate purposes, a number of other factors have to be taken into account in a full analysis of the contemporary capitalist class. For one thing, the production of relative surplus value and the development of monopoly production go hand in hand. Thus, profits are made up not only of relative surplus value in the money form but also of monopoly profit per se. To my knowledge, there is no way of statistically breaking down capitalist income into these two components. Secondly, the contemporary ruling class bases itself in part on the production of absolute surplus value at home and abroad (for example, sweatshops in the competitive sector of the home economy controlled by monopoly capital, on the one hand, and branch plants of the giant corporation located in foreign "cheap labor havens," on the other). Again, I do not think that there is any way to separate empirically capitalist income drawn from relative surplus value, from income drawn from absolute surplus value. Finally, capitalists organize the production of both absolute and relative surplus value *simultaneously*. For example, if worker productivity is measured by an index of 100, and if a worker is forced to increase the intensity of his work by 10 percent, surplus value increases by 10. If his productivity is an index of 1,000, surplus value increases by 100. The point is, however, that in the long run there are definite limits to the production of absolute surplus value, as the monopoly capitalist class and capitalist governments have realized for many decades.

in the typical industrial corporation are no longer owned by the industrial capitalist per se, who does own these claims? That is, Who owns and/or controls the financial institutions? At the turn of the century, most major industrial corporations were closely held by the financial giants of the day. The industrial corporation was a relatively new device and there was little or no widespread ownership of stock. John Moody in his classic study of the "masters of capital" estimated that the Rockefeller and Morgan groups shared ownership and control of corporate empires in excess of $20 billion, or about one-fifth of the national wealth at that time. Today, as we suggested above, these same groups of capitalists, together with a number of others, exercise control of the financial institutions. This is demonstrated beyond all shadow of a doubt by Menshikov.[11] Industrialists have become "bankers" in order to mobilize capital from the population as a whole and in order to insure that they participate fully in the appropriation of surplus value. And bankers have become "industrialists" because they realize that in the long run their financial claims are worthless unless surplus value is produced and realized in industry on a continuous basis. By and large, the same people organize or supervise the production and realization of surplus value and the appropriation of surplus value. Although financial and nonfinancial companies are formally separate, the American ruling class does not consist of "bankers" on the one hand and "industrialists" on the other. Rather, the dominant stratum of this class is made up of rich capitalists who own and/or control both kinds of institutions. This class puts a large share of its stockholdings in trust, and the managers of their banks represent these holdings in their role of fiduciaries. In turn, their industrial corporate managers deposit corporate funds in the same banks (Fitch and Oppenheimer neglect to point out that about 70 percent of total demand deposits consist of roughly a hundred thousand corporate accounts amounting to over $100,000 each). To insure that their operating companies have access to sufficient money capital, most large corporations are given preferential positions in the "capital market." To insure that the broad experience of top bank managers is available to their operating companies (and to try to insure against "inside" managers feathering their own nests at the expense of financial capitalists), these managers serve as directors of nonfinancial corporations. And to insure maximum coordination between industry and banking, the presidents and chairmen of the boards of directors of the industrial companies serve as directors of the big banks. Finally, to insure that competition between financial institutions does not get out

11. Menshikov, *Millionaires and Managers*, chap. 6.

of hand, these institutions "do not operate independently, but rather are intricately interwoven in a web of de facto economic alliances."[12] The production and realization of surplus value require that industrial companies are run efficiently and profitably; but the appropriation of surplus value requires that bank representatives stand at the beginning and the end of the classic process—M-C-M'.

3. THE GOALS OF MONOPOLY CAPITALISTS

What goals will financial institutions holding financial claims on surplus value in the form of stocks and bonds adopt? In principle this question has a clear-cut answer in the event that there are two groups of people, one holding corporate debt and the other holding corporate equities. For the group or institution holding equities, interest charges on loans (both working capital loans and bonds) add to costs. For the group holding corporate debt, interest charges add to income or revenues. It is obvious that the level of interest rates is a source of potential or real conflict between the two groups (just as interest rates divided the old-fashioned banker and industrialist years ago and continue to divide the small businessman and finance capitalist today). More, conflicts that reach well beyond the question of interest charges can arise (and have arisen) between debt holders and equity holders. For example, decades ago American bankers were preoccupied with the financial side of overseas economic expansion and actively sought the cooperation of other capitalist powers with the aim of expanding world trade as a whole. On the other hand, independent industrialists were interested mainly in expanding their own exports, not world trade.

Today, most conflict between financial and nonfinancial companies is confined to those sectors of the economy that are poorly integrated into the dominant monopoly capitalist empires. The integration of industrial and bank capital in most large-scale industry has muted or eliminated conflicts arising from interest charges. This special kind of vertical integration also has helped to create a more or less uniform view within the ruling class as a whole over the questions of foreign trade and investment, tariff policy, and related matters. In short, the fact that every monopoly capitalist group and most of their financial institutions hold or control *both* corporate equities and debt instruments means that the "conflict" between "bankers" and "entrepreneurs" (or industrial capitalists) that dominates Fitch and Oppenheimer's world

12. Barber, *The American Corporation*, p. 62.

64   THE CORPORATIONS AND THE STATE

view is largely a figment of their imagination.[13]

What then are the motives of the monopoly capitalists or finance capitalists? What goals do they seek? How do they harmonize their short-term and long-term aims? How and why do they decide to appropriate surplus value in the particular ways that they do? What kind of trade offs are they faced with? As these questions suggest, and as Fitch and Oppenheimer recognize (III:46), the issue is enormously complex. Moreover, there is very little analysis of the subject in either the bourgeois or Marxist economic literature.

Unfortunately, Fitch and Oppenheimer's own thoughts on the subject are not very enlightening. They begin with the claim that "just as production and sales are no longer ends in themselves, neither are industrial profits—at least for the stratum of the bourgeoisie that controls the giant corporation" (III:46). But in no stage of capitalist development were "production and sales . . . ends in themselves." They have always been the means to the end of profits. The authors continue to say that "the key point . . . is that the pursuit of financial profits can be partially dissociated from the pursuit of industrial profit. Dividends, for example, can be increased without a proportionate increase in industrial profits—even, perhaps, at the expense of future industrial profitability." There is no question that dividends "can be increased" without an increase in industrial profits, but the authors do not tell us why or under what conditions finance capitalists will in fact increase dividends. More so-called examples of the dissociation of financial and industrial profits follow: "Or the board of directors dominated by bondholders may decide upon a profit strategy designed chiefly to maximize the security of their bondholdings. Or such a board may decide that even though equity financing (common stock) is cheaper and will increase industrial profits more substantially, the corporation should pay for its expansion program by increasing its indebtedness to the interested

13. For example, see II:85. The authors cite the split in the Republican party as evidence of the "conflict" between "bankers" and "industrialists." They write that the split "pits the Eastern financial establishment led by the Rockefeller-Lodge-Scranton axis against their regional and entrepreneurial capitalist enemies like California's Henry Salvatori, South Carolina's Milliken family, and the scores of Texas and California oil millionaires without sizable foreign holdings" (II:95–96). Although there is always some conflict between the main body of financial capitalists and new upstarts, Menshikov writes that "analysis of forty-nine of the new fortunes shows that only seven have served as a basis for creating new independent financial groups [and that] the prevailing tendency is the readiness of the new plutocracy to join the existing system of the financial oligarchy" (p. 68). In my view, the split is explicable mainly in terms of the conflicts between capitalists whose wealth depends mainly on the appropriation of surplus value *directly* (e.g., Rockefeller) and capitalists who appropriate surplus value *indirectly* via the state budget (see above, pp. 39–42).

bankers. Or the directors may decide to guide the corporation into an 'unprofitable' sales agreement with another corporation because the directors have a financial interest in the other corporation" (III:46).

Let us consider these three points in the order presented by the authors. In the first place, as Gabriel Kolko and other historians have shown, stability, predictability, and security always have figured importantly in corporate decision making in America. And in economic theory, the standard "textbook entrepreneur" devotes considerable attention to the problem of minimizing risk and uncertainty. Clearly, if bondholders seek maximum security for their bondholdings, they will avoid any policy that might impair "future industrial profitability." On the contrary, they will strive for maximum security of *industrial* profits. Fitch and Oppenheimer's second example is not an example of *finance* capitalist control of industrial corporations, but rather of *bank* capitalist control. If bankers controlled the black pieces on the chessboard of American capitalism, and industrialists controlled the white pieces, under certain circumstances bankers might drive a corporation into increasing indebtedness "even though equity financing is cheaper." But, as we have seen, finance capitalists control both the black and white pieces. Finally, there is no question that directors who have financial interests in more than one corporation may "guide [one] corporation into an 'unprofitable' sales agreement with another corporation." In principle, this is hardly a novel situation: in every large corporation, the directors at one time or another "guide" one *branch* of the corporation into " 'unprofitable' " agreements with other branches. But this does not prove that the directors are not interested in industrial profits. The example merely suggests that finance capitalists are less interested in industrial profits in any particular corporation making up part of their empire than in industrial profits in the empire as a whole.

I do not claim to have a final answer to the question of the goals of the monopoly capitalists. The remarks that follow are thus meant to be suggestive, not definitive. In the first place, it is clear that as money-lenders and bondholders, finance capitalists favor high interest rates. It is equally clear that as stockholders in industrial firms, finance capitalists must be devoted to maximum productivity consistent with maximum industrial profits. Further, as "industrialists" capitalists favor low interest rates—everything else being equal—because interest charges are a cost item. I believe that a case can be made that their industrial interests normally take precedence over their banking interests. As "industrial capitalists" they seek to organize the production and realization of maximum surplus value; as "bankers" they seek to appropriate as much surplus value as possible. But surplus value that is not produced cannot be appropriated.[14] Thus, although at first glance it appears that finance capitalists have conflicting interests, in fact they do not.

Next, let us return to the original distinction between absolute and relative surplus value. A century ago absolute surplus value was a relatively more important source of profit than it is today. When capital was predominantly in the form of unskilled labor power and primitive machinery, capitalists who organized the production of surplus value depended upon a sweated, low-paid work force.[15] At the time, the idea that high and increasing productivity was the secret of industrial wealth was comparatively novel: the prototype was the American steel industry before Carnegie rationalized the entire work process from beginning to end. In the absolute surplus value "stage" of capitalist development, there was one certain way to become very rich and powerful. The first step was to acquire as many financial claims on surplus value as possible; the second step was to drive up the price of these claims well beyond the actual exchange value of existing plant and equipment. Put another way, getting wealthy meant promoting industrial mergers and acquisitions, watering the stock, speculating in stock, developing the fine points of "insider" trading, and so on. One consequence of all this activity was the frequent neglect of physical plant and equipment, administration and management within the industrial firm, and other productive features of the victimized company. But whether or not productivity was impaired by financial wheelings and dealings was a matter of relative indifference to the early speculator, in part because productivity and the total volume of surplus value were small in absolute terms and in part because the individual speculator had few if any *institutional* or *class* interests.

14. It should be clear at this point that the Fitch-Oppenheimer analysis of the relationship between financial and nonfinancial institutions (and any similar analysis) complements, not substitutes for, Baran and Sweezy's analysis of the industrial economy in *Monopoly Capital.* Baran and Sweezy are concerned with the absorption of the "economic surplus"—in other words, the realization of surplus value. Fitch and Oppenheimer are chiefly concerned with the appropriation of surplus value that already has been produced and realized. To be sure, Baran and Sweezy concentrate their fire on the ways that surplus value is realized (e.g., via the "sales effort"). But Fitch and Oppenheimer are silent on *both* the question of the work process (i.e., surplus value production) and the problem of marketing and sales (i.e., surplus value realization).

15. The American ruling class skillfully synthesizes the two modes of surplus value production. Domestic skilled labor was used to build up a highly productive industrial complex; immigrant labor was used to keep wages low and working conditions poor. The steel industry under Carnegie pushed unit costs so low that one European observer christened the industry "the eighth wonder of the world." The industry was so efficient because Carnegie simultaneously introduced the most modern plant and equipment and the most oppressive kind of labor relations, keeping labor productivity up and wages low.

Today, increases in surplus value are mainly relative. Modern industrial production is highly complex, machinery is very advanced, production techniques are scientific, and labor power is relatively skilled. In contemporary capitalism, not only is it possible to become very rich by organizing the production, realization, and appropriation of relative surplus value (without having to engage in potentially destructive speculation), but also no financial capitalist group in its right mind would engage in any activity that might have ruinous consequences for the productivity of its profitable enterprises. The volume of surplus value is too great and there is too much at stake. I hasten to say that it is still possible to become very wealthy by financial speculation—many if not most of the new oil, savings and loan, real estate, and other millionaires got where they are today by buying and selling real property and financial claims on this property.[16] I also hasten to add that I realize that stock prices have tended to rise considerably faster than the increase in total production (to a large degree because pension funds, mutual funds, insurance companies, and so on, have mobilized masses of working-class savings and channeled these savings into the stock market, driving up prices). My point here is that in the old days stock speculation was the only way to get really rich (putting aside traditional mercantile and real estate activity)—and a man got rich by riding the ups and downs in the stock market, ups and downs created by trading on inside information, watering stock, rumors. Today, most stock trading consists of buying and selling *between* the large financial institutions —a very closed community, as Fitch and Oppenheimer imply throughout their work—institutions that have every reason in the world to keep speculation under control. Precisely because financial claims on surplus value are concentrated in a handful of giant financial institutions, it becomes more and more difficult to unload large amounts of stock at *any* price in a falling market. Thus, for example, during the stock exchange "crisis" of 1962, the mutual funds stayed out of the market and refrained from selling large amounts of stock, which buoyed up the market and helped to prevent a bust.

Fitch and Oppenheimer no doubt would be quick to reject the lines of analysis presented above, not to speak of my criticisms of their own analysis. Even in an epoch when productivity is the key to secure wealth and power, they believe that "finance capital" control is used to milk

16. I agree with Fitch and Oppenheimer when they write that "a final reason for the fantastic increase in external debt is this: the suppliers of external finance . . . see the opportunity to create and profit from a speculative boom by financing take-overs" (II:82). What I disagree with is the authors' claim that "suppliers of external finance" are so preoccupied with speculation that they neglect industrial productivity and profits.

industrial profits—that is, to appropriate industrial profits at the expense of productive capacity and efficiency. In some passages, they express their views as certainties: "Unable to maintain itself profitably in the technologically mature monopoly industries, finance capital destroys them through cannibalization of their assets, disguised as 'diversification' " (II:72). In other passages, they hedge their bets: for example, they refer to corporations with external debt as being "forced into potentially ruinous indebtedness" (III:75). Whatever the degree of certainty with which the authors hold these views, they do try to support them with factual materials drawn from the transportation, communications, electrical power, and other industries. Thus, even though I have tried to explain why I reject most of their theoretical analysis, I still am obliged to consider their evidence and examples.

The authors devote more attention to the Penn Central case than to any other firm or industry. Because it is impossible in a review to explore every important aspect of the relationship between the directors of Penn Central and the New York finance capitalists, I will confine my comments to one crucial question: as Fitch and Oppenheimer show, Penn Central has neglected to modernize its rail facilities and has engaged in a diversification program that itself has turned out to be quite unprofitable. The question is, Did the directors of Penn Central neglect its productive facilities because the railroad could not *afford* a modernization program (that is, because the line was overextended financially as a result of heavy borrowing to finance the diversification program) as Fitch and Oppenheimer claim? Or can the neglect be attributed to the unprofitability of the railroad business *independent of the relationship between Penn Central and the financial institutions,* as I believe? The question is not whether or not the railroad was saddled with a big debt, but rather the underlying causes of the neglect. The first question that must be cleared up is the difference between "economic efficiency" and "technical efficiency." Neglect of physical facilities is not necessarily a sign of economic inefficiency: for example, New England is covered with abandoned textile mills that proved to be unprofitable from an economic point of view, even though they were efficient from an engineering point of view. The owners of the mills abandoned them because labor costs were too high. Similarly, finance capitalists "abandoned" the railroads because labor costs and other operating expenses were too high in comparison with revenues. And to a large degree, the diversification programs of the railroads (and utilities) were the rational response of rational capitalists seeking the highest return on their capital.

At times, Fitch and Oppenheimer come close to recognizing this:

at one place, they write that the Penn Central directors "saw the railroad as a dying man whose vital organs could be transplanted to other,
more promising patients" (II:112). On the other hand, they insist that

> profits haven't fallen because rail transport is outmoded. Passenger trains
> may be empty, but forty-one per cent of all freight and by far the great mass
> of bulk commodities—steel, coal, petroleum—continue to be shipped by
> rail. New forms of transport—trucks and airplanes—have not even begun
> to compete for this vital segment of rail revenues. In fact, total rail revenues,
> as distinct from profits, have increased substantially since 1963. Yet thanks
> to the [diversification program], the railroads are starved for capital.
> [III:51]

This passage contains the sum and substance of Fitch and Oppenheimer's claim that the railroads remain a viable private investment—
if only the banks would stop ripping them off. However, a close examination of their argument reveals that their claim is unfounded. In the
first place, the authors neglect to mention that the volume of rail profits
has gone down not only because interest charges have risen but also
because wage and other operating costs have gone up. Second, they fail
to discuss the relationship between the railroads and the Interstate
Commerce Commission. In 1951 the ICC refused to relieve the railroads from umbrella rate-making practices designed to protect the
traffic of rival carriers. In effect, the ICC told the railroads that they
were forbidden to compete with water and other carriers. The Transportation Act of 1958 granted the railroads a small measure of relief,
and railroad rates subsequently declined. The average cost of shipping
freight by rail fell by about 15 percent. Despite the relief, rail traffic
declined in comparison with water, truck, and air traffic—stabilizing in
1962 at about 43 percent of total ton miles (down from more than 75
percent in 1926). It is an open question whether or not rail traffic would
rise significantly if the ICC permitted the railroads to cut their rates
even more. Third, although Fitch and Oppenheimer claim that "new
forms of transport . . . have not even begun to compete for [the bulk
commodity business]," the fact is that the railroads transport no natural
gas, which to a large degree has replaced coal and other fuels that rails
used to handle. To be sure, the railroads' share of total tonnage over
years has declined less than railroad revenues, precisely because the
railroads retain *low value* bulk commodities. Finally, the *rate* of profit
in railroading (in contrast to the volume of profits) actually *rose* during
most of the 1960s—jumping from 1.97 percent in 1961 to 3 percent
in 1967, chiefly as a result of the rate reductions. Nevertheless, finance
capitalists believed (in most cases, accurately) that higher rates of return
were available elsewhere. Indeed, the unprofitability of railroad invest-

ments explains why the roads have been nationalized in nearly every country in the world—a fact that the authors forgot to include in their account.[17]

Although Fitch and Oppenheimer aim their big guns at the relationship between financial institutions and the utilities and transportation industries (which have had a symbiotic relationship for a long time), they fire a few scattered shots at the ties between banks and manufacturing corporations. One of their main theses is that "Wall Street . . . regulates the rate of capital accumulation throughout the economy, retarding it in the mature industries—telephone, railroads, textiles, steel—and over-accelerating it in the new industries—computer software, electronics, franchise foods" (III:75). Needless to say, this description of the allocation of capital resources is perfectly consistent with the conclusions of accepted economic theory: capital moves from declining to expanding sectors of the economy in search of the highest rate of return, and competition between industrial capitalists or financial groups frequently leads to overinvestment in the expanding sectors. Putting this aside, the reader is surprised to learn that Fitch and Oppenheimer fail to mention even one example of a bank ripping off a manufacturing company at the expense of productive capacity and industrial profits. Early in their article, the authors imply that Chrysler has been so victimized. They write that "conventional corporate critics might counter that the Penn Central is an anomaly—a throwback to a vanished era. . . . Several corporations with assets larger than the Penn Central's have come close to playing out the same drama, with only a few of the lines changed" (I:76). In a footnote, they say, "Chrysler, the nation's sixth largest corporation, with four directors representing Manufacturers Hanover, has gone through a protracted crisis brought on by a profit decline. The various stages of the crisis have been marked by a purge of inside management by outside directors, a liquidity crisis, and a rescue operation led by Manufacturers Hanover." What the authors do not say is that the profit decline was not attributable to bank control but rather to the fact that in

17. In fairness, it should be pointed out that the Bureau of Accounts of the ICC has warned that potential abuses in railroad conglomerate mergers include underinvesting in road maintenance and low capital spending for road facilities. But it should also be pointed out that the ICC is the (poorly managed) cartel of the railroad, water carrier, and interstate trucking industries, and its functionaries speak in the name of their special interests, not in the name of finance capitalists, capitalist economic rationality, or the "public interest."

comparison with GM and Ford, Chrysler has small production runs and thus has been stuck with obsolete production capacity, owing to the Big Two's policy of introducing annual model changes. They also fail to tell the reader that the purge of inside management in 1960 was sparked by management's attempt to enrich itself at the expense of the corporation, thus abusing the trust of the company's monopoly capitalist owners.

In my view, the process of capital accumulation in American industry is far more complicated than Fitch and Oppenheimer allow. The steel industry can serve as an example. There is no question but that when steel passed into the hands of financial men in 1901, the industry ceased to be obsessed with the problem of lowering unit labor costs. However, the main reason was not that the monopoly capitalists were preoccupied with "financial profits" and ceased to take an interest in industrial production and industrial profits, but rather that the era of competition had ended, and U.S. Steel exercised considerable monopoly control in product markets. So long as this monopoly position was secure, finance capitalists under normal conditions could count on a regular flow of industrial profits without being excessively preoccupied with productivity. For more than a decade after World War II, steel passed on wage increases in the form of higher prices without overly troubling itself with modernization. But with the revival of international competition, and with the danger of permanent inflation, steel entered into a vast capital construction and modernization program—with large help from the banks. At present, the steel industry has about $5 billion of outstanding debt (up more than 100 percent since 1960). Long-term loans have been used to finance the vast rebuilding program of the 1960s, suggesting that the banks are hardly indifferent to the problems of modernizing capacity, elevating productivity, and expanding industrial profits. In this connection, it should also be pointed out that even the most cursory glance at the productive capacity and level of productivity in the major industries—autos, rubber, glass, plastics, chemicals, aluminum, copper, electrical machinery, food processing—reveals that American capitalism is still a marvel of technological and engineering efficiency.

4. MONOPOLY CAPITALISM AND MICROECONOMICS

According to Fitch and Oppenheimer, the allocation of economic resources (composition of production and investment, price structure, and so on) in modern capitalism bears little resemblance in practice to the textbook theory of competition. I agree fully. Most Marxist and many bourgeois economists agree that the competitive model is a highly inaccurate representation of the workings of modern capitalist markets. "In many a sphere of economic activity," Tsuru writes, "the market is no longer a place where buyers and sellers . . . gather and compete with each other. . . . It has come to partake more of the character of a sales department of a monopolist."[18] On the other hand, Fitch and Oppenheimer seem to think that the coordination and control of supplies, production, transportation, communication, and prices within and/or between industries is a new historical phenomenon. I disagree. After all, the principal example of "reciprocity" that the authors use in their debate with the "Marxist managerialists" was ended by a court decision more than a decade ago (at least, the presumption is that the practice was ended). In other words, their own example is out of date (the authors show how the DuPont interests used their financial power to force U.S. Rubber to sell tires to General Motors—in which DuPont had more stock than in U.S. Rubber—at prices little above costs in order to increase GM's—and thus DuPont's —profits).

Further, I don't think that coordination and control within and/or between industries can be attributed primarily to the "domination of finance capital." At times, monopoly capitalists use their banks to coordinate industry; at other times, coordination is exercised by the directors of industrial corporations (as in the electrical equipment industry price-fixing case). An important reason why the banks are needed to coordinate the plans of industrial corporations is that the Clayton Act forbids interlocking directorships between companies that compete in the same market. The monopoly capitalists have used the banks to escape this limitation: the Act does not forbid associates in a single banking house from serving as directors of competing corporations as long as each associate serves on the board of a different company.

Unfortunately, neither Marxist nor bourgeois economists have

18. Shigeto Tsuru, "A Road to Socialism," *Monthly Review* 19, no. 9 (February 1968): 13.

studied the economic effects of cross-industry planning in any detail, especially in the newer conglomerates.[19] Personally, I do not believe that such control is exercised primarily for "financial" motives. In general, the importance of interlocks and reciprocity for economic planning, as opposed to financial planning, is twofold: first, to minimize the costs of selling in the capital goods sector of the economy; second, to coordinate investment plans with the aim of reducing or preventing overinvestment in productive capacity. In specific, considering the authors' example of reciprocity, I think that a good case can be made that DuPont was less interested in a financial rip-off than in giving GM a head start in production and sales. After all, the auto giant's ability to buy cheap tires meant that GM could hold down costs and prices and hence make more sales and industrial profits. In point of fact, in Fitch and Oppenheimer's own discussion of the battle between finance capitalists and Howard Hughes, the authors admit that "the giant corporation is . . . forced to pursue a strategy of forward and backward integration. . . . Finance capital performs this function by abolishing the market and 'socializing' industrial decision-making" (II:89). According to the authors, Hughes the industrialist collided head-on with the Eastern "syndicate" when Hughes attempted to win independence for himself and free TWA from "tribute" in the form of interest charges to the "syndicate." Although the other big airlines went to banks for financing, Hughes sought to bankroll TWA from profits generated by his own company, Hughes Tool. The struggle (which Hughes lost) is used by the authors as an example of the eternal conflict between industrialists and bankers. In Fitch and Oppenheimer's own words, "The entrepreneur wants to make profits, and the bankers want to make profits, but the banker can make profits only at the expense of corporate profits" (II:85). This statement is inaccurate in principle, and probably also inapplicable to the Hughes case. It is theoretically unsound for two

19. The staff of the Antitrust Subcommittee of the House Committee on the Judiciary wrote that

there is virtually no reliable current information available that will demonstrate either acceptable or undesirable effects that have resulted from the fact that common management personnel participated in, or influenced, particular business transactions. Without factual information concerning the actual operation of interlocks, "common-sense" presupposition, reliance on past proof, and abstract reasoning have been predominant in the analysis of both the virtues and evils attributed to corporate interlocks." [U.S., Congress, House, Committee on the Judiciary, Antitrust Subcommittee, *Interlocks in Corporate Management,* 92nd Cong., 1st sess., 12 March 1965 (Washington, 1965), p. 229]

Although this was written several years ago, we remain largely ignorant of the "actual operation of interlocks" insofar as production, investment, industrial location, costs, and prices are concerned.

reasons: first, banks coordinate economic activity as well as financial activity and thus help to produce surplus value, as well as appropriate surplus value; second, bank loans can and do stimulate production and sales, and thus indirectly activate the production and realization of surplus value. It is probably inapplicable to the Hughes case (I say "probably" because I do not have all of the facts) because the "syndicate" represents not bank capitalists but finance capitalists, who control capital in all of its forms, both money and industrial forms. Thus, it may be that Hughes was seen as a threat not because "bankers" wanted to milk profits from TWA, but mainly because Hughes threatened the finance capitalist monopoly on *industrial* capital and *industrial* profits. In other words, finance capitalists, not bank capitalists, entered the lists against Hughes, and it is reasonable to assume that strictly financial motives took second place to considerations of industrial monopoly and profits—that is, to the production and realization of surplus value.

Returning to the problem of reciprocity, it makes little difference whether a corporation forces one branch to sell cheaply to another branch, or whether finance capitalists compel one of their corporations to sell cheaply to another.[20] In both cases, it pays to increase efficiency consistent with profit maximization. Thus, it would have been in Du-Pont's long-run interests to improve efficiency in U.S. Rubber in order to buy tires even cheaper—just as it pays U.S. Steel or Alcoa to keep up productivity in their captive mines. Nor does it make much difference whether monopoly capitalists force their industrial enterprises to engage in price fixing, or whether corporations adopt a policy of price leadership on their own initiative. The forms of administered pricing are different in these two cases, but the economic effects are the same. Finally, it is hard to take Justice Brandeis's classic argument for opposing corporate interlocks seriously (as Fitch and Oppenheimer do)— namely, that "no man can serve two masters." The reason is that interlocked directors within and between financial and nonfinancial companies in fact serve *one* master—the monopoly capitalist interests.[21]

20. By way of contrast, Sloan of General Motors introduced organizational changes treating the various divisions as *separate* corporations in order to insure maximum efficiency in the allocation of capital. This strategy is commonplace today, whether employed by banks, newer conglomerates, or older multiproduct firms like GM.

21. I also believe that the authors exaggerate the importance of interlocks for the monopoly power of the investment banks. They write that
sources of very large blocs of long-term capital are fewer than might be supposed. One prime source is the investment banking fraternity, which maintains close relations with the commercial banks. . . . It would seem plausible that if a corporation was offered terms it disliked by one investment bank, it could always turn to another. But United States finance doesn't work this way. . . . Typically, each powerful investment banking firm has achieved a monopoly on the securities business of certain

The existence of "one master" does not mean that industrial competition is outdated. Each corporation operates in a specific environment, some features of which are of the owners and managers of the corporation's own making, and others of which are not. Whatever the precise mixture of these features in any particular industry, the evidence is overwhelming that Chrysler, General Electric, and other companies that Fitch and Oppenheimer would claim are "dominated by finance capital" and which operate in oligopolistic industries producing consumer durable goods in fact place as much stress on new product development, model and style changes, advertising, forced obsolescence, and the "sales effort" in general as do their counterparts with relatively weak ties with the financial institutions (such as Ford Motor Company). As Baran and Sweezy showed, the "sales effort" is indispensable for maintaining and expanding aggregate demand. Further, the evidence is also overwhelming that corporations such as Alcoa, U.S. Steel, Uniroyal, and Anaconda Copper, operating in oligopolistic industries producing capital goods, place enormous stress on efficiency and productivity. These features of modern capitalism were described and analyzed by Baran and Sweezy in *Monopoly Capital*. In a nutshell, the behavior of the giant corporation largely is determined by the market structure—the degree of competition, type of competition, product produced, costs, government contracts if any, and so on, to-

---

corporations, and its monopoly is respected by other investment bankers. [II:77–79] In the same section, the authors cite the *Investment Bankers* case:

In 1953 the United States government charged seventeen investment bankers . . . with having organized a conspiracy to monopolize the securities business. . . . Investment bankers were alleged to have controlled the financial affairs of securities issuers through such devices as interlocking directorates and syndicates. [The court argued] that interlocking directorates actually promoted competition and that the government's case was without merit. In a sense Medina's dismissal was justified. The government presented a shamefully inept case, drawing primarily on old evidence and calling only one key witness.

The reader is left with the impression that Medina dismissed the case for negative reasons —that is, because the government failed to provide any solid proof of its allegations. In fact, the court itself prepared independent evidence of a positive kind, which Fitch and Oppenheimer fail to relate. What happened was that "the government contended that the directorship charts showed that when a security issue was made and a bank representative was on the issuer's board, the defendant who had a man on the board acted as either manager or comanager in 86 per cent of the cases. The court, however, found that the Government's charts, and their use, were unsatisfactory because no attempt was made to relate the material to 'attendant circumstances.' . . ." (House Antitrust Subcommittee, *Interlocks in Corporate Management,* pp. 74–75) Moreover, "as a result of his dissatisfaction with the Government's charts, the Court prepared one of his own. The Court's chart shows that [only] 12.5 per cent of the defendants' business in the management of new issues, during the 15-year period 1935–1949, was obtained from issuers upon whose boards there was any partner, officer, or employee of a defendant at the time of issue" (ibid.).

gether with the condition of the economy as a whole. Two more recent
empirical studies serve to drive this point home. One study demonstrates that "management-controlled companies" (that is, finance capi-
talist-controlled companies) and "owner-controlled corporations" earn
the same rates of profit—and that total assets, total sales revenues,
barriers to entry, and industrial growth rates "explain" nearly all variations in profit rates.[22] This study suggests that finance capitalists allow
their corporations to make what they can, and to reinvest profits in
accordance with market criteria of profitability. A second study shows
that large corporations have higher profit rates than medium-sized and
small corporations regardless of the degree of market concentration
(that is, monopoly power in specific product markets).[23] As Fitch and
Oppenheimer show, large corporations seek relatively more external
financing than smaller companies—but far from draining industrial
profits, as the authors imply, external financing appears to be the road
to *greater* profits.

Finally, we need to say a few words about Fitch and Oppenheimer's
discussion of the recent conglomerate movement—that is, the tendency
of many corporations to diversify into seemingly (and, at times, actually) unrelated product lines. The authors are dead certain that the
conglomerates are motivated solely by the desire for a fast buck. In one
place, they write that " 'immediate financial gain' is exactly what the
conglomerate merger 'movement' was all about, and exactly what the
railroad and utility 'diversification' efforts are aimed at achieving"
(II:114). In another passage, we read that "finance capital's . . . hunger
for quick speculative profits creates industrial monstrosities—the conglomerates—whose assets make no more pretense to industrial integration than those of a mutual fund" (III:75). Unfortunately, space and
time limitations do not permit a full discussion of the conglomerate
merger movement at this time, but I would like to point out that these
mergers have many purposes, of which speculation and "immediate
financial gain" are but one. In no particular order of importance, some
of these purposes are:

1. To create a pool of investment capital that can flow in any
direction that promises a superior return. At any particular time,
conglomerate funds are frozen in particular assets that seem profitable, but these assets will be liquidated when they lose their luster.
Traditional one-product firms such as steel companies are diversify-

22. David Kamershen, "The Influence of Ownership and Control on Profit Rates,"
American Economic Review 58, no. 3 (June 1968): 432–447.
23. Courtesy of the author of the study (research still in progress), Professor Marshall
Hall, Washington University.

ing with the aim of more rational financial planning (as opposed to immediate financial gain), which has been made possible by modern systems analysis. These companies are putting their money into industries in which the rate of return on capital is highest, which is precisely what the textbooks say that capitalists will do in a competitive capital market.

2. To create, consolidate, and capitalize on positions of control in marketing. During most of the 1960s, the single most frequent kind of merger was the "product extension" merger—that is, the combining of firms manufacturing products that are marketed in the same outlets. For example, the new chemical-drug-cosmetic conglomerates bring together production units that depend on the same marketing facilities. As the 1960s wore on, monopoly capitalists increasingly became preoccupied with marketing and sales. The reason is that they faced expanding product competition, not only from overseas trade and as a result of the new productive facilities added by corporate expansion programs, but also as a consequence of the conglomerate movement itself. In fact, a good case can be made that conglomerate mergers increase competition in the high-profit industries that are the merger targets. In the words of one businessman, "In the good old days all the emphasis was on the product, rather than on the market and its needs. Production and finance told the sales department what they had to get for the product. Today and even more so in the future, marketing will tell finance and production the cost range in which they must operate to sell in the marketplace."[24]

3. To get tax write-offs. Under present tax laws, different tax rates are applied to different industries. An integrated corporation can purchase a firm in an industry that is taxed at a relatively low rate, charge the acquired firm low prices for supplies produced and sold by another branch of the corporation, and come out way ahead on the deal.

4. To get the benefits of cross-fertilization of technical-administrative know-how. The skills and abilities of systems experts, scientists, engineers, and administrators can be used to more advantage in multiproduct companies. Principles of research and development, production planning and control, and scientific management in general can be applied to many different lines of production.

5. To integrate production and distribution facilities horizontally and vertically. For example, many utilities are acquiring land

24. *Business Week*, 17 October 1970.

for new home construction (and thus new utilities customers).[25] Bethlehem Steel is diversifying mineral exploitation and going into ocean shipping. These are forms of forward and backward integration. Further, there are a large number of "compatibility" mergers, which resemble horizontal integration. Magazine publishing companies have gone into the book business and have bought TV stations, can companies have merged with or acquired firms manufacturing paper containers, and so on.

6. To get a piece of low-risk, cost-plus government business by acquiring military contractors.

7. To diversify operations with the aim of spreading risks and reducing uncertainty. For example, modern research and development decreases the time lag between the invention and marketability of a new product. Possibilities of unforeseen discoveries in the lab motivate a company to go into a new field as a hedge against competing firms developing new products in their labs.

8. To keep up and accelerate corporate growth rates. The conglomerate merger is one way for a company to prevent its rate of expansion from slowing down, by getting into fast-growing fields.

9. To hedge against inflation. Inflation helps to finance mergers, which provide a new source of corporate earnings. Clearly, the big upsurge in mergers and acquisitions from 1966 to 1969 can be attributed largely to growing inflation.

Taking these and other considerations discussed above into account, it is difficult to take Fitch and Oppenheimer seriously when they write that " 'immediate financial gain' is exactly what the conglomerate merger 'movement' was all about," and that "the conglomerator depletes industrial capital in order to create new paper values." A few years ago, I wrote that "the picture of a few finance capitalists manipulating stock, acquiring huge overnight profits, and frantically putting together and taking apart industrial empires with an eye to immediate financial gain is simply not consistent with what is known about managerial decision making in the vast majority of large corporations today."[26] Fitch and Oppenheimer quote this passage—disapprovingly. But despite the authors' best efforts, I see no reason at this time to rewrite the passage or to change its basic conclusion.

25. *Wall Street Journal,* 7 July 1970.
26. O'Connor, "Finance Capital or Corporate Capital?" p. 32.

PART III
THE STATE

CHAPTER FIVE

*Scientific and Ideological Elements
in the Economic Theory of
Government Policy*

*"In our time . . . faith in the manipulative omnipotence of the State has all but
displaced analysis of its social structure and understanding of its political and
economic functions."—Paul A. Baran, "On the Political Economy of Backwardness"*

*"In no other field [than public finance] has the intrusion of metaphysics done
so much harm as here."—Gunnar Myrdal,* The Political Element in the
Development of Economic Theory

1. INTRODUCTION

There is a large and growing body of economic doctrine on the subject
of state expenditures and taxation which attempts to lay down guidelines for state fiscal policy. "Such studies," Peacock and Wiseman have
written, "attempt to set up criteria for the size and nature of government expenditures and income by utilizing techniques usual in the
study of market economics. Starting from some concept of economic
welfare, defined in terms of individual choice, they attempt to specify
the taxing and spending activities of government that would conduce
to the ideal condition of such welfare."[1]

The general questions that are raised are: How large should the
state budget be? How should budget expenditures be allocated be-

1. Alan T. Peacock and Jack Wiseman, *The Growth of Public Expenditures in the United
Kingdom* (New York, 1961), p. 13.

tween alternative ends? What should be the burden of taxes on various groups? Put another way, What elements should make up a normative theory of "public finance"? Immediately we can see that the conventional phrase "public finance" reveals the ideological content of bourgeois economic thought by prejudging the question of the *real* purpose of state expenditures. In other words, it remains to be shown just how "public" are the real and financial transactions that take place in the state economic sector.

Our first task is to develop a rough statement of the two main lines of orthodox theory, one based upon neoclassical microeconomic theory, the second based on Keynesian macroeconomic theory. It should be said at the outset that although many bourgeois economists consider the analysis of public finance to be concrete, practical "precepts for action," others are aware that the theory is devoid of any significant social and political content, and hence represents little more than a formal exercise.

Our second task is to briefly review the critique of orthodox microeconomic theory, or welfare economics, developed by orthodox economists themselves. This critique is based solely on the lack of internal consistency or logical clarity of the theory, and in no way challenges its underlying assumptions. These underlying assumptions, as we shall see, are based on the criteria of competitive markets and welfare maximizing. In turn, these criteria take for granted the system of private ownership of the means of production and the economic, social, and political institutions that go with private ownership. We believe that these criteria are based on a one-dimensional view of human beings and their real potentialities, and, moreover, on a historically specific and short-lived mode of production.

Thus, our third task, and our purpose, is to develop our own critique of orthodox public finance, one which challenges the assumptions of both micro- and macro-theory and goes beyond an attempt to reveal certain logical inconsistencies or contradictions implied by it. We do not, however, attempt to answer the question, What should the state do? We do not attempt to reconstruct the normative theory of state finance, because that would take us into a different subject altogether, the political economy of socialism. What state revenues and budgetary expenditures should be in a noncapitalist society would depend on the specific type of socialism to emerge from United States capitalism, the circumstances surrounding the struggle for socialism, the coalition of forces which lead the struggle, and so on. These questions would obviously take us well beyond the scope of our subject matter.

2. TRADITIONAL WELFARE ECONOMICS

In its approach to the role of the state under capitalism, welfare economics, based on microeconomic analysis, adopts the principle of "neutrality." It is contended that the state (including state tax policy) should refrain from disturbing the pattern of resources allocation determined by private market relationships except in the event that the existing allocations are at odds with the competitive norm—the types of allocations which prevail in a regime of perfect competition—with "welfare maximizing."

The concept of ideal output is central to the normative theory of public finance. We have no intention of doing anything like full justice to the range and complexity of problems arising from, and variations on, the idea of ideal output, but rather make a simple and somewhat old-fashioned statement of it. Pigou in his *Economics of Welfare* defines ideal output as that composition of production such that "no alternative output which could be obtained by means of reallocation among the various industries of the economy's resources would leave the community better off than before." To put it differently, ". . . any reallocation of the resources employed in producing the ideal output will so affect the various members of the economy that those who are better off as a result of the change will be unable to compensate those who are worse off as a result of the change and at the same time make a net gain for themselves. . . ."[2]

The question next arises, When will private market relationships depart from ideal output? or, to put it differently, When will the private

2. Formally: Assume no externalities in production (a situation where a firm's costs of production depend not only on the size of the firm, but also on the size of the industry) and externalities in consumption (a situation where an individual's satisfaction depends not only on the quantity of a commodity he consumes, but also on the quantity of a commodity other individuals consume) and assume a constant income distribution and level of employment. What is the relationship between competitive and ideal outputs? One equilibrium condition under competition is $P_x/P_y = MPC_x/MPC_y$.

In the absence of externalities, private costs correspond to social costs, or $MPC_x = MSC_y$ and $MPC_x - MSC_y$. Next consider a transformation curve between x and y. The slope of the curve must be $MSC_x/MSC_y/$ because MSC_x/MSC_y is equal to the decrease in the production of x associated with a given increase in the production of y (or vice versa). Competitive equilibrium thus requires that the output combination be one for which the slope of the transformation curve be equal to the slope of the price line. Ideal output is where the indifference and transformation curve are tangent. Thus ideal output corresponds with competitive output. If private market relationships lead to an output which departs from ideal, then the state's task is to encourage (or discourage) the production of commodities which are undersupplied (or oversupplied).

market misallocate economic resources, thus providing the "justification" for state intervention?

First, markets organized along monopolistic rather than competitive lines may lead to a misallocation of resources. Monopoly tends to keep prices higher and outputs lower than those prevailing under competition. Thus a tax to force the monopolist to lower the price, or a policy to restructure the market in order to bring the price down, is justified. In the event that the marginal social cost exceeds marginal private cost, however (the case of heroin production, for example), monopoly restrictions may improve the allocation of resources, and an attack on the monopoly by the state would not be "justified."

Second, there is the more general case of the existence of externalities in production. The full-blown name for the concept is "technological economies or diseconomies of scale," which arise in many industries where the costs facing the firm depend not only on the size and efficiency of the firm itself, but also on the size and efficiency of the industry in which the firm operates. Marshall was the first to formalize this concept, and limit it to "technological" (compared with pecuniary) economies and diseconomies.[3]

For example, in the fishing industry, the more operators that are engaged in fishing, the higher will be the costs facing any individual operator. In this case, there are said to be external diseconomies of production. Because of these diseconomies, marginal social costs *(MSC)* will exceed marginal private costs *(MPC)*. Thus the price of the commodity will be lower than it would be if the divergence between *MSC* and *MPC* were to be eliminated. Here, orthodox theory argues that a tax is in order, to discourage private production, and thus reduce social costs to the point where there is no disparity between social and private costs.

A good example of an industry in which there are considered to be external economies of scale is education. It is argued that social costs fall well below private costs because the educated individual contributes more than the uneducated to capitalist society's growth and political stability. The same kind of argument is made regarding transportation facilities. In these cases state subsidies are in order, or even public ownership.

A third departure from ideal output is the presence of increasing returns to scale in the production of a commodity. If a commodity is produced under conditions of increasing returns (air transport, for

3. In classical economics, at least in Smith, Walras, and Wicksell, there is no place for externalities, and even though Say and Mill recognized the possibility of their existence, they do not figure in their public policy recommendations.

example), then just as in any industry, marginal revenue should be set equal to marginal costs to maximize profits and hence welfare. But marginal costs will be below average costs because average costs by definition are declining. Thus, in order to have an efficient resource allocation, the industry must be subsidized. Otherwise, the firm must restrict output to cover average costs and thus command a higher price. On the other hand, taxes should be imposed on decreasing return industries; in these sectors, a policy of pricing to cover costs will mean that marginal costs are higher than average costs, signifying a misallocation of resources.

The extreme example of decreasing costs or increasing returns is the case of the "public good." The public good is defined as an activity where the additional cost of extra use is zero, or to put it another way, where my consumption does not reduce what is available to you. Standard examples are radio and television programs, lighthouses, and the Defense Department. Welfare economics teaches that for public goods price should be zero or near zero. With a price in excess of zero, ideal output exceeds actual output because more people could be better off and no one made worse off by an expansion of output.

It should be noted that the concept of a public good has little or nothing to do with whether the facility is owned by private capital or the state. Theoretically, private capital could own and manage lighthouses and the state could subsidize private capital so that prices could be set at zero and profits still made. To put it another way, lighthouses and television can be priced on the basis of private market principles; for example, radar could be placed on lighthouses to prevent freeriders by means of electronic scrambling of signals. And there is, of course, pay television. There is a category of public goods, however (military goods are given as the main example), in which the problem of "revealed preferences" arises. One could choose whether or not to pay to see a television program. But in the case of a military establishment, it is thought that there would be a general tendency to underpay via voluntary contributions because once "defense" is provided, everyone is "protected" whether or not he wants the protection. It is not possible to bomb North Vietnam in the name of some Americans and not others. In these cases, private ownership of the means of production—in our example, the means of destruction—is not warranted because there is no entrepreneurial function provided. Thus public goods, no matter what their special character, should be either heavily subsidized or owned publicly.[4]

4. Is it any accident that orthodox economists tend to conclude from their surveys of current-day economic activity that on orthodox criteria the great bulk of such activity is

There is a fourth category of market imperfections which "justify" state interference in the private economy. This is a catchall category which includes the following special cases: first, the case of neighborhood effects or spillovers. To take one or two examples: My unwillingness to conform to quarantine laws or mosquito control will affect everyone in the community, and thus it is justified for the state to coerce me to conform. Or the existence of a public highway may raise property values locally. Thus, the state is justified in paying transit deficits with property taxes. Or situations where one firm affects the efficiency of the employment of resources by other firms. Suppose, for instance, that a farmer on a mountainside cuts down trees to cultivate his land, affecting adversely the ecological cycle by flooding the valley. These are not true technological externalities because the scale of the industry per se has nothing to do with the increase or decrease in the costs of the specific firm. Other examples come to mind in the capitalist labor market. For example, capitalists may have short-time horizons and hire workers with lifetime horizons, such that work time is "optimum" in the short run but shortens a man's working life in the long run. Historically, hours laws can be traced to the irrationality of individual capitalists in the labor market, and the need for the state to preserve labor power for all capitalists from the depredations of individual capitalists.

A final case is a situation where external economies or positive spillovers are so vast, and hence costs and prices under competition are so high, that the commodity does not even get produced. In this event, few people are even aware of the possible "advantage" to society. Good examples are import-substitute activities in underdeveloped capitalist countries which may benefit the economy greatly in the long run but which are not begun in the absence of protective state policy.

We offer so many examples of cases which do not fit neatly into the standard orthodox categories only to emphasize the fact that faced with real concrete situations it is often possible to "justify" any particular government interference after the fact—justify it in terms of orthodox criteria. Thus, the idea of consumer sovereignty and welfare maximization (or ideal output) implies state intervention but offers few clear criteria. Because these criteria are so abstract, the dictum that taxes should be "neutral" except in the event that they are consciously designed to improve resource allocation is somewhat empty. More impor-

---

"justified"? For example, Bator concludes that 96.8 percent of public purchases are public or semipublic "goods and services" (Francis M. Bator, *The Question of Government Spending* [New York, 1960], p. 100). Bator is truly a Pangloss.

tant, there is nothing in normative theory to tell us whether or not the dictums are realistic in a political sense—or to suggest precisely what externalities the state can be expected to capture and which cannot be.

3. TRADITIONAL CRITICISMS OF WELFARE ECONOMICS

The traditional perspective on welfare maximizing and state policy has come under increasing fire from contemporary orthodox economists, not because there are so many cases which do not fit neatly into the increasing cost or externality categories where the "correct" state policy is relatively straightforward and unambiguous, but rather because of the internal logic of the traditional view itself. Modern welfare economics rejects any partial analysis (an analysis restricted to one industry or branch of the economy) which purports to show that any given sector of the economy should be expanded to seize externalities in production. The arguments of contemporary welfare economists are highly mathematical and we cannot reproduce them here. The gist of the main argument is that given external economies and necessary equilibrium conditions for the economy as a whole, it can be shown under certain assumptions no more or less arbitrary than those used by the traditional school that expanding sectors of the economy where there are no externalities may increase output even more than expanding sectors where there are. Further, there is the argument that there is no way to know whether a tax to correct an external diseconomy is better than some alternative measure, including the alternative of doing nothing.[5]

One of the latest words on the subject has been said by Professor Baumol, who wrote that if "external economies are . . . strong . . . and persistent, it will indeed pay society to increase all activity levels indefinitely."[6] Moreover, in the past decade there has been a sustained critique, again from an orthodox standpoint, of the theory of consumer behavior on which welfare economics is based.[7]

Three major points have been made. First, consumers may not be consistent in their choices, and thus it is not possible to say that they

5. See, for example, Ralph Turvey, "On Divergencies Between Social Cost and Private Cost," *Economica,* n.s., no. 30 (August 1963): 119; William J. Baumol, "External Economies and Second-Order Optimality Conditions," *American Economic Review* 54, no. 4 (June 1964), pt. I, pp. 358–372.
6. Baumol, "External Economies," pp. 366–367.
7. I. M. D. Little, *A Critique of Welfare Economics* (London, 1967); J. de Graaf, *Theoretical Welfare Economics* (London, 1957).

are better off in one situation than in another. Second, externalities in consumption, or collective aspirations and well-being, have no place in traditional theory. Third, the argument is made that if the community is made up of one set of persons at one time, and another at another time, how can it be said when and if the community is better off?

We can safely conclude from this brief review of the critics of traditional theory that welfare economics, even one based on the assumption that capitalism as a system is eternal, offers no firm criteria for state policy.

4. A MARXIAN CRITIQUE OF WELFARE ECONOMICS

The reason is that the critics of traditional welfare economics, as well as its few remaining defenders, accept criteria based on values which are in turn derived from a system based on the domination of private capital. To put it another way, any notion of economic rationality which is independent of the "rationality" of the private market is still taboo.

For this reason, claims by some economic theorists that value judgments have no place in their analysis are without any real foundation. Many traditional and modern welfare economists may claim that they attempt merely to determine the circumstances in which people with given economic interests may pursue these interests more "efficiently" by broadening the role of the state in the economy. But, at the same time, the theorist accepts these interests as valid—as worth defending and realizing. In the event that he rejected the given private interests, he would hardly waste time deducing from them implications for state action under varying sets of circumstances. It follows that the welfare economist ideologically supports the dominant private interests at the expense of the politically weakest private interests.

Another technical school of economics is the positive school. The positive economist views himself as a *technician* who rules out explicit normative theorizing and, finally, accepts the preferences of the "authorities" as given. The customary role of the positive economist is as either an adviser to the state or some private group or a technician faced with a "maximization" problem chosen by himself.

In the first case, the economist claims a certain neutrality with respect to the wisdom or lack of wisdom of some change proposed by the state, and confines himself to formulating alternative means to a given end. Needless to say, the positive economist accepts without question the desired end and, moreover, ordinarily fails to consider *all* possible alternative means to this end. There are no economists, for example, currently employed to work out the economic implications of nationalizing the drug industry or the oil interests, even though on pure efficiency criteria alone many economists would be compelled to give these industries very low marks. Thus the economic technician is to one degree or another merely a normative economist in disguise.

This is not a surprising conclusion; what is surprising is the economists' claim that they are merely "objective" analysts. If anything, the positive economist-technician adviser is less objective today than in the past. It can no longer be written as confidently that "economists treating government influences on the economy have largely neglected the essential institutional and procedural aspects of government action. That is why their analyses and recommendations are often characterized as utopian and unrealistic by the specialist in public finance."[8] Today the "objective" economist is more willing to dispense with independent critical judgments than in the past, and, conversely, to accept more constraints ("institutional and procedural aspects of government action") in his analysis.

In the second case, the economist analyzes an economic maximization problem chosen by himself; for example, the "optimum" investment in some new water resource. If all existing constraints—physical, legal, administrative-budgetary, and so on—are incorporated in the analysis, then the economist is bound "to exclude the interesting solution," to quote Otto Eckstein. What is meant by this is that a given market situation determines a certain set of prices, level of investment, and so on, and thus in order to put his apparatus to work, the economic technician must ignore at least one political, property, financial, or other given relationship. The choice of which constraint to "assume away" is, of course, a normative judgment. Even here, the economist's values are in the center of his work.

5. THE DISTRIBUTION OF INCOME

The only important issues of state economic policy which the traditionalist does not refer to the welfare norm are the distribution of income, economic stabilization (including international stabilization), and economic growth. So far as the distribution of income is concerned,

8. Gerhard Colm, "Why Public Finance?" *National Tax Journal* 1, no. 3 (September 1948): 196.

after many decades of debate, contemporary orthodox economists by and large reject the neoclassical fiction of "tax justice." The economist *qua* economist is powerless to make comparisons of "interpersonal utility" and thus cannot justify a progressive tax structure, or any other tax structure, without reference to given legal norms, precedent, "public opinion," and so on. Among orthodox economists the general consensus appears to be that the market distributes income more or less "fairly" in advanced capitalist countries—even though there is some recognition that everyone does not have equal access to the capital market (e.g., higher education)—although the more sophisticated writers are fully aware that this is not a necessary attribute of the market. For example, Samuelson rebuts those who accept the marginal productivity doctrine as a normative theory of income distribution between economic classes in the following way: "Under appropriate conditions of demand and technology, a marginal productivity theory might impute 99 percent of the national income away from labor, which would be exploitation enough in the eyes of radical agitators."[9]

Thus it would appear that contemporary economics has traveled a long way to go (admittedly) a very short distance, yet on one crucial question the subject remains in the Dark Ages. We refer to the tendency to separate the ("ethical") question of income distribution from the ("scientific" or "objective") question of resource allocation and market efficiency. From the standpoint of formal *logic,* this separation is objectionable because price determination and income distribution are inseparable. Further, an analysis of the political economy that ignores the actual connections between distribution and allocation is unreal. Clearly, economic efficiency depends on the distribution of output and income, and thus it is impossible to develop any fully satisfactory norms for resource allocation independent of the given distribution of income. Furthermore, it is not at all certain that a more equal income distribution would not automatically be accompanied by an increase in social consumption at the expense of private consumption as status symbols and material emulation in general would figure much less prominently in the social economy.[10]

In a world of conspicuous consumption, for example, leveling income may greatly increase welfare. For another thing, if the satisfaction that one individual gets from his consumption depends in part on another individual's consumption, then changing the income distribu-

9. Paul Samuelson, "Economic Theory and Wages," in David McCord Wright, ed., *The Impact of the Union* (New York, 1956), p. 328.
10. "Review of the Month," *Monthly Review* 10, no. 9 (January 1959): 337–344.

tion will change ideal output and hence welfare.

Lastly, in order to promote what *some* economic classes and groups consider to be an equitable distribution of income, it might be necessary to abandon the private market system altogether, or at the very least, modify it to the degree that its foundations are undermined. Needless to say, bourgeois economics defines "ethical" and "equitable" without reference to this alternative.

Complicating matters, the normative theory of state expenditure assumes that everyone benefits equally from a given expenditure (e.g., the police). The assumption is made that there is no link between the distribution of income and the welfare impact of state expenditures; for example, that individuals who cannot afford to travel benefit from highway expenditures as much as those who can. In the private market, bourgeois economists often justify inequalities in income distribution on the basis of "preserving incentives." No economist would ever dare say in public that inequalities in the welfare impact of "public" expenditures are required to preserve incentives.

6. TRADITIONAL MACROECONOMIC THEORY

Next we turn to macroeconomic fiscal theory, again beginning with an exposition of the main lines of the theory. Macroeconomics, like economics generally, uses the postulate-deductive form of equilibrium theory which begins with a few simple axioms and combines them to form a group of concepts that are logically interrelated. These concepts provide the basic terms of the system and describe the primary general relations between them.

The purpose of macroeconomic, or income, theory is to analyze the determinants of aggregate or total spending on commodities. The elementary concept is the utility of objects for individuals; the general relation is the principle of maximization of utility for individuals and returns (profits) for firms. A million light years, however, separate individual utility and demand for commodities from aggregate demand for commodities, and in macroeconomic theorizing, individual utility is ordinarily lost sight of. This means that macroeconomics in no sense can be considered "pure" economic theory.

In a simple macroeconomic model total income, or the value of total production (Y), is constituted by consumption spending (C), investment spending (I), and government spending (G) $(Y = C+I+G)$. The level of employment is determined by the level of income or production $(E = E(Y))$. The price level (P) is assumed to be unchanged up to the point of full employment. When full employment is reached, the price level is determined by the level of spending.

Macro-theory does not independently investigate the determinants of consumption, which is made to depend on income via the "marginal propensity to consume" (MPC). The simplest form of the consumption function is $C = a + bY$, where a is the volume of consumption when income is zero, and b is the propensity to consume, or the proportion of income consumed. Income itself, and hence employment and prices, are thus determined by investment spending and government spending.

There are almost as many theories of investment as there are investment theorists. A simple theory views investment as depending on the anticipated rate of profit (p), the money supply (M), and society's preference for holding assets in liquid (cash) form (LP). Government spending is determined by the political authorities and is not subject to economic laws.

Some elementary functional relations of the system are (a) the higher the MPC, the higher the level of income and employment; (b) the greater the stock of money, the lower the rate of interest, the higher the volume of investment, and the higher the level of income and employment; (c) the weaker the preference for holding assets in the form of cash, the greater the demand for bonds, the higher the price of bonds, the lower the rate of interest, and the greater the level of investment, income, and employment.

The system is said to be in equilibrium when the volume of production at current prices equals consumption, government spending, and intended investment. Actual investment equals intended investment when inventories of commodities are no lower or greater today than capitalists expected them to be yesterday, i.e., when today's sales equal yesterday's production. In this event, the market is cleared; there is no excess demand or supply. The peculiar characteristic of this model is that the system may be in equilibrium even though there may be a sizable amount of unemployment (or, alternatively, inflation).

Thus to increase employment, income must be increased. Income may be increased directly by raising the propensity to consume (e.g., by deflating the economy and increasing the real value of savings, and hence liberating savings for consumption), by raising investment (e.g., by subsidies to capitalists), and by government spending or tax reductions. Income may be increased indirectly by increasing the supply of money, lowering the rate of interest, and hence raising the level of investment.

It should be obvious from this discussion that macro-theory was formulated with an eye to macro-policy—that in no sense can macro-theory be considered pure theory, or value-free theory. The orientation of macro-theory is toward the *control* of income, employment, and prices via state economic policy. Thus macro-theory, fiscal theory (the analysis of the effects of government spending, taxation, and borrowing), and fiscal policy (applied fiscal theory) all boil down to fundamentally the same phenomenon—how to make capitalism a viable economic and social system by keeping unemployment and inflation within reasonable bounds.[11]

7. CRITIQUE OF MACROECONOMIC THEORY

Macro-theory of the type discussed above, i.e., theory that places primary emphasis on demand, has been popular during two historical eras—during the late mercantilist period and today, the epoch of monopoly capitalism. In both periods the state plays a central role in the economy. During the era of laissez faire, income theory was banished by the classical and neoclassical economists. Brought to life by Keynes, today it dominates economic thought in the advanced capitalist countries.

The main point is that macro-theory is at one and the same time the science and ideology of the ruling class—or, more precisely, the dominant stratum of the ruling class, the corporate oligarchy. The corporate oligarchy has long ago accepted the inevitability and desirability of economic self-regulation—or what is euphemistically called government intervention in the economy. What is more, the corporate oli-

11. The foregoing are the elements of the theory of income and employment determination in the short run—when the capital stock, technology, and the labor force are assumed to be unchanged. Neo-Keynesianism, or growth theory (the theory of secular changes in income), bases itself on an analysis of the relationship between changes in income and spending and changes in the capital stock, or productive capacity. Put simply, neo-Keynesianism argues that if the addition to productive capacity due to yesterday's investment spending equals the change in total spending, the system will be in dynamic equilibrium. Put another way, the increment to spending from one period to another is just sufficient to absorb the extra commodities which yesterday's investment spending has made it possible to produce. If the increment to capacity is greater than the increment to spending, neo-Keynesian policy calls for state encouragement to consumption spending. If the increment to capacity is smaller than the increment to spending, neo-Keynesian policy calls for state encouragement to investment spending. For example, during the 1950s increments to income went to consumption and government spending. James Tobin and other neo-Keynesians thus convinced Kennedy to squeeze consumption and push investment, in order to keep increases in productive capacity in line with increases in consumer income and spending.

garchy is the only segment of the ruling class which is in a position to effectively *control* macro-fiscal policy. I do not think that this assertion requires elaborate proof. There is a growing historical literature describing the sources and development of a class consciousness on the part of the corporate rich, and there is a sociological literature describing the modes of control by the corporations of the quasi-private planning and policy organizations such as the Committee for Economic Development, and the process of ideology formation in which these organizations play a decisive role (see Chapter Six). Even if such a literature did not exist, it is easy to understand why fiscal policy *must* be formulated in the interests of the hundred or so dominant corporations, because the health of the economy depends almost exclusively on the health of these giants.

Income theory, then, is a *technical* science to the degree that it has practical value to the corporations. To put it another way, income theory is "scientific" insofar as it is useful to preserve and extend monopoly capitalism as a system and perpetuate class divisions and class rule. On this criterion, for example, neo-Keynesian theory is more "scientific" than Keynes' original doctrines. A fiscal policy for growth is more practical than one for economic stabilization because of its bias in favor of investment, and hence profits.

On the other hand, income theory is not a *critical* science because it constitutes itself on the given economic and legal foundations of capitalism. It fails to make the foundations of capitalism themselves a subject for analysis. At best, then, income theory offers only a description of the *mechanics of operation* of advanced capitalist economies. A critical science is not a science of mechanics, but of real causes, historical causes; the variables are not abstractions such as the interest rate, or supply of money, but rather they are *human* agents.

Thus over the past thirty years there has developed an elaborate analysis of the determinants of income, employment, and production —an analysis which has proven to have great practical value in helping the state underwrite business investments and business losses or, to use the long-current euphemism, in helping the government to stabilize the economy and encourage it to grow. What is more, its practical value to the corporations and business in general is greatly enhanced by the fact that business increasingly takes it for granted that income theory *is* an accurate description of the economy.

On the other hand, few would place much confidence in the explanations of the ultimate causes of fluctuation and growth which are integral to income theory. These explanations run in terms of individual psychological motivations and responses and abstract completely from the ever-changing, concrete socioeconomic setting which decisively conditions consumer and business behavior. The concepts of "propensities," "preferences," and "anticipations and expectations" seem to Marxist economists to be very fragile foundations for such an elaborate structure as income theory. The alternative, and correct, path, in my view, is to submit consumption, investment, and government spending to a *structural* determination, i.e., to deduce the implications for the volume of and changes in investment (or consumption) in the context of the *actual* behavior of large corporations operating in oligopolistic markets.

Perhaps an analogy will be useful at this stage. A good one is the relationship between medicine, on the one hand, and biochemistry, biophysics, and other sciences which attempt to understand the body as a whole, on the other. To a surprising degree, there is frequently a great gulf separating medicine from the body sciences. The diagnosis and treatment of some diseases—a good example is mental illness—often remain unchanged when the body scientists advance their understanding of the causes of illness, for the simple reason that medicine remains an excellent description of the mechanics of the body. In fact, it is well known that in psychotherapy a priori statements about which technique will produce results with any given patient are very hard to come by. Often, the therapist is not even aware of why he has achieved results. One could make the same statement about some economic policy makers.

Income theory is neither right nor wrong—in the sense of being close to or distant from the real causes of economic change—because income theory does not pretend to investigate real causes. It is only more or less useful—more useful if the mechanics of operation of the economy are accurately specified, less useful if not. The main criterion of success is *results.*

Income theory can achieve good results even though its theoretical foundations may be weak. But it could get better results if it were scientifically based on real causes, as we will suggest below. The point which needs emphasis, however, is that it is impossible for an economic theory which exists to maintain capitalism and class rule to be based on real causes. The reason is that a causal science is a critical science, one which subjects the foundations of capitalism—as well as the transitory economic manifestations of these foundations—to analysis. Clearly, a theory that is designed to perpetuate the social and economic relations (and indirectly the taboos and superstitions) of capitalism will be of little value to anyone who wishes to question these relations and taboos and superstitions.

If the economic theory questioned its own assumptions, it would negate itself; and since income theory is first and foremost ruling-class theory, a critical theory would imply that the ruling class would have to question itself, its own right to rule, or negate itself. Let me illustrate with a simple example in the form of a hypothesis: Suppose that inflation is caused by the groups or classes which benefit from inflation; suppose further that anti-inflation policy is in the hands of those who caused the inflation. The anti-inflation policy will leave some groups or classes worse off and some better off. Among those who will be better off will be the group which was the prime mover behind the inflation, the original beneficiaries. Now suppose that the ruling class employs economists to study inflation—indeed, not only study inflation, but find acceptable ways to cause inflation. Clearly, a critical science of inflation would require that economists study not only their employers but themselves.

The economics profession adamantly refuses to do this—to consider itself systematically as part of the experimental field. But it is obvious that economics as a technical science is a *social* phenomenon—and it may be true that only economists are in a position to comprehend their own social role. In fact, we believe it can be shown that the economist's tools have made it possible in the past to have a little unemployment and a little inflation, an optimal situation for the corporations. For example, two famous economists, Paul Samuelson and Robert Solow, wrote an article entitled "Our Menu of Policy Choices," in which "we" are given the "choice" of a little unemployment and a little inflation, or, alternatively, a little inflation and a little unemployment! Abolishing both unemployment and inflation is impossible given the fact (for bourgeois economists, the eternal fact) that employment depends on the growth of income, which in turn depends on investment, which in turn requires at least a slight profit inflation (that is, prices rising faster than money wages).

In short, income theory does not seek to remove the extremes of society—unemployment and inflation (and capital and labor, rich and poor, privileged and underprivileged, rulers and ruled)—but rather, to quote Marx, it attempts to "weaken their antagonisms and transform them into a harmonious whole." Marxists believe this to be impossible. And hence a critical bourgeois social science, including income theory, is for this reason impossible.

8. BUDGETARY POLICY AND ECONOMIC GROWTH

Let us now turn to the treatment that public finance affords the relationship between budgetary policy and economic growth. "Growth models in their present form," Peacock and Wiseman write, "cannot be treated as anything more than exercises in a technique of arrangement." The basic reason that income and growth theory is unrealistic is the failure to include a theory of state expenditures. Evsey Domar once noted that government expenditures can be dealt with in one of three ways: they can be assumed to be "exogenous" to the system, they can be merged with consumption expenditures, or they can be assumed "away altogether." The latter alternative is completely unsatisfactory, and to assume that government expenditures are determined by "outside" forces is tantamount to an admission that they are beyond the realm of comprehension. Merging all government spending with private consumption merely substitutes fiction for fact.

Paradoxically, government spending is increasingly placed in the middle of discussions of growth and stagnation. Most economists view the state as a kind of *deus ex machina* and assume that government spending not only can but should make up the difference between the actual volume of private expenditures and the level of spending which will keep unemployment down to a politically tolerable minimum. State expenditures in this way are incorporated into models of fluctuations and growth. However, the *actual* determinants of government spending are not considered; rather, what is considered is the volume of spending and taxation necessary to achieve certain goals given certain assumptions and characteristics of the given model.

The reason why economists do not know the actual determinants of government expenditure is not hard to find. There are no markets for most goods and services provided by the state, and hence it is not possible to lean on the doctrine of revealed preferences. Thus a theory of state expenditures requires an examination of the forces influencing and conditioning demand. But utility theory forbids any inquiry into these forces—putting aside statistical "explanations" such as the age-mix of the population, climatic conditions, and the like. The logical reason is that an equilibrium model must assume that demand is independent of supply. Thus it is forbidden to raise the question: How does supply or production condition demand?

This line of thinking leads to the conclusion that before fiscal theory can lay claim to being a critical science, the laws which govern the determination of the volume and composition of state expenditures, and the relation between expenditures and taxes, must be uncovered. This means that fiscal theory must have a clear notion of the character of the state under monopoly capitalism—fiscal theory is then a branch of the theory of the state.

9. BUDGETARY PLANNING

One important tributary of both the micro- and macro-theories of the state finances is budgetary planning. The outlines for an "optimal" budget plan have been presented by Musgrave[12] and others. It is assumed that the scale of social wants is predetermined and that the state is responsible to the "people." The need for "national planning" arises from the historical expansion of the role of the state in the economy and the growing recognition of the need to establish economic objectives as an essential basis for the formulation of economic and fiscal government programs. Musgrave's "optimal" budget is the logical extension of this position.

Musgrave assumes that the state has three main economic functions: the improvement of the allocation of resources, income redistribution, and economic stabilization. From this it follows that there should not be one budget but three: an allocation budget which is formulated so that traditional welfare goals are realized; a distribution budget which distills "society's" idea of equity into a concrete set of transfer payments; and a stabilization budget which insures an appropriate level of aggregate spending or effective demand.

These are the "real" budgets; the consolidated budget should be merely considered as an administrative device. "Consolidation [of the budget]," Musgrave writes, "to be sure, presents no dangers in our imaginary model of efficient budgeting. It is . . . an uninteresting clerical operation undertaken after each of the subbudgets has been formulated on its own merits." But Musgrave is concerned that "in the real world the matter is regarded differently [since] there the tendency is to view the budget in consolidated terms from the outset, and thus confuse the underlying issues in the planning stage." Musgrave of course refers to the underlying issues as defined by policy makers oriented to the needs of the large corporations. From the standpoint of small businessmen or the working class, the absolute size of the budget may itself be an "underlying issue."

What is more, it would seem to confuse the issue to formulate the subbudgets "on [their] own merits," for the reason that for the "loser" the redistribution budget, to take an instance, has no merits. And even accepting Musgrave's own terms of reference, it is difficult to see how

12. Richard Musgrave, *The Theory of Public Finance* (New York, 1959), chaps. 1 and 2.

the subbudgets can be formulated on their own merits because of the interrelationships between them. For example, an income distribution which Musgrave might consider to be "fair" with full employment may be considered by him to be "unfair" with a substantial unemployment rate.

Finally, it should be pointed out that when Musgrave says these are the three "functions" of the state there is the implication that these are *real* functions, and not merely Musgrave's opinion of what the state should have as functions. To be sure, the state may affect the allocation of resources, income distribution, and aggregate demand, but these may be the indirect effects of the *real* functions.

10. THE CORPORATE REVISIONISTS

It is safe to conclude that traditional economics offers no important criteria for state economic policy independent of the welfare norm other than the precept, "a little unemployment, a little inflation." Inevitably, even some bourgeois economists have been unhappy with this state of affairs. The most articulate spokesman of the bourgeois "revisionists" is John Kenneth Galbraith, whose *The Affluent Society* attempts to develop a concept of economic rationality which is partly independent of market rationality. Galbraith's writings represent a sharp break from the traditionalist school in that he *emphasizes* sources of waste under capitalism which cannot be taxed out of existence and sources of gain which subsidies to private interests will fail to bring into being. Not that traditional welfare economics is unaware that these kinds of waste—two favorite examples are the resources used to form a cartel and to circumvent tax laws—arise under capitalism, but they are considered to be "exceptional" or "off the beaten track." What distinguishes the Galbraithian school is the single-minded focus on one source of irrationality—namely, the "artificial" creation of wants by private producers, together with a generalized ideological and financial bias against the public sector and state-provided goods and services.[13]

Put briefly, Galbraith reasons as follows: The demand for public goods in advanced capitalist economies increases more rapidly than the supply of public goods and, given the absence of a price mechanism, there is no tendency for demand and supply to ever reach an equilib-

13. Several well-known policy economists accept Galbraith's main theses. For example, see W. W. Rostow, "The Problem of Achieving and Maintaining a High Rate of Economic Growth: A Historian's View," in *Papers and Proceedings,* American Economic Association 50, no. 2 (May 1950).

rium. Put another way, there is perpetual shortage, growing ever more severe, of public goods and services.

The sources of expansion of demand are located in the growth of urbanization, the social and industrial division of labor in a complex economy, the rise in average income, and so on. These tendencies all add up to an increase in the per capita demand for roads, schools, public health facilities, utility services, urban planning, and the like. On the other hand, there are three related drags on the supply of public goods. First, a general ideological bias against "government" limits the expansion of the public sector; the "conventional wisdom" in the past held that state activities were inherently unproductive and that the need for rapid capital accumulation was first and foremost on the economic agenda. Present thinking about the public sector is irrational because it is conditioned by the prevalence of economic scarcity in the past.[14] Second and third, the operation of markets for private goods under advanced capitalism leans heavily on selling costs to "synthesize" or artificially create demand and thus prevents the accumulation of taxable surpluses by consumers. Private production and consumption is pushed beyond a rational level because it is "the process of satisfying wants that creates wants." The process places consumers in a financial bind (i.e., deep in debt) which in turn sharply limits state expenditures.

Galbraith's opponents fall naturally into one of two camps—critics from the right and critics from the left. Henry Wallich and F. A. Hayek can be cited as representative of the former.[15] Wallich is an exponent of a more or less undiluted form of traditional normative theory. Referring to actual changes in various types of private and public spending, he shows, for example, that both private *and* collective savings for old age have risen more rapidly than total output. Of total expenditures on health and medical care, more than three-quarters were private in 1960. Even in the sphere of education, about one-fifth of total outlays on education were nongovernmental. From these and other data, Wallich asserts that public needs have not been necessarily neglected, nor are they necessarily intrinsically public in character. What may be required, he concludes, is better *private* spending, rather than more pub-

14. The truth of this proposition is a historical question that is inappropriate to consider fully here. Galbraith is in fact quite wide of the mark; in the past the propertied interests feared the state and therefore forbade the state to acquire productive assets. For this reason, the working class either resented or was indifferent to the state because the state was physically and financially unable to meet working-class economic needs and demands.

15. Henry C. Wallich, "Public versus Private: Could Galbraith Be Wrong?" *Harper's Magazine,* October 1961:12–25; F. A. Hayek, "The Non Sequitur of the 'Dependence Effect,'" *Southern Economic Journal* 27, no. 4 (April 1961): 346–348.

lic spending; the aim of the state should be to encourage private business to seize objective opportunities to provide social needs, thus retaining free choice in the marketplace. For bourgeois economists this position—close at home to the competitive norm as it is—has a certain security and familiarity to recommend it. But it hardly comes to grips with Galbraith's main point—economic waste caused by synthesizing demand.

The same complaint cannot be made about Hayek's critique, which purports to meet Galbraith's argument head on. The gist of Hayek's position is that the small value of something is not proven merely because people do not feel the need for it until it is produced. Readers of novels could hardly be aware that they would enjoy *Crime and Punishment* until it was actually written. If Galbraith believes that wants are "passively" created by the production process by which they are satisfied, then his thesis is no more than a truism; if he claims that wants are "deliberately" (Galbraith uses both words) created, then he might have a case, but, in this event, he displays little understanding of the nature of the market system. Individual producers cannot influence wants, Hayek reminds us, much as they may try, because they are faced with competition from others trying to do the same thing.

What escapes Hayek is that it is precisely the inability of any producer to influence his consumers which gives the characteristic of *necessity* to the whole process. It is the net effect of the process of want synthesization (or the selling system) that is important—not the gains and costs to any given producer of advertising and other sales efforts. Put another way, the point is not that the wants which are created are those which any specific producer desires to create, but merely that in general wants are "deliberately" created. To the extent that books and paintings, for example, are transformed into commodities, wants are "deliberately" created in the above sense; the art world is governed by necessity (that is, is not subject to conscious human control). The question whether a writer or painter himself "deliberately creates wants" is an altogether different, and for our present discussion, mainly irrelevant, matter. Thus we can safely conclude that Hayek's criticism is wide of the mark, given the fact that corporations purposefully synthesize wants in order to sell commodities in general, not necessarily the product of their own work.

Galbraith's critics from the left rest their case on two fundamental points.[16] First, it is readily conceded that there exists a "conventional

16. "Review of the Month"; Paul Baran, "Discussion," *Papers and Proceedings,* American Economic Association 50, no. 2 (May 1950).

wisdom" which throws up a bias against the public sector (or at least certain activities of the public sector), but that this masks private material *interests,* which are as powerful now as in the past. Thus an expansion of the public sector requires far more than the popularization of a new *idea;* it is required to curtail the power of those whose interest it is to maintain the old ideas. But Galbraith fails to propose any means of accomplishing this. Clearly, people must be educated to the need for public services; simultaneously attempts by private producers to instill ever greater desires for private goods must be thwarted. On this question, as well, Galbraith is silent, although it is only fair to point out that other liberals use the cold war as a crutch for arguments in favor of "structural changes" in the economy in order to pursue a more "effective" foreign policy.[17]

Putting this possibility aside, the editors of *Monthly Review* correctly write: "It would seem that there is nothing left for liberals to do but take their pens in hand and go forward to do battle for the public mind against capitalism's growing army of open and hidden persuaders. We wish them luck but fear that the contest is an unequal one. It is not that liberals can expect no successes . . . [but] under capitalism liberal reform is a labor of Sisyphus. It never ends, and relative to needs and possibilities it makes little if any progress."

The second main point refers to the sources of financing of an expanded public sector. There are three broad possibilities: (1) the bill can be shifted to the working classes, but it is precisely their interests the enlargement of the public sector is designed to serve; (2) although it is theoretically feasible to appropriate the private product of the propertied classes, public services would then grow at the expense of profits, meeting with dogged resistance on the part of private interests (what would increase the resistance of private business even more is the idea of taxing itself in order to subsidize its own competition [e.g., state insurance and public housing]); (3) a larger public sector can be financed out of economic growth, and a subsequent expansion and rationalization of federal subsidies to state and local governments. This latter possibility is in fact foremost in the thinking of most contemporary students of public finance, chiefly because of the fatal drawbacks of the other two approaches. Yet it is not as politically "neutral" an approach as would appear at first glance. It places the burden of promoting economic growth on the state, which, however, is forbidden to acquire and reproduce productive assets. Thus, state economic policy is necessarily directed toward promoting *private capital accumulation* and

17. David T. Bazelon, *The Paper Economy* (New York, 1965).

hence raising the profit share of national income; in effect, we are told that the distribution of income must be worsened before it is possible to correct the imbalance between private and public goods and services. Actually, one main task of the capitalist state has *always* been to promote private accumulation, and therefore it is readily understandable why the "growth school" of public finance is so popular among bourgeois economists.

To this critique, we add two observations: First, Galbraith, as well as the traditionalists, lacks any theory of the *distribution* of public goods and services. It can be shown that in middle-class communities there is an approximation of an "optimal" bundle of private and public goods, but not in urban working-class communities. Thus, what Galbraith (together with some Marxist writers) mistakes for a generalized shortage of public goods is often in fact inequalities in their distribution.

Second, Galbraith does not tell us whether we should correct overcrowded highways by building more highways, or developing mass transit, or both. In general, he fails to provide any criteria for public spending, excepting impressionistic references to "unsatisfied public needs." The problem is not that the values of the economists figure in their scientific work; quite the opposite. The problem is that they fail to have any strongly felt values, and hence substitute the ruling values for their own.

The "revisionists," of which we take Galbraith as the key representative, depart from the traditional school in two fundamental and related respects: first, as we have seen, Galbraith locates *important* irrationalities in advanced capitalism which do not fit easily into traditional externality concepts; second, Galbraith is led by this position to introduce the state as a *deus ex machina;* the state "solves problems" when they arise without reference to the source or nature of the problem. Between the two varieties of bourgeois thought, then, there is a quite different assessment of the possibilities of social and economic change in a capitalist society. The traditional school, represented by Baumol, describes individual needs and desires as they are transfigured by a voting process into state economic activity. The state economy is reduced to the totality of personal needs; therefore, assuming that individual behavior is rational and well informed, what is possible is what exists; today's allocation of resources within and between the "private" and "public" sectors is in general the only possible one.

Galbraith's state, on the other hand, is the creation of objective reason—as opposed to the rationality of the market—and submits to reasoned argument by enlightened citizens. But as to how the state attained the independence to play the role assigned it, and as to how the role is played concretely, we are left in the dark.[18]

One reason that both the traditional and Galbraithian schools offer no concrete independent criteria to guide state policy is attributable to the lack of any coherent theory of the capitalist state.[19] As Buchanan has put it, neither school has made "explicit their assumptions concern-

18. In his earlier work on "countervailing power," Galbraith also assigns the state a certain mysterious independence. It should not surprise us that Keynes and his followers share a similar perspective. Keynes looked to the state "not to do things which individuals are doing already, not to do them a little better or a little worse; but to do those things which at present are not done at all" (quoted in Lionel Robbins, "The Economic Functions of the State in English Classical Political Economy," in Edmund S. Phelps, ed., *Private Wants and Public Needs* [New York, 1962], p. 97).

Walter Heller advances a closely related view. To paraphrase his position very roughly: The role of the economist in government is to rationally blend the service, stabilization, and income-transfer "functions" of government. We must note the assumption that these are truly "functions" and that the state with the right advice can and will correct irrationalities and inequities.

19. John F. Due is a well-known student of public finance and the author of the leading basic textbook in the field. He is also a man who in this book not only cannot separate science from ideology or fact from value, but also is not even aware of the difference.

In Chapter 1 of his text, *Government Finance: Economics of the Public Sector,* rev. ed. (Homewood, Ill., 1962), his purpose is a "preliminary review of the reasons *why* the governments have undertaken various forms of economic activity" (p. 3, italics added). He thus poses a scientific question: Why do military, education, and highway expenditure make up the vast share of government spending? On page 6, this scientific perspective becomes less sharp. An explanation of the trend of increasing state activity "must be based upon a consideration of the extent to which a free market society attains or fails to attain the goals of economic welfare which are accepted by society." Note too that he *assumes* certain "goals" that are "accepted by society."

But immediately a certain ambiguity creeps in: *"To the extent that* the undertaking of economic activity by government is based upon the desires of the community, it reflects dissatisfaction with the adequacy of the market economy in obtaining optimum welfare" (italics added). But he does not describe the conditions under which the government will *not* undertake economic activity based on the desires of the community.

Pages 7–13 are devoted to an analysis of the *reasons* for state economic activity. The "reasons" are taken out of the pages of the books of *normative* economists! Thus science for Due consists of the following steps: first, hypothesize a competitive economy with welfare maximizing as "society's goal" (as if the average person either knew or cared about the precepts or counsels of normative economics!); second, "explain" state economic activity on the basis of departures from these idealized goals (e.g., externalities, public goods, internal economics of scales, monopoly, a "fair" income distribution, high employment without inflation). That is, Due makes a very unsubtle shift from positive science to normative economics.

His choice of language is one clue. He frequently uses the expression "the task of the government is to. . . ." This obscures his real meaning. If he stuck to the scientific question, he would write, "the government *does* such and such *because.* . . ." If he understood the difference between science and economic game playing he would write, "the government *should* do such and such because. . . ."

In Chapter 2 he switches gears altogether, admitting the irrelevance of the criteria of normative economics. The government is no longer the embodied will of "society," but rather the interpreter of this will. "The task of determining community consensus about the desirability of the various degrees of attainment of the goals, and thus of the relative importance attached by society to the activities, rests upon the government."

ing the form of the polity."[20] Wicksell caught the problem from almost the right perspective when he wrote that "much of the discussion in fiscal theory proceeds on the implicit and unrecognized assumption that the society is ruled by a benevolent despot." It is probably more accurate to say that one welfare theorist's benevolent despot is another's arbitrary dictator.

We conclude with the reminder that few modern orthodox economists concern themselves very much with the question of the real relationships between the private and public sectors. The public sector "exists" on the basis of a priori reasoning, or it is assumed to exist in a vacuum. One exception to the rule is Buchanan, who appreciates that "any approach to a complete or satisfactory treatment of the public economy must examine as a central feature the way in which collective decisions are made." It is clear from the above analysis, however, that the important questions revolve around the real functions of the state under monopoly capitalism. It is only by taking the step toward a reconstruction of the theory of the state and the state finances that we will have a basis for a complete critique of bourgeois economic science.

20. James B. Buchanan, *Fiscal Theory and Political Economy* (Chapel Hill, N.C., 1960), p. 4. Even Buchanan, who among bourgeois economists is one of the most aware of the need for some solid sociological foundations for public finance theory, fails in these essays to go beyond a critique and to reconstruct the theory. When he attempts to do so in a book coauthored by Gordon Tullock, he cannot give up the traditional extreme utilitarian assumptions.

CHAPTER SIX

The Fiscal Crisis
of the State

This essay is a contribution to the analysis of the development of the present-day world capitalist economy as a whole. The starting point is summarized in Georg Lukács's remark that "all economic or 'sociological' phenomena derive from the social relations of men to one another." In Lenin's words, Marx selected "from all social relations the 'production relations' as being the basic and prime relations that determine all other relations." Marx termed the production relations—the social relations between human beings in the process of production, distribution, and exchange—"the economic structure of society."

The relations of production in capitalist society are antagonistic. Marx demonstrated that the antagonism springs from the basic contradiction of capitalism: on the one hand, capitalist production is intrinsically social in character; on the other hand, the means of production are monopolized by private owners —that is, production is for profit, not for use.

Since Marx wrote Capital *the world capitalist system has undergone a tremendous advance in the development of the forces of production and important changes in the relations of production, some of them foreseen by Marx, others not.*

On the one side, production has become much more social; an incredibly complex world network of economic interdependency has developed (see Chapter One). The advanced social character of production in turn has led to higher forms of social integration—for example, the modern corporation integrates labor power drawn from dozens of different countries, and applied to thousands of specific tasks (see Chapters Seven and Eight). On the other side, the means of production have become concentrated in fewer and fewer hands; industrial capital and bank capital have merged into large-scale monopoly or finance capital. The basic contradiction of capitalism has therefore intensified; and since this contradiction gives rise to class struggle, class struggle has also intensified.

World capitalism has undergone other changes, changes in the arenas in which the class struggle is fought, and changes in the forms of struggle. In short, the class struggle has been diffused, fragmented, and displaced. The reason that the class struggle has been displaced is the higher form of social integration that has accompanied the intensified social character of production.

The corporate ruling class in the United States (like European and Japanese ruling classes in past eras) displaces the class struggle abroad by establishing the dollar as a world reserve asset, by exporting unemployment through the use of foreign aid, by establishing branch plants of industrial corporations abroad, and by many other methods. The revival of French nationalism pitted against the United States, West Germany's new independence, Japan's fresh interest in "traditional" American markets in Latin America, and, above all, national liberation struggles in Asia, Africa, and Latin America are all in part responses to the American ruling class's attempts to export its economic and social problems.

At home, the black revolution, rank and file struggles within the unions and directed against union leadership, the student revolt, the women's movement, and the youth movement all signify new arenas and new forms of struggle.

This essay takes up the question of the growing movement of employees of the state, clients of the state, and others who must look to the state for that which they cannot provide for themselves, and which private capital cannot provide. Its major thesis is that the fusion of economic base and political superstructure in the current era has extended the class struggle from the sphere of direct production to the sphere of state administration, and transformed the forms of struggle.[1] It also argues that the state is unable to contain these struggles in formalized relations among labor unions, workers, clients, and state agencies such as welfare institutions.

1. INTRODUCTION

At present, the United States federal government employs about 2.5 million civilian workers in eighty departments and agencies and nearly 4 million members of the armed forces, and total state and local government employment is roughly 8.5 million. In the federal government, employment is greatest in military and international relations agencies and the postal service, which employ 1 million and 600,000 workers, respectively. At the state and local level, employment is concentrated

1. Norman Birnbaum's criticism of classical Marxism in this sphere is too moderate: ". . . the bourgeois state has become so embedded in the economy proper . . . [that] the classical Marxist theorems on the relationship between base and superstructure require emendation" ("The Crisis in Marxist Sociology," *Social Research* 35, no. 2 [Summer 1968]: 350). Rudi Dutschke's criticism may be too severe:

The problem of the intervention of the State in the socio-economic process becomes a problem for neither Lenin nor Lukács. But precisely this . . . ought to have been subjected to revolutionary/scientific investigation. . . . Only thus could there have been a materialist theory of crises with revolutionary implications in the period after the world war. Uncritical retention of the 'time-tested formulas' of the classics degraded the revolutionary struggle to the level of unthinking praxis, blind activity. [Bergmann et al., *Rebellion der Studenten, oder die neue Opposition* (Hamburg, 1968), p. 50]

in the fields of education (4 million workers), health and hospitals (1 million), highways (550,000), and police protection (450,000).[2] In brief, a sizable part of the "new working class" employed in nondirectly productive, service, and similar occupations is employed by the state.

In addition to the 11 million workers employed directly by the state, there are countless wage and salary earners—perhaps as many as 25 to 30 million—who are employed by private capital dependent in whole or in part on state contracts and facilities. Workers in such industries as military and space, branches of capital goods, construction, transportation, and others, are *indirectly* employed by state capital. Further, tens of thousands of doctors, welfare workers, and other self-employed and privately employed professionals and technicians who use facilities provided by the state are also dependent in whole or in part on the state budget. Finally, tens of millions of men and women are dependent on the budget as clients and recipients of state services; these include nearly all students at all levels of education, welfare recipients, and users of public health, hospital, recreational, and other facilities.

There is no way to measure the total number of people who are related to each other through the state budget, and who are dependent on the budget for their material well-being; everyone is in part dependent on the state, and for millions of poor people, particularly minority people, this dependence runs very deep. Perhaps one-quarter to one-third of the labor force is wholly dependent on the state for basic necessities. And, historically, more and more people have looked to the state for that which they cannot provide themselves. Schools and colleges are bulging at the seams, the welfare roles expand, and state employment holds out the only hope of employment for millions of blacks, young people, retired workers, and women—between 1950 and 1966 the state sector accounted for 25 percent of the total growth of employment in the United States.

During recent years of high taxes and inflation, real wages and salaries of state workers have declined.[3] Better known is the fact that federal, state, and local welfare, health, and education budgets are being frozen or cut across the entire country. And the growing poverty of the state spills over into the private sector, not only in the form of rising taxes that cut into real income, but also in rising prices for

2. U.S. Department of Commerce, *Chart Book on Governmental Finances and Employment, 1966* (Washington, D.C., 1966), p. 15.
3. Although the state employs many workers with the same kinds of skills required in the private sector, there is little competition for state jobs originating from the work force in the private sector.

services. Because of the absence of new facilities constructed by the state, for example, hospital fees rose by 100 percent from 1957 to 1967, and are expected to rise more than 200 percent from 1968 to 1975.[4]

Progressively tighter budgets, constant or falling real wages and salaries of state employees, and declining welfare expenditures and social services in general have unleashed a torrent of criticism against the state by employees, dependents, and others. Public employee unions grow by leaps and bounds. The American Federation of State, County and Municipal Employees grew from 150,000 members in 1950 to 400,000 today. Unions are calling more strikes, and strikes are fought for longer periods: in 1953 there were only 30 strikes against state and local governments; in 1966 and 1967, 152 and 181 strikes, respectively. In 1967–1968 the American Federation of Teachers alone conducted 32 major walkouts and mini-strikes that involved nearly 100,000 teachers.[5] In Massachusetts state employees have created an organization that cuts across occupational and agency lines, and that has mounted a demand for a 20 percent wage and salary increase. In New York 25 percent of the city's union membership are public employees. In the past few years, whole towns and cities have been brought to a standstill as a result of general strikes of municipal employees.

Practical criticism of the state has not been confined to local general strikes, still less to traditional labor union activity. State clients and dependents have been compelled to conduct their struggles around budgetary issues in highly unorthodox ways. Today there are few sectors of the state economy that remain unorganized. Welfare recipients have organized hundreds of welfare rights groups; student organizations have conducted militant struggles in small or large part over the control of the state budget for minority studies programs, student activities, and so on; blacks are struggling in countless ways to force the state to intervene on their behalf; public health workers, doctors, probation officers, prisoners, even patients in public mental hospitals have organized themselves, and seek better work facilities or better treatment and more finances and resources for themselves and the people whom they serve.

A serious revolt against high taxation is also developing. The forms of the present tax revolt are many and varied; the core cities are demanding that suburban commuters pay their "fair share" of city expenditures, and the suburbanites are resisting attempts to organize their

4. Bureau of Labor Statistics study, cited in *Missouri Teamsters,* 5 April 1968.
5. *American Teacher* 52, no. 10 (June 1968).

communities into metropolitan governments; working-class residential districts organize tax referenda against downtown business interests; and property owners vote into office politicians who promise to reduce property tax burdens.

All of these activities—the demands mounted by state workers and dependents, on the one hand, and the tax revolt, on the other—both reflect and deepen the fiscal crisis of the state, or the gap between expenditures and taxation. Yet, by and large, these struggles have not been fought along class lines, and therefore do not necessarily pose a revolutionary challenge to the United States ruling class. In fact, the popular struggle for the control of state expenditures has been led by liberal forces, and, to a much lesser degree, by militant black and radical forces. And the tax revolt has been all but monopolized by the right wing.

Nevertheless, the state has been unable to develop traditional ad-ministrative solutions to these struggles, struggles in which the state itself is one of the contending parties. The state has not yet been able to encapsulate these struggles, nor has it been able to channel frustra-tion, anger, and energy into activities which potentially do not threaten ruling class budgetary control. Whether or not the state can succeed in ameliorating these struggles, whether or not the state can prevent large numbers of people coming together in radical organizations around budgetary issues, and whether or not the contradiction between right-wing leadership of the tax revolt and liberal-left leadership of the fight for the control of expenditures can be resolved—these are some of the questions raised here.

2. A POLITICAL FRAMEWORK FOR BUDGETARY ANALYSIS

The developing economic struggles against the state are rooted in the structural contradictions of United States capitalism. Full compre-hension and evaluation of these struggles requires a political frame-work for an analysis of the state budget. Budgetary theory is a branch of the theory of the state, and thus a brief sketch of the nature of state power is needed.

How do the main production relations in the United States express themselves politically? In the first place, the state is the economic instru-ment of the dominant stratum of the ruling class—the owners and controllers of the large corporations, who have organized themselves along both interest group and class lines.

Interest group organization, activity, and participation in the state have been studied by McConnell, Hamilton, Kolko, Engler, and others.[6] In Hamilton's words, "there are currently associations of manufacturers, of distributors, and of retailers; there are organizations which take all commerce as their province; and there are federations of local clubs of businessmen with tentacles which reach into the smaller urban centers and market towns. All such organizations are active instruments in the creation of attitudes, in the dissemination of sound opinion, and in the promotion of practices which may become widespread."[7]

In essence, these organizations are self-regulatory private associations which are ordinarily organized along industry rather than regional or other lines, owing to the national character of commodity markets. More often than not, these industry groups use the state to mediate between their members, as well as to provide needed credits, subsidies, technical aid, and general support. Some of the key industry and interest groups are the highway lobby (automobiles, oil, rubber, glass, branches of construction, and so on), the military lobby, oil, cotton textiles, railroads, airlines, radio and television, public utilities, banking and brokerage. In agriculture, wheat, cotton, sugar, and other growers, together with cattlemen, are also organized into industry associations.

These and other interest groups have appropriated numerous small pieces of state power through a "multiplicity of intimate contacts with the government."[8] They dominate most of the so-called regulatory agencies at the federal, state, and local levels and many bureaus within the Departments of Agriculture and Interior, the Bureau of Highways, and a number of congressional committees. Their specific interests are reflected in the partial or full range of policies of hundreds of national and state government agencies, for example, the Interstate Commerce Commission and other regulatory bodies, Department of Defense, Corps of Engineers, United States Tariff Commission, and Federal Reserve Bank. "What emerges as the most important political reality," McConnell writes in a summary of the politics of interest groups,

> is an array of relatively separated political systems, each with a number of elements. These typically include: (1) a federal administrative agency within the executive branch; (2) a heavily committed group of Congress-

6. Grant McConnell, *Private Power and American Democracy* (New York, 1966); Walton Hamilton, *The Politics of Industry* (New York, 1957); Gabriel Kolko, *Railroads and Regulation, 1877–1916* (Princeton, N.J., 1965); Robert Engler, *The Politics of Oil* (New York, 1961).

7. Hamilton, *The Politics of Industry*, p. 9.

8. McConnell, *Private Power and American Democracy*, p. 279.

men and Senators, usually members of a particular committee or subcommittee; (3) a private (or quasi-private) association representing the agency clientele; (4) a quite homogeneous constituency usually composed of local elites. Where dramatic conflicts over policy have occurred, they have appeared as rivalries among the public administrative agencies, but the conflicts are more conspicuous and less important than the agreements among these systems. The most frequent solution to conflict is jurisdictional demarcation and establishment of spheres of influence. Logrolling, rather than compromise, is the normal pattern of relationship.[9]

By itself, interest group politics is inconsistent with the survival and expansion of capitalism. For one thing, "the interests which keep [the interest groups] going," Hamilton writes, "are too disparate, and the least common denominator of action is too passive to bring into being a completely cohesive union."[10] For another, interest consciousness obviously leads to contradictory policies; enduring interest groups require a sense of "responsibility"—that is, class consciousness. For example, the attempt by regulatory agencies to maintain profitable conditions in a particular industry tends to freeze the pattern of resource allocation, establish monopoly conditions, and so on, which in turn retards capital accumulation and expansion in the economy as a whole. Foreign economic expansion thus becomes increasingly important, as a key mode of economic growth and as a way to transform interest group conflict into interest group harmony. And foreign expansion clearly requires a class-conscious political directorate.

The *class* organization of corporate capital—both its private activity and participation in the state—have been studied by Williams, Weinstein, Kolko, Domhoff, Eakins, and others.[11] These writers have shown that increasing instability and inefficiency attendent upon capitalist production increased investment risk and uncertainty, contributed to crises and depressions, and led to a deficiency of aggregate demand. By the turn of the century, and especially during the New Deal, it was apparent to the vanguard corporate leaders that some form of rationalization of the economy was necessary. And as the twentieth century wore on,

9. Ibid., p. 244.
10. Hamilton, *The Politics of Industry*, p. 9.
11. William Appleman Williams, *The Contours of American History* (New York, 1961); James Weinstein, *The Corporate Ideal in the Liberal State, 1900–1918* (Boston, 1968); Gabriel Kolko, *The Triumph of Conservatism, 1900–1916* (Glencoe, Ill., 1963); G. William Domhoff, *Who Rules America?* (Englewood Cliffs, N.J., 1967); David Eakins, "The Development of Corporate Liberal Policy Research, 1885–1965" (Ph.D. diss., University of Wisconsin, 1966).

The theoretical issues in the analysis of ruling classes, interest groups, and power elites are discussed in W. Wesolowski, "Class Domination and the Power of Interest Groups," *Polish Sociological Bulletin,* no. 3–4 (1962): 53–65; "Ruling Class and Power Elite," *Polish Sociological Bulletin,* no. 1 (1965): 22–33.

the owners of corporate capital generated the financial ability, learned the organizational skills, and developed the ideas necessary for their self-regulation as a class.

Thus, it was a class-conscious corporate directorate which controlled the War Industry Board during World War I, parts of the NRA and AAA, and the Office of War Mobilization, the last of the World War II planning agencies. Class-conscious corporate capital today profoundly influences or controls the Department of Defense, agencies within the Commerce and State departments, Treasury Department, Council of Economic Advisers, and Bureau of the Budget. Owing to the necessity of reconciling and compromising conflicts within the corporate ruling class and to the complex and wide-ranging nature of the interests of this class, policy is not dictated by a single directorate but rather by a multitude of private, quasi-public, and public agencies. Policy is formulated within the highly influential Business Advisory Council, in key ruling class universities and policy planning agencies such as the Foreign Policy Association and the Committee for Economic Development, and by the corporate-dominated political parties, and translated into law through legislation written and introduced by the federal executive. The president and his key aides thus have the supreme task of interpreting corporate ruling class interests, and translating these interests into action, not only in terms of immediate economic and political needs, but also in terms of the relations between corporate capital on the one side, and labor and small capital on the other.

This is the second way the production relations are expressed politically: the regulation of the social relations between classes in the interests of maintaining the social order as a whole. Around the turn of the century, labor, socialist, and populist forces posed a potentially serious threat to American capitalism. In a series of political moves designed to prevent popular movements from "removing the extremes of society"—capital and wage labor—the corporate leaders and the political directorate sought, in Marx's words, "to weaken their antagonisms and transform them into a harmonious whole." Lelio Basso writes that "capitalism can function only thanks to the permanent intervention of the state to organize the markets and ensure the process of accumulation."[12] The political meaning of this "permanent intervention" is that all elements of the population must be integrated into a coherent system, not rejected by it. Far

12. Lelio Basso, "*State and Revolution* Reconsidered," *International Socialist Journal* 5, no. 25 (February 1968): 82.

and away the most important element is organized labor, which was taught a responsible attitude toward corporate capital and society as a whole. Specifically, this required regular cooperation between the leaders of organized labor, the corporations, and the state to head off mass social movements, transform collective bargaining into an instrument of corporate planning, guarantee a high level of employment and wages commensurate with productivity advances, and maintain labor's reproductive powers, with regard not only to the level of private consumption, but also to social insurance, health, education, and general welfare.

Class conflict thus tends to be bureaucratized, encapsulated, administered; qualitative demands originating on the shop floor are transformed by union leaders into quantitative demands that do not threaten "managerial prerogatives"; contradictions between labor and capital at the point of production are displaced or deflected into other spheres. Corporate capital's agencies for regulating the relations between organized labor and the unemployed and poor and themselves are numerous—the National Labor Relations Board, National Mediation Board, Federal Mediation and Conciliation Service, Department of Labor, Social Security Administration, Department of Health, Education and Welfare, congressional committees and subcommittees, and state employment agencies are some of the most important.

The state also regulates the relations between big capital and small capital, between capital based in different regions, and between capital in expanding sectors of the economy and capital in contracting sectors. Monopoly capital requires the political support of local and regional capital for its national and international programs, and thus cannot afford to antagonize the latter needlessly; subsidies must be granted to declining industries and to capital in underdeveloping regions. Deeply involved in managing relations within the ruling class as a whole, and permanently engaged in financing small capital support for monopoly capital, are, among other agencies, the Department of Agriculture, the Department of Commerce, many congressional committees, and federal grant-in-aid programs.[13]

13. There is a final aspect of state power, the financial dependence of the state on the banks and other financial institutions whose cooperation is necessary to float the state debt. Only in times of national emergency has this dependence dissolved; for example, during World War II when the Treasury compelled the Federal Reserve system to support federal bond prices. At the state and local level, the dependence of the state on finance capital for capital funds is total.

3. STATE CAPITALIST BUDGETARY PRINCIPLES AND CONTROL

Many of these aspects of state power, which are not unique to monopoly capitalism, but which have taken special forms in the twentieth century, are extremely expensive. Further, excepting interest group economic needs, to which the elected branch is highly responsive, the new functions of the state require a strong executive branch, supportive class-conscious elements in the Congress, and executive control of the state budget, because they require overall planning. The growth of, and centralization of power within, the executive branch, the multiplication of its functions, the decline of congressionally initiated legislation, the growth of bureaucratically managed governments at the state and local levels, the development of city manager governments, and the spread of the giant supramunicipal authorities—that is, the major trend of our times that signifies the removal of decision making from politics and the substitution of bureaucratic and administrative rule—constitute a familiar story.

Less familiar, but of equal importance, are the corresponding changes in budgetary control. Therefore a review of the changing state budgetary principles, in particular the process through which the executive appropriated control of the budget, is required.

In the late nineteenth and the twentieth centuries, technological innovations in production and the need to harmonize and stabilize production relations revolutionized the state finances and the budgetary principles on which they were based. The development of science and organized technology, the accumulation of large blocks of capital, and the concentration and integration of the work force needed to be regulated and controlled. As state capitalism and monopolistic industry developed, the budgetary principles of the liberal state were gradually discarded.

One change was the substitution of direct for indirect taxation; another was the surrender of the principle of balanced budgets; still another was the acceptance of an inconvertible paper monetary standard and a new role for loan finance. But most important, there was a steady expansion of state expenditures and an increase in the number and variety of state economic functions.

The evolution of the state budget as an increasing source of monopoly profits has gone hand in hand with the development of the state bureaucracy as the administrative arm of the giant corporations. This is particularly the case in the military, space, foreign loan, and research and development fields, where the lion's share of investment and production costs is borne by the general taxpayer while the profits accrue to the corporations. Further, there is the assumption of government rather than individual risk associated with the operation of the economy. The state underwrites business losses sustained during economic crises and arising from the anarchy of capitalist production. Direct lending, indirect lending via intermediaries, and loan insurance and guarantees socialize business risk and create huge government liabilities that can be guaranteed only by further private capital accumulation and growth—and hence more loans, subsidies, and guarantees. State capitalism is no temporary phenomenon that will be dismantled once capitalism finds its way back to "normalcy," but rather is the integrating principle of the modern economic era.

A brief review of the changing relationships between the representative and executive branches of the state is needed to fully comprehend the character and significance of the revolutionary change in the budget principles of monopoly capitalism. In Britain the budget was transformed into an instrument of the financial control of the crown by the rising middle classes during their struggle for political representation and, finally, political dominance. In the United States revolutionary warfare eliminated the crown, removing any analogous development. From the very beginning, a certain harmony between Congress and the executive existed because both represented more or less perfectly the interests of local and regional capital. The budget was from the start the expression of the material interests of the planter and merchant classes and, later, the farmers, and was always a source of private profit. By the late nineteenth century, the ascendancy of national capital and the giant regional interest groups began to drive a wedge between the representative and executive branches of the federal government. The latter became more and more responsive to national capital while the former still largely represents small, regional and local capital, as well as trade union and community interests.

Especially since the turn of the century, the control exercised by the representative body over appropriations has become increasingly imperfect. The ways in which Congress has disabled itself include the establishment of revolving funds, the creation of government corporations, the refusal to prohibit transfers between appropriations, the authorization of the use of departmental receipts without limitation of amount, and the voting of lump-sum appropriations.[14] The attempt to reestablish control by way of large numbers of specific appropriations,

14. Lucius Wilmerding, Jr., *The Spending Power: A History of the Efforts of Congress to Control Expenditures* (New Haven, Conn., 1943), p. 193.

"far from securing to Congress that completeness of financial control which is . . . its constitutional birthright, has served only to make the law less certain and to satisfy Congress with the name, rather than the substance of power."[15] Congressional control after funds have been appropriated has been equally imperfect. It is instructive to compare the situation in the United States with that in Britain, where parliamentary control after appropriations is relatively secure and the House of Commons is able to ensure that its policies are carried out "accurately, faithfully, and efficiently."[16]

Meanwhile class-conscious elements within the executive branch of the federal government have been eager to transform the budget into an instrument of national economic planning in accordance with the needs of national capital. With this aim in mind, the executive has hurried along the consolidation of its own financial powers by mingling appropriations, bringing forward the unexpended balance of former appropriations and backward the anticipated balance of future appropriations, and by incurring coercive deficiencies.[17]

Changes in the formal character of the state budget, however, have been the major steps toward executive financial control. At least three budgetary changes deserve mention. The first was the introduction of the "administrative budget," which coordinates expenditures proposed by the executive, and the creation of the Bureau of the Budget by the Budget and Accounting Act of 1920. The administrative budget is the basic instrument that coordinates the various activities of the congressional committees, which in turn are responsive to the specific industrial, regional, and other interests of private capital. It is the chief mode of "management and control by the Executive and Congress over activities financed with federal funds . . . which [once approved] becomes a tool of Executive control over the spending of the various departments, agencies, and government corporations."[18] In effect, the Act took the initiative away from Congress and gave it to the president. The class-conscious, corporate-dominated Institute for Government Research led the way. Many decades passed before Congress was willing to support the idea of coordinated executive expenditure proposals, and historically the individual executive departments had dealt directly with the specific congressional committees. Thus it was not until well into the twentieth century (putting aside the post-Revolutionary War period) that the state was sufficiently independent of specific private

15. Ibid., p. 195.
16. Basil Chubb, *The Control of Public Expenditures* (London, 1952), p. 1.
17. Wilmerding, *The Spending Power,* p. 194.
18. David S. Ott and Attiat F. Ott, *Federal Budget Policy* (Washington, D.C., 1965), p. 6.

interests to begin to impose its own discipline on the private economy.

The second change in the increasing executive domination of the budget is the gradual substitution of "line-time" budgets with "program" budgets. Line-time budgets are the net result of many specific competing forces, and classify expenditures in terms of the items to be purchased, while program budgets classify outlays on the basis of outputs and the resources necessary to yield certain outputs, and hence require some measure of resource costs—that is, some planning. The idea of program budgeting was first put forth in 1912 by the Taft Commission on Economy and Efficiency and the first applications were made by the Tennessee Valley Authority and the Navy Department. Beginning in 1961, program budgeting was introduced in the Department of Defense. For fiscal year 1968, twenty-three major departments and agencies were instructed to prepare program budgets, and many other departments were encouraged to do so.[19]

From an administrative point of view, program budgeting lays the basis for the application of marginal analysis and hence is attractive to many economists. Smithies, for example, writes that "budgeting is essentially an economic problem in solving as it does the allocation of scarce resources among almost insatiable and competing demands."[20] In supporting program budgeting, this school of thought denies that budgetary issues are political issues and sees little or no difference between the allocation of resources by the household or business firm and the state. Critical analysis of the state and the state budget per se is replaced by an implicit acceptance of the given balance of private interests as reflected in the given composition of the budget. As one defender of program budgeting writes, "marginal analysis points to the need for continual reassessment of the pattern of expenditure *at the margin*, rather than being beguiled by arguments concerning the over-all 'necessity' of a particular program."[21] Other economists, however, clearly understand that the real significance of program budgeting is that it strengthens the executive office of the president in relation not only to the federal agencies but also to the Congress. The program budget, according to Burkhead, "becomes a technique, not for management at the operating level, but for the centralization of administrative authority."[22]

19. David Novick, ed., *Program Budgeting: Program Analysis and the Federal Budget* (Cambridge, Mass., 1965), passim.

20. Arthur Smithies, *The Budgetary Process in the United States* (New York, 1955), pp. xiv–xv.

21. James R. Schlesinger, *The Political Economy of National Security* (New York, 1960), p. 109.

22. Jesse Burkhead, *American Economic Review* 56, no. 4 (September 1966), review of Novick, *Program Budgeting*, p. 943.

The third step toward executive control of the state finances was taken in 1963 when for the first time the budget contained an analysis of expenditures and receipts on a national income accounting basis. The national income budget is a more accurate measure of the impact of federal spending on general economic activity because it excludes purely financial credit transactions and it accounts for receipts and expenditures at the time of their economic impact rather than when cash receipts and payments are actually made. The national income budget represents an explicit recognition of the integral relation between the budget and the private economy and is a necessary precondition for overall fiscal planning.

In Congress there was for years no immediate sense of a loss of power. Congressional procedures for appropriating federal funds have remained unchanged for decades and the budget is still viewed by the representative branch as a set of individual and unrelated parts. It remains true that "taxes and expenditures are decided separately by the separate committees in each house, and although the bills on taxes and appropriations are passed by vote of the whole House and whole Senate, there is little evidence that the two groups of bills are related closely to each other when they are considered."[23] Similarly, the benefits and costs of the programs authorized in the specific appropriations bills are never analyzed or judged in relation to each other. Nor are the bills discussed or studied in detail by the full committees, and full House debate is rare. Each subcommittee of the House Appropriations Committee, for example, is still concerned with a different division of the government and "it is quite natural that a group of men familiar with a particular division of the executive branch will be inclined to take a parochial interest in its welfare."[24] In any event, only about 30 percent of federal expenditures is within congressional discretion to change from year to year. Finally, in recent years the military budget and weapons policies have been determined by the Department of Defense and the Armed Services committees without any real critical examination by the Congress.

In one sense, Congress still effectively "represents" the various parochial interests. But the executive increasingly interprets and coordinates these interests. This is an extremely subtle process and has few formal expressions, even though informal control is substantial. For one thing, any bill initiated by an individual congressman without "legislative clearance" from the Budget Bureau faces enormous obstacles.

23. Ott and Ott, *Federal Budget Policy*, p. 36.
24. Schlesinger, *National Security*, p. 111.

The Bureau has considerable control over the direction and timing of federal obligations incurred because it is the apportioning authority, hence augmenting its powers even more. During the Kennedy years, the Bureau, the Treasury, and the Council of Economic Advisors were organized into an informal group with the responsibility for overall fiscal planning, and began to exercise a powerful influence on the budget and general fiscal decisions. Thus, increasingly, budget policy is formulated by the executive without any attempt to revolutionize or "modernize" the appropriations process in the Congress itself. The effect of this shift in financial control to the executive has been succinctly described by Schlesinger:

> The Congress, secure in its belief that the basic legislation has established policy, may view its annual consideration of the budget formulated by the experts simply from the standpoint of assuring the most economical attainment of legislative goals. Thus policy formulation, which is so intimately connected with the appropriations levels, may slip into organizational limbo and finally be unconsciously seized by the Bureau of the Budget—the one organization that, in theory, should be concerned with economy and efficiency, and should be divorced entirely from policy formulation.[25]

The general result is that budget issues cease to be political issues, and the budget becomes a more reliable planning instrument for the executive. In the past two decades, no major program introduced during previous administrations has been eliminated. The Republican administration in the 1950s even failed to reverse the upward trend of federal spending, including the expansion of outlays in the health, education, and welfare fields. In the contemporary period, only the executive can interpret the needs of private capital and private interests as a whole, and effectively act on these interpretations.[26] So far as the operation of

25. Ibid., p. 107.
26. The process that we describe above is also characteristic of state government finances. State and local governments have little or no financial independence and hence the scope for independent financial activity even in the legislatures is severely restricted. We are fortunate to have a careful study of the state finances of Illinois (Thomas J. Anton, *The Politics of State Expenditures in Illinois* [Urbana, Ill., 1966]), which demonstrates this proposition:
> Despite its formal authority over appropriations, the 1963 General Assembly was virtually powerless in the determination of state expenditures.... The legislature had no criteria of its own to apply to [appropriations] bills other than the fact that they were appropriations and therefore worthy of passage. In the absence of such criteria legislative behavior could only produce a stamp of acceptance for decisions made elsewhere. As an institution the legislature was incapable of doing more. [p. 246]
Elsewhere Anton writes that "decisions with regard to large [expenditures] increases, and all other major decisions made in 1963 were determined by the Governor, or persons acting in his name. Deference to the Governor on all 'big' decisions was in part a function of his control over a centralized budgetary mechanism and in part due to his unique ability to take the actions necessary to balance the budget." (p. 247)
The responsiveness of local government to the needs of large-scale capital has been

bourgeois democratic institutions is concerned, there is no need to add anything to the conclusion of one economist: "The relationship between the legislative and executive branches largely determines the success or failure of democratic government. Hence, the budget, because it is at the same time the most important instrument of legislative control and executive management, is at the very core of democratic government."[27]

4. SOCIAL CAPITAL EXPENDITURES

The budget reflects the particular and general economic needs of corporate capital, on the one hand, and the general political needs of the ruling class as a whole, on the other. Preliminary to an investigation of these needs, and their budgetary reflections, it should be stressed that there are no specific budgetary items that mirror *exclusively* any particular or general need. There are no hard-and-fast theoretical categories applicable to the analysis of the budget because there are no precise, real, historical budgetary categories. Individual expenditure items do not reflect with absolute precision any particular interest; quite the contrary, a particular item may express imperfectly a multitude of interests. To cite one outstanding example, state-financed railroad construction in the nineteenth century was determined by a combination of related economic and political factors.

Today there are few state expenditures that fail to serve a number of different, although related, ends. Johnson's War on Poverty aimed to simultaneously insure social peace, upgrade labor skills, subsidize

noted in other countries. In Japan, local governments are "clerks" for monopolistic enterprise and "promote works exclusively for the interests of great enterprise at the expense of local inhabitants" (Kiyoharu Nishikawa, "Local Governments and their Financial Administration in Post-War Japan," *Public Finance* 18, no. 2 [1963]:116–117). The responsiveness of national governments to large-scale capital in other countries has also been noted. France provides an extreme case. After the war, one ideologist of monopoly capital argued for the rationalization of the state budget machinery to take into account "national needs." He deplored the fact that there are "countries with a parliamentary government where the executive is not vested with so much authority and where the annual vote for credits . . . offers Parliament an opportunity, which it seldom allows to slip, to question again the principle of the plan itself or to modify its contents." He concluded by favoring the reorganization of public institutions "which still bear the stamp of liberalism" (Robert Jacomet, "The Adaptation of Public Finance to the Economic Function of the State," *Public Finance* 3, no. 1 [1948]: 56). For a discussion of the decline of parliamentary control over the budget in France, see Andrew Shonfield, *Modern Capitalism* (New York, 1965), pp. 130, 143. For example, Mendès-France's *loi programme* in 1954 was in effect a "super budget" that would go on regardless of short-term decisions by parliament on the use of public funds.

27. Harold D. Smith, "The Budget as an Instrument of Legislative Control and Executive Management," *Public Administration Review* 4, no. 3 (Summer 1944): 181.

labor training for the corporations, and help finance local governments. Highway expenditures complement private investments in manufacturing and distribution facilities, encourage new private investments, link up the major metropolitan centers in accordance with the needs of the Department of Defense, facilitate the mobility of labor, and provide a kind of social consumption—or goods and services consumed in common. Outlays on other forms of transport, communications, water supplies, utilities, and the like, also simultaneously provide inputs to private capital and services to the working class. Nevertheless, it is useful to categorize specific expenditures into four major groups, not for purposes of exposition, but rather because there is always a preponderant set of social forces determining the amount, type, and location of the particular facility.

The first major category of expenditures consists of facilities that are valuable to a specific industry, or group of related industries. These are projects that are useful to specific interests and whose financial needs are so large that they exceed the resources of the interests affected. They also consist of projects in which the financial outcome is subject to so much uncertainty that they exceed the risk-taking propensities of the interests involved. Finally, these are projects that realize external economies and large-scale production economies for the particular industries.

These projects fall into two subcategories: *complementary* investments and *discretionary* investments. Both types of investments, like private investments, increase the productive forces. But the first consists of facilities without which private projects would be unprofitable.[28] Complementary investments are determined completely by the rhythm of private capital accumulation, or by the spheres that private capital has chosen to expand, and by the technical relations or coefficients between private investment and complementary activities. Complementary investments are thus a special form of private investment: their determination rests squarely on the determination of private commodity production and accumulation. And since private accumulation is increasingly social—since the economy is increasingly interdependent—there is no economic or technical limit on state expenditures for facilities which complement private facilities. The most dramatic exam-

28. A further distinction can be made between state investments required to maintain or augment the production system at the current rate of profit, and state investments required to maintain the distribution system. These distinctions are not academic, but extremely important in the analysis of the generation and absorption of the economic surplus. The author is engaged in research in this area, which goes beyond the subject of this essay.

ple of complementary investments are infrastructure projects in backward capitalist economies that specialize in the production of one or two primary commodities for export. The relationship between state and private capital is seen here in its pure form. Private investments in agriculture and mining completely determine the location, scale, function, and degree of flexibility of infrastructure projects. Railroads, ports, roads, and communication and power facilities are oriented to serve one or two industries making up the export sector.

The purpose of discretionary investments is to provide incentives for private accumulation. In practice, there is no hard line drawn between complementary and discretionary investments; highway extensions, for example, facilitate the movement of goods and also encourage new investments. While complementary investments are part of the normal rhythm of capital accumulation, discretionary investments are ordinarily made during times of crisis—when profitable opportunities for capital as a whole are lacking, or in the event that declining industries depress certain regions. Both kinds of investments are oriented by profit, although the latter may or may not raise the rate of profit.

In the context of the federal system and the fiscal crisis, which compels local governments to compete with one another for new tax-producing industrial and commercial properties by providing low-cost or free facilities to specific investors, and in the context of an industrial structure dependent on the state for contracts and subsidized to develop new technical "solutions" for "crime control," institutional administration, transportation systems, and so on, more and more discretionary investments are being financed by the state.

The most important state investments serving the interests of specific industries are highway expenditures.[29] Domestic economic growth since World War II has been led by automobile production and suburban residential construction, which requires an enormous network of complementary highways, roads, and ancillary facilities. Rejecting public transportation, on the one hand, and toll highways, on the other, the state has "socialized intercity highway systems paid for by the taxpayer —not without great encouragement for the rubber, petroleum, and auto industries."[30] From 1944, when Congress passed the Federal Aid to Highways Act, to 1961, the federal government expended its entire transportation budget on roads and highways. Today approximately 20 percent of nonmilitary government spending at all levels is destined for

29. Weapon expenditures fall partly into this category, but since their ultimate determinant lies elsewhere discussion of military spending is postponed until later.
30. Payntz Taylor, *Outlook for the Railroads* (New York, 1960), p. 91.

highways; inland waterway and airport expenditures total less than $1 billion yearly; and railroads and local rapid transit receive little or nothing. And in area redevelopment schemes, highways receive the lion's share of the subsidies; more than 80 percent of the funds allocated by the federal government to Appalachia for economic development, for example, has been destined for road construction. The reason was that the federal planners needed the cooperation of the local governors, who together with electric power, steel, and other companies combined to block other "solutions."[31] The power of the "auto complex" has been documented many times; two more examples will suffice. In 1962 the combined forces of the truckers, port groups, and barge companies blocked legislation that sought to give the railroads more freedom to cut rates; in 1965 an attempt by Johnson to compel truckers to pay higher user charges failed completely.

Initiated and supported by the auto complex, sometimes along, and sometimes allied, with other industries, road transport nevertheless receives powerful support from the large part of private capital as a whole, as well as from the suburbs. From the standpoint of private capital the availability of truck transport is the key factor in location decisions.[32] For the car-owning commuter, the transportation budget constitutes a giant subsidy, for two reasons. First, although the determinant of highway construction is found in the auto complex, highways have technical characteristics—mainly free access and unused capacity —that afford easy use by the car owner.[33] Second, because "the auto owner enjoys a low marginal price per mile by auto once he commits himself to ownership" (because, in turn, he must meet fixed car payments), his use of public transportation is minimal.[34]

The social cost of auto transport is extraordinarily high, hence the

31. *Wall Street Journal,* 28 June 1965.

32. According to a *Business Week* survey, the availability of truck transport was mentioned by 75 percent of the businessmen questioned, and was the most frequently mentioned requirement ("Plant Site Survey, A Study among *Business Week* Subscribers," *Business Week* Research Reprint, 1964). The State of Michigan, controlled by the auto industry, boasts the largest continuous stretch of interstate freeway in the country. Serving the auto industry directly, Michigan's highways are also used to advertise that state's transportation advantages for private capital in general (for example, see Consumers Power Commission advertisement in the *Wall Street Journal,* 24 February 1966).

33. A provocative thesis is that the argument that roads "benefit" everyone in a capitalist society is the same as the argument that slave quarters "benefit" eveyone in a slave society. Both roads and slave quarters, because of their physical features, can be used for recreation. The political consensus that developed in the 1950s—grand era of road building and suburbanization—thus is attributable partly to the technical features of roads, and so on, not to any consciously designed plan for promoting the general well-being.

34. Roger Sherman, "A Private Ownership Bias in Transit Choice," *American Economic Review* 57, no. 5 (December 1967): 1211–1217.

enormous fiscal burden on the state. In the United States, about 20 percent of total product is spent on transportation (in the Soviet Union, roughly 7 percent), chiefly because of the high capital requirements of moving people from one destination to another, together with the existence of vast unused physical capacity—partial underutilization of highways during nonpeak hours and autos in transit, and full underutilization of autos during working hours.

Costs, and the fiscal burden, are also rising; it has become a standard complaint that the construction of freeways does not end, but rather intensifies congestion. The basic reason is that auto use is subsidized; hence expanding the freeway system leads to the expansion of the demand for its use. Furthermore, the state cannot free itself fiscally by constructing more freeways, because the freeway system has spawned more and more suburban developments—where road expenditures per capita are much greater than in the cities—at greater distances from the urban centers.

Further, road transport intensifies the fiscal crisis of the cities, owing to the removal of land from the tax rolls for freeways, access roads, and ancillary facilities. Simultaneously, the cities' commuting population places an extra burden on city expenditures in the form of traffic control, parking facilities, and the like.

For all of these reasons, not only does the social cost of transportation steadily rise, but also transport costs borne by capital itself increase. Local capital and the state itself are responding to the monster created in Detroit, Akron, and other centers of the auto complex with programs for public transport, two of which have been implemented in San Francisco and Washington. But far from solving the transportation problem, these and other efforts are bound to add to the total irrationality of transportation patterns, and to the fiscal crisis. At present, there are more than thirty agencies at the federal level regulating or promoting particular modes of transport. Many of these agencies are in competition with one another, paralleling the competition for state funds among different branches of industry. To date, the federal government has been unable to rationalize and streamline transportation, because it has not been able to acquire sufficient independence from the conflicting and contradictory interests of particular industries to deprive the state agencies representing these specific interests of their independence.[35] Another reason to expect the transportation budget to rise in the future is that the development of rapid transport will push the suburbs out even further from the urban centers, and put even more distance between places of work, residence, and recreation. Far from

35. *Wall Street Journal,* 23 July 1965.

contributing to an environment that will free suburbanites from congestion and pollution, rapid transport will simply displace the traffic jams
to the present perimeters of the suburbs, thereby requiring still more
freeway construction. The only general solution is planned urban development as a whole, and neither corporate capital nor local capital is
willing or able to take this step.

Integrally related to transport outlays are urban renewal expenditures, which figure more and more in local, state, and federal budgets,
and which are the main response to the decline in profits of downtown
business interests. The decline in profitability in turn is attributable to
the profoundly exploitative relationship that has developed between
the suburb and the city.

It is in this context that urban renewal should be interpreted. The
market still determines the contours of urban and regional development. More important, the supramunicipal authorities and quasi-public
regional development agencies that control urban renewal *reinforce* the
"decisions" of the market. The state budget has thus contributed to the
dynamism of the downtown sections and the decay of the remainder of
the city. Urban renewal expenditures are thus bound to expand in the
future because they do not correct the irrationalities of capitalist development, but rather intensify them.[36]

Specifically, spending on urban reconstruction takes the form of
multiproject investments that harmonize the specific expenditure items
in the interests of local capital as a whole. The main aspects of urban
renewal include reconstruction of downtown areas in the interests of

36. For example, Detroit is the top candidate for HUD's "demonstration city"
program. Detroit's plan calls for $2.5 billion in federal funds over a ten-year period.
Nearly all of the proposed expenditure items will have the effect of *reinforcing* the existing
social structure and pattern of resource use. Public transportation receives no attention
in the plan; instead, $300 million is requested for freeways and city streets. Nor does
new working-class housing rate attention; instead, Detroit wants $50 million for slum
clearance in order to make room for five industrial development areas, and $73 million
for middle-class recreational and cultural facilities in order to reverse the middle-class
migration to the suburbs. While the largest request is $1.7 billion for schools, the key
to the entire plan is the neighborhood family centers. These appear to be giant settlement
houses, which will provide employment services, "delinquency control teams," clinics,
staff homemakers, hobby, education, and other activities. Clearly, Detroit's plan, considered by HUD to be the best proposal put forth by any city, confirms and *formalizes* the
existence of the ghetto, inequality, and the class system (*Wall Street Journal*, 1 January
1966).

A similar conclusion can be drawn about rural redevelopment expenditures. In 1965
Congress voted over $3 billion to "depressed areas." According to the administration
bill, "the bulk of the money would be earmarked for federal grants to public works
projects such as water works, waste treatment plants, industrial streets and roads, airport
and other facilities useful in attracting private industry (*New York Times*, 2 June 1965).
In the absence of planned, directly productive investments this kind of program will only
make the depressed areas more depressed.

retailers suffering from sharp suburban competition; stadium and other recreational investments that seek to give restaurants, clubs, and so on, a new lease on life; multiplication of parking and other facilities for suburbanites working in downtown office buildings; deceleration of the deterioration of middle-class neighborhoods, and acceleration of the decline of working-class neighborhoods;[37] in general, the re-creation and intensification of profitability conditions for builders, banks, utilities, retailers, brokers, and land speculators. To the degree that urban renewal reconstructs cities that complement suburban development, the development of the suburbs and the underdevelopment of the cities are intensified; to the degree that urban renewal reconstructs cities that compete with the suburbs, the underdevelopment of the cities is deaccelerated, at the expense of the duplication and multiplication of facilities of all kinds. In either case, urban renewal heaps new, expanding fiscal burdens on the state budget.

The second major determinant of state expenditures stems from the immediate economic interests of corporate capital as a whole. The budgetary expression of these interests takes many forms—economic infrastructure investments, expenditures on education, general business subsidies, credit guarantees and insurance, social consumption, and so on. In the United States, most of these forms appeared or developed fully only in the twentieth century, although in Europe state capitalism emerged in an earlier period—in France, during the First Empire, generalized state promotion buoyed the private economy; in Germany, state economic policy received great impetus from political unification and war; in Italy, laissez faire principles did not prevent the state from actively financing and promoting accumulation in the major spheres of heavy industry; and everywhere liberal notions of small,

37. The practical experience and the literature on this subject are vast, and the general conclusions widely accepted. Urban renewal means people removal, especially black removal, owing to the transfer of families from the downtown periphery to deteriorating districts elsewhere in the city, the blighting of neighborhoods by freeway construction, and the chaining of public housing to slum clearance and, thus, the impossibility of using open spaces. As Charles Abrams has written, "since the welfare of the building industry had won equal place with the people's welfare in the 1949 Housing Act, it seemed inevitable that sooner or later the interests of lower-income families would be forgotten. When the entrepreneurial and the general welfare are bracketed in the same legislation, it should not be surprising that the social purpose will be subordinated. It was." (*The City Is the Frontier* [New York, 1966], p.85)

Martin Anderson's *The Federal Bulldozer* (Cambridge, Mass., 1964) analyzes the coalition of banks, newspapers, department stores, downtown real estate owners, academic intellectuals, city planners, and city politicians who have made urban renewal what it is. Originally introduced at the expense of both the urban working class and small business, urban renewal began to protect the latter in 1964 when Congress passed a housing bill which provides concessions and compensation to small business.

balanced budgets and indirect taxation came face to face with the fiscal realities of wartime economies.

In the United States the budget remained small throughout the nineteenth century; transportation investments were chiefly private, and natural resource, conservation, public health, education, and related outlays were insignificant. The state served the economic needs of capital as a whole mainly in nonfiscal ways—land tenure, monetary, immigration, tariff, and patent policies all "represented and strengthened the particular legal framework within which private business was organized,"[38] State subsidies to capital as a whole were confined to the state government and local levels and were largely the product of mercantile, rather than industrial capital, impulses.[39]

In the twentieth century, however, corporate capital has combined with state capital to create a new organic whole. Corporate capital is not subordinated to state capital, or vice versa, but rather they are synthesized into a qualitatively new phenomenon, rooted in the development of the productive forces and the concentration and centralization of capital.[40] More specifically, the rapid advance of technology has increased the pace of general economic change, the risk of capital investments, and the amount of uncontrollable overhead costs. Further, capital equipment is subject to more rapid obsolescence, and there exists a longer lead time before the typical investment is in full operation and thus is able to pay for itself.[41] The development of the production relations has also compelled corporate capital to employ state power in its economic interests as a whole, and socialize production costs. The struggles of the labor movement have reinforced the general tendency for the rate of profit to decline, and have thus compelled corporate capital to use the state to mobilize capital funds from the liquid savings of the general population. And, finally, the onset of general realization crises has forced large-scale business to use the budget to subsidize the demand for commodities.

The most expensive economic needs of corporate capital as a whole are the costs of research, development of new products, new produc-

38. Henry W. Broude, "The Role of the State in American Economic Development, 1820–1890," in Harry N. Scheiber, ed., *United States Economic History: Selected Readings* (New York, 1964).

39. Louis Hartz, *Economic Policy and Democratic Thought: Pennsylvania, 1776–1860* (Cambridge, Mass., 1948), pp. 290–291.

40. This synthesis of corporate and state capital has profound implications for the generation and absorption of the economic surplus, and therefore indirectly for the fiscal crisis. Following up this line of analysis, however, would lead us too far away from the framework of the present essay, but see Chapter Two.

41. Good general discussions of these tendencies can be found in Shonfield, *Modern Capitalism*, p. 192, and John Kenneth Galbraith, *The New Industrial State* (Boston, 1967), passim.

tion processes, and so on, and, above all, the costs of training and retraining the labor force, in particular technical, administrative, and nonmanual workers. Preliminary to an investigation of the process of the *socialization* of these costs,[42] a brief review of the relationships between technology and production is required.

The forces of production include available land, constant capital, labor skills, methods of work organization, and, last but not least, technology, which is a part of, but not totally identified with, the social productive forces. The advance of technology, the uses of technology, and its distribution between the various branches of the economy are all determined in the last analysis by the relations of production.[43] The transformation from a labor-using to a labor-saving technology in mid-nineteenth-century Europe was caused not only by competition but also by the disappearance of opportunities for industrial capitalists to recruit labor "extensively" from the artisan and peasant classes at the given wage rate. During the last half of the nineteenth century, the established industrial proletariat faced less competition, their organizations were strengthened, and they were better able to win wage advances. Thus, it was partly the class struggle that compelled capital to introduce labor-saving innovations.[44]

42. All or even a majority of education expenditures are not determined by corporate capital's drive to socialize these costs. A large part of the education budget consists of social consumption for middle-class children; that is, education is required to complement private consumption, and as a way to create and maintain prestige and status for middle-class and ruling-class families. Further, the main purpose of elementary education is to structure personalities, behavior patterns, and thoughts in accordance with the need for maintaining the social order as a whole. And, lastly, to the degree that education teaches consumer and related skills, there is obviously a large element of economic waste in the education budget. All of these functions of education, however, excepting the last one, are traditional. In our discussion of the education budget we concentrate on what is new and unique, namely, the socialization of production costs. To put it another way, the practical element in education has become of crucial importance. Veblen was one of the first to take note of this: business "feels the need of a free supply of trained subordinates at reasonable wages," parents "are anxious to see their sons equipped for material success," and youth "are eager to seek gainful careers" (*The Higher Learning in America* [New York, 1957], p. 144). According to studies now in progress by Herbert Gintis, the *practical* element in education today is precisely "personality structuring" in accordance with the need to produce "human capital."

43. Rather than vice versa. Technology by itself determines nothing. Ideas such as Galbraith's "industrial state" thesis, based on the "imperatives of technology," seem to be objective, but in fact are fetishistic. They place technology above man, and make man a slave to technology. Various theories of the "convergence" between the United States and the Soviet Union make the same fundamental methodological error.

44. The change in technology then "works back upon" or modifies the relations of production, but not mechanically or owing to any "imperative." The immediate decision to accelerate labor-saving technology belonged to capitalists; the ultimate decision lay in the production relations. The acceleration of labor-saving techniques had the long-term effect of stratifying the working class into many unskilled, semiskilled, and skilled layers. Broad-based working-class organizations, the development of class consciousness, and class unity were subsequently more difficult to achieve.

Despite the rapid advance of technology during the first half of the twentieth century, until World War II the industrial corporations trained the largest part of their labor force, excluding basic skills such as literacy. In the context of the further technological possibilities latent in the scientific discoveries of the nineteenth and twentieth centuries, this was a profoundly irrational mode of social organization.

The reason is that knowledge, unlike other forms of capital,[45] cannot be monopolized by one or a few industrial-finance interests. Capital-as-knowledge resides in the skills and abilities of the working class itself. In a free labor market—that is, in the absence of a feudallike industrial state that prohibits labor mobility, a flat impossibility in the capitalist mode of production—no one industrial-finance interest can afford to train its own labor force or channel profits into the requisite amount of research and development. The reason is that (excepting the patent system) there is absolutely no guarantee that their "investments" will not seek employment in other corporations or industries. The cost of losing trained manpower is especially high in those corporations that employ technical workers with skills that are specific to a particular industrial process.

World War II provided the opportunity to rationalize the entire organization of technology in the United States. As Dobb writes, "a modern war is of such a kind as to require all-out mobilization of economic resources, rapidly executed decisions about transfer of labor and productive equipment, and the growth of war industry, which ordinary market-mechanisms would be powerless to achieve. Consequently, it occasions a considerable growth of state capitalism. . . ."[46] The intervention of the state through government grants to finance research programs, develop new technical processes, and construct new facilities, and the forced mobilization of resources, converted production to a more social process. The division of labor and specialization of work functions intensified, industrial plants were diversified, the technical requirements of employment became more complex, and, in some cases, more advanced. The end result was a startling acceleration of technology.

At the end of the war, corporate capital was once again faced with the necessity of financing its own research and training its own technical work force. The continued rationalization of the work process required new forms of social integration in order to enable social production to

45. As Marx demonstrated, capital takes many forms, among them labor power itself. Thus, if technical knowledge is a form of labor power, it is also a form of capital.
46. Maurice Dobb, *Capitalism Yesterday and Today* (New York, 1962), p. 75.

advance still further. The first step was the introduction of the GI Bill, which socialized the costs of training (including the living expenses of labor trainees) and eventually helped to create a labor force that could exploit the stockpile of technology created during the war. The second step was the creation of a vast system of lower and higher technical education at the local and state level, the transformation of private universities into federal universities through research grants, and the creation of a system exploiting technology in a systematic, organized way that included not only the education system, but also the foundations, private research organizations, the Pentagon, and countless other federal government agencies. This system required enormous capital outlays, a large expansion of teaching and administrative personnel, an upgrading of teachers at all levels, together with programs of specialized teaching training, scholarships, libraries; in short, vast new burdens on the state budgets. In turn, this reorganization of the labor process, and, in particular, the free availability of masses of technical-scientific workers, made possible the rapid acceleration of technology.[47] With the new, rationalized social organization of technology and the labor process completed,[48] technical knowledge became a main form of labor power and capital.

The continued substitution of "mind" work for manual work is bound to place a growing burden on state budgets at local, state, and

47. It is instructive to compare the labor process in the United States and Europe. While all governments in the advanced countries finance the vast majority of industrial research, government financing of education in Europe is relatively underdeveloped. Most technical workers are promoted from the factory floor, not hired from the colleges and universities. The main reasons are (1) the comparative financial weaknesses of European corporations and governments; (2) the survival of pre- and early capitalist educational systems; and (3) the relative absence of competition which renders it profitable for European capital to leave technological possibilities unexploited. The main effect is technological backwardness in the new, expanding, high technology industries such as computers, electronics, and so on.

48. This is an overstatement. The federal system prevents the full rationalization of the labor process from the standpoint of profitability. Ordinarily, local business dominates the boards of local and state institutions of higher learning; further, junior colleges are normally financed at least in part from local taxes. Owing to the mobility of labor and the existence of market-determined wages, there is a tendency for local capital to underinvest in education, and rely instead on high wages and salaries to attract technical labor trained in other localities and states. This is probably why technical and trade schools located in working-class districts tend to be underfinanced, and frequently oriented toward training people for skills that are no longer needed by private capital.

Thus, higher organs of the state, which are able to act in the name of larger strata of capital, are beginning to rationalize the education process still further. A number of states, including New York, are imitating California's Master Plan. North Carolina, a growing industrial state with few traditional industrial interests to fight against "modernization," has established a statewide system of twenty industrial education centers that today enroll more than 40,000 students. Again, federal aid to education can only result in more federal control, and thus overall rationalization of local education systems.

federal levels. Equally important, the increased demand for higher education will add to the fiscal crisis. Education remains "private property" in the sense that the material benefits from training accrue not to society at large but to the technical worker himself.

Another rising expense facing corporate capital as a whole consists of investments in economic infrastructure—plant and equipment for education and research; water, power, and similar projects; and harbor, air, and other transportation facilities. Specific industries or groups of related industries normally do not provide the political impetus for these expenditures; rather regional or corporate capital as a whole does. These kinds of economic infrastructure ordinarily serve a wide variety of industries, either precede or coincide with private capital accumulation, and generate many-sided, long-term economic effects. They are also capital-intensive projects that are characterized by large "indivisibilities"; they require large original capital outlays and normally are constructed in large, discrete units. To cite one example, the Boeing 747 jetliner makes many existing air terminal facilities obsolete, and will require the construction of entirely new airports, rather than a gradual modernization of existing facilities.

These projects place a growing burden on the state budget for three reasons: first, their absolute size is increasingly large, owing to their capital-intensive and "indivisible" character; second, monopoly capital needs more economic infrastructure, because of the increased complexity and interdependence of production; and, third, state and local governments seeking to attract branch plants of large corporations by subsidizing infrastructure projects tend to produce an oversupply of projects. For all these reasons, federal outlays and grants-in-aid and state and local bond issues for "capital improvements" will continue to expand.

5. SOCIAL EXPENSES OF PRODUCTION

Still another fiscal burden heaped on the state by corporate capital is the *expenses of selling*. From a theoretical standpoint, the need for state spending destined to underwrite private commodity demand is limitless. Capital "accumulates or dies" and in the absence of regular increases in private commodity demand, which in the current era require fresh state subsidies, accumulation comes to a halt. Moreover, a few particular commodities receive the greatest share of state subsidies. Highways and education receive the most direct subsidies and private suburban housing and development receive the greatest indirect subsidies. Politically, it is difficult for the state to shift resources from highway construction to other modes of transportation, from suburban residential development to urban housing, and from social consumption in the suburbs to social consumption in the cities. This introduces an element of *inflexibility* in the budget, and tends to intensify the overall fiscal crisis.

The uncontrolled expansion of production by corporate capital as a whole creates still another fiscal burden on the state in the form of outlays required to meet the *social costs of private production* (as contrasted with the socialization of private costs of production, which we have discussed above). Motor transportation is an important source of social costs in the consumption of oxygen, the production of crop- and animal-destroying smog, the pollution of rivers and oceans by lead additives to gasoline, the construction of freeways that foul the land, and the generation of urban sprawl. These costs do not enter into the accounts of the automobile industry, which is compelled to minimize its own costs and maximize production and sales. Corporate capital is largely unwilling to treat toxic chemical waste or to develop substitute sources of energy for fossil fuels that pollute the air. And corporate farming—the production of agricultural commodities for exchange alone—generates still more social costs by minimizing crop losses (and thus costs) through the unlimited use of DDT and other chemicals that are harmful to crops, animals, water purity, and human life itself.

By and large, private capital refuses to bear the costs of reducing or eliminating air and water pollution, lowering highway and air accidents, easing traffic jams, preserving forests, wilderness areas, and wildlife sanctuaries, and conserving the soils. In the past these costs were largely ignored. Today, owing to the increasingly social character of production, these costs are damaging not only the ecological structure, but also profitable accumulation itself, particularly in real estate, recreation, agriculture, and other branches of the economy in which land, water, and air are valuable resources to capital. The portion of the state budget devoted to reducing social costs has therefore begun to mount.

Another major category of state expenditures consists of the expenses of stabilizing the world capitalist social order: the costs of creating a safe political environment for profitable investment and trade. These expenditures include the costs of politically containing the proletariat at home and abroad, the costs of keeping small-scale, local, and regional capital at home, safely within the ruling corporate liberal consensus, and the costs of maintaining the comprador ruling classes abroad.

These political expenses partly take the form of income transfers and direct or indirect subsidies, and are attributable fundamentally to the unplanned and anarchic character of capitalist development. Unrestrained capital accumulation and technological change create three broad, related economic and social imbalances. First, capitalist development forces great stresses and strains on local and regional economies; second, capitalist growth generates imbalances between various industries and sectors of the economy; third, accumulation and technical change reproduce inequalities in the distribution of wealth and income and generate poverty. These imbalances not only are integral to capitalist development, but also are considered by the ruling class to be a sign of "healthy growth and change." What is more, the forces of the marketplace, far from ameliorating the imbalances, in fact magnify them by the multiplier effects of changes in demand on production. The decline of coal mining in Appalachia, for example, compelled other businesses and able-bodied workers to abandon the region, reinforcing tendencies toward economic stagnation and social impoverishment.

The political containment of the proletariat requires the expense of maintaining corporate liberal ideological hegemony, and, where that fails, the cost of physically repressing populations in revolt. In the first category are the expenses of medicare, unemployment, old age, and other social insurance, a portion of education expenditures, the welfare budget, the antipoverty programs, nonmilitary "foreign aid," and the administrative costs of maintaining corporate liberalism at home and the imperialist system abroad—the expenses incurred by the National Labor Relations Board, Office of Economic Opportunity, Agency for International Development, and similar organizations.

The second major cost of politically containing the proletariat at home and abroad (not to speak of the socialist world) consists of police and military expenditures required to suppress populations in revolt. These expenditures place the single greatest drain on the state budget. A full analysis of these expenditures would require detailed development of the theory of imperialism, which cannot be undertaken here. However, we can identify those factors in the arms race, the structure of the "military-industrial space complex," the wars against national liberation struggles abroad, and the physical suppression of revolutionary movements at home that are likely to force the ruling class to expand the military budget in the foreseeable future.

First, the continuous expansion of social production, the extension of capitalism into the Third World, and the proletarianization of the world population enlarge the arena both for capital accumulation and for class conflict. The increasing instability of the world capitalist social order, the transformation of nationalist movements led by compromise-minded national bourgeoisies into national liberation struggles led by revolutionary armies, and the birth of new socialist societies have all required greater levels of military expenditure in the "mother country."

Second, a large and growing military establishment is needed to initiate technological advance in *civilian* production.

Third, not only is the economy as a whole more dependent on rising military expenditures, but also the major "private" military contractors have established permanent beachheads in the state budget, and thus have a permanent stake in the arms race itself. The largest fifty defense contractors received 58 percent of all military orders during World War II, 56 percent during the Korean War, and 66 percent in 1963–1964.[49] In military production, "the initiative, risk-bearing and similar manifestations of enterprise appear to have become characteristics of the buyer rather than the seller,"[50] and thus the big military contractors cooperate readily with government defense programs independent of the rationality of these programs for overall ruling class interests.

The final expense of stabilizing the world capitalist social order consists of the funds needed to keep local and regional capital securely within the corporate liberal political consensus at home and the costs of maintaining the comprador ruling classes abroad. The latter take the form of foreign aid: in particular, balance-of-payments assistance through the International Monetary Fund; infrastructure loans by the World Bank and AID that economically strengthen export industries in the Third World and politically harden the rule of local bourgeoisies whose economic interests are based on export production, processing, and trade; and outright military and nonmilitary grants-in-aid.

At home corporate capital must make alliances with traditional agricultural interests (especially those of the Southern oligarchy) and small-scale capital. In the Congress, the votes of Southern and Midwestern farm legislators and other representatives bound to local and regional economic interests—for example, shipping, soft coal mining, and the fishing industry—are indispensable for the legislative victories of corporate liberal policies. Support for federal programs in the areas of urban renewal, education, health, housing, and transportation by state legislators, municipal governments, and local newspapers, TV stations, and other "opinion makers" is equally important.

49. William Baldwin, *The Structure of the Defense Market, 1955–1954* (Durham, N.C., 1967), p. 9.

50. Murray Wiedenbaum, "The Defense-Space Complex: Impact on Whom?" *Challenge,* April 1965, p. 46.

The political support of small businessmen, farmers, and other local and regional interests is extremely costly. Billions of dollars of direct and indirect subsidies are required by the farmers, especially the large growers who dominate the farm associations and many local and state governments. Subsidies in various forms—in particular, allowances to finance the relocation of small business—are also required to placate small-scale capital adversely affected by corporate-oriented urban renewal programs.

6. FINANCING THE BUDGET

In the preceding sections, we have attempted to analyze state expenditures in terms of the development of the forces and relations of production. We have seen that the increasingly social character of production requires the organization and distribution of production by the state. In effect, advanced capitalism fuses the "base" and "superstructure"—the economic and political systems—and thus places an enormous fiscal burden on the state budget.

In the next section, we attempt to submit the major sources of state *financing* to a similar structural analysis. Is it possible for the state to continue to expand traditional sources of financing to meet its growing fiscal needs? Can the state find new sources of financing? Or does modern capitalism produce a permanent "fiscal crisis of the state"?

In general, there are three possible ways that the state can meet the fiscal burdens that modern capitalism heaps on it: the development of profit-making state enterprise, together with the introduction of other measures to increase productivity in the state sector, the creation of a new state debt, and the expansion of taxation. Each of these possibilities requires underlying changes in social relations, either in the production relations between labor and capital or in the relations within the capitalist class.

The first possibility consists of the development of productive, profit-making enterprise within the state sector, and the mobilization of the surplus produced by the workers in these enterprises to finance general budgetary expenditures. From a strictly economic standpoint, there are no barriers to the accumulation of state capital in the directly productive spheres of the economy. Within the state sector there is no shortage of scientific, technical, skilled, or unskilled labor, nor is there an absence of overall organizational and management "know-how."

Within the federal government there exists an abundance of knowledge and experience in the areas of labor relations, financing, marketing, and other spheres of modern production. Moreover, lands presently owned or leased by federal and state governments could yield
sufficient raw materials, fuels, and other necessary resources.

In fact, these "economic" possibilities are impossible politically. In
capitalist society, state investments are confined to non-profit-making
spheres. It is in the interests of private capital to seize all possible
profit-making opportunities for itself, and resist the encroachment of
state capital on its own "natural territory." Private capital also has every
reason to compel the state to remain dependent on tax revenues by
depriving the state of opportunities to accumulate wealth in order to
weaken or "pauperize" it and thus reduce the possibility for popular
governments to redirect the allocation of economic resources on the
basis of popularly determined, rather than corporate capital, priorities.
Finally, from an ideological standpoint, private capital normally
monopolizes profit-making activities in order to perpetuate the myth
that the state is incompetent to manage directly productive capital.

There have been crisis periods (in particular, World War II) when
corporate capital has used the state to develop and manage productive
wealth in the interests of general economic efficiency. But with the
return to "normalcy" the state is rapidly stripped of its capital assets.
From 1946 to 1949, for example, the cumulative percentage decline
of state-owned producer durable assets exceeded 40 percent. In the
wake of the Hoover Commission investigations and follow-up recommendations by the director of the Bureau of the Budget in the 1950s,
the federal government abandoned more commercial activities to private capital.[51] Even in the climate of corporate-dominated federal
policy and working-class quiescence of the early Johnson administration, the government was compelled to promise to sell off the few
remaining enterprises competing with private business (for example,
nuclear fuel production) in order to win a "business consensus" for its
(probusiness) policies.[52]

51. A 1963 Bureau of the Budget directive warns civil servants proposing to use
public enterprises for the provision of a product of service:
   The existence of the government-owned capital assets is not in itself an adequate
   justification for the government to provide its own goods and services. The need for
   continued government ownership and operation must be fully substantiated.... Even
   the operation of a government-owned facility by a private organization through
   contractual arrangement does not automatically assure that the government is not
   competing with private enterprise. This type of arrangement could act as a barrier to
   the development and growth of competitive commercial sources. [Cited in Shonfield,
   Modern Capitalism, pp. 298–299]
52. M. J. Rossant, *New York Times*, 7 June 1965. In late 1969 the Atomic Energy

The problem of financing the budget reduces itself to the problem of increasing taxes, specifically the problem of intensifying tax exploitation of the working class, owners of small businesses, and self-employed professionals.

The issue of taxes has always been a class issue; it is still true that "external protection and power, and the enrichment of some classes at the expense of others [are] the purpose of the tax system."[53] Every important change in the balance of class forces has always been registered in the tax structure.

In advanced capitalist states tax exploitation cannot be openly applied or instituted without some kind of ideological justification. Taxes can be either concealed, which is difficult to accomplish in the modern era, or justified on some basis of "tax fairness or equity." Failing this, there is the danger of a tax revolt, in the form of tax evasion or organized political opposition.

Even in the feudal era, the ruling class was compelled either to conceal or to justify tax exploitation. Taxes contained an "equity" criteria when they first appeared in the budgets of the feudal nobility. But they were based on the principle that different persons and classes had different rights and duties. "The nobility of eighteenth century France were serenely certain," Louis Eisenstein has written, "that they contributed special benefits to society that called for a special immunity

Commission was ordered to prepare to sell its three uranium enrichment plants to private capital. Thus, "what started as total government ownership and control of the 'industry of the future' has become an industry dominated by and organized for private profit with the public paying most of the costs" (Lee Webb, "U.S. to Sell Vast Uranium Complex," *Guardian,* December 1969).

The growth of state capitalism is evidenced by the fact that state capital makes up a growing share of the total capital stock in the United States. From 1902 to 1946 the government's share of the value of total national capital assets (excluding military assets) rose from 6.6 percent to 20.6 percent (Solomon Fabricant, *The Trend of Government Activity in the United States Since 1900* [Princeton, N.J., 1950], p. 19, table 3; p. 20, table 4x). The greatest part of government assets, however, consists of noncommercial assets. Goldsmith has estimated that in 1955 the government's share of "total reproducible tangible assets" was about 13 percent and that only 2 percent of all assets was operated directly by government enterprise (Raymond W. Goldsmith, *The National Wealth of the United States in the Postwar Period* [Princeton, N.J., 1962], p. 98, table 24; p. 99). The state's share of the total stock of producer durable goods was only 3 percent, or $5.9 billion of a total of $199.9 billion; its share of total structures was about 20 percent (ibid., pp. 117–118, table A–5). The proportion of total land operated or managed by the state was 13 percent, but private interests monopolized the ownership of livestock, and the greatest part of state-owned land consisted of parks, reserves, and other non-income-producing properties. It is interesting to note that prior to the federal property inventory report of June 30, 1956, issued by the Committee on Government Operations, public domain lands were listed as having "no value."

53. Rudolf Goldscheid, "A Sociological Approach to the Problem of Public Finance," in Richard A. Musgrave and Alan T. Peacock, eds., *Classics in the Theory of Public Finance* (New York, 1958), p. 203.

from taxes. They . . . had incentives that had to be preserved for the welfare of others."[54]

In nineteenth-century America, the ruling class concealed tax exploitation. The working class was small and a personal income tax was not feasible; the only wealth tax was the property tax. The tariff became the most important source of revenue, one that was hidden from view because it took the form of higher commodity prices. (Because they are easy to conceal, import and export taxes today are held up as models of taxation in underdeveloped countries. Economists have written of the political "advantage" of export taxes because they hide the burden that falls on peasants engaged in export production.)[55]

Today the false reasons given to justify tax exploitation revolve around two ideas—the old concept of "incentives" and the new idea of "ability to pay." Put briefly, the "incentive" rationale asserts that if profits are taxed too heavily, the accumulation of capital, and thus the growth of employment, will diminish. Similarly, the "incentives" of investors, wealthy families, and others who monopolize the supply of capital must not be "impaired." Such statements are in fact true within the framework of capitalism because those who make them threaten to sabotage production if they do not realize acceptable profits. Again in brief, the doctrine of "ability-to-pay" assumes that the benefits of state expenditures accrue to everyone more or less equally, and therefore that everyone should pay taxes according to ability, normally measured by the level of personal income. This doctrine obviously has no basis in reality, and is false, not because of its logic, but because of its premise.

Tax exploitation is still concealed—there are roughly 150 taxes hidden in the price of a loaf of bread, and about 600 taxes concealed in the purchase of a house.[56] Excise and sales taxes still remain important sources of revenue at state and local government levels. But, of more importance, tax exploitation is accepted because the ideology of corporate capital is still accepted. Only recently has this ideology been subject to challenge. Thus, both workers and the individual capitalists identify their interests closely with those of the state; and workers therefore identify their interests with those of capital.[57]

54. Louis Eisenstein, *The Ideologies of Taxation* (New York, 1961), pp. 222–223.

55. R. Jackson, "Political Aspects of Export Taxation," *Public Finance* 12, no. 4, (1957): 291.

56. These were the conclusions of a study by the Tax Foundation, cited by Sylvia Porter, *San Francisco Chronicle,* 29 November 1966.

57. The situation is different in Europe and the underdeveloped countries where bourgeois ideological hegemony is relatively weak.

Concealing and justifying taxes are of crucial importance in the contemporary era because the fiscal burden that the owners of corporate capital place on the state is not accompanied by any willingness to shoulder the burden themselves. Superficially, it appears that the ruling class taxes itself in a number of ways—there are corporation income taxes, property taxes, and inheritance taxes, besides the individual income tax, which place extremely high marginal tax rates on high incomes. In fact, corporate capital, for the most part, escapes taxation altogether except during periods of national crisis (for example, in 1936–1939, when Congress legislated an undistributed profits tax, and during World War II, when corporate capital had to pay an excess profits tax).

First, the corporate managers completely shift the corporate income tax to consumers—mainly wage and salary earners—in the form of higher prices. Although corporate gross rates of return doubled between the 1920s and 1950s, net rates of return remained the same, even though the corporation income tax rate rose from 5 percent to 52 percent during the same period. In effect, the corporation income tax is similar to a general sales tax, levied at rate in proportion to the profit margin of the corporation.[58]

Second, the property tax falls mainly on the working class, not on the business class. One reason is that within the core cities residential properties assume the larger share, and commercial land and buildings the small share of the total property tax burden. Property values in the central city show a relative decline owing to the "suburbanization of industry" and to the spread of freeways and the expansion of public parking facilities, office buildings, and other structures that have taken lands off the tax rolls. The flight of well-to-do workers and the middle classes to the suburbs has reduced local revenues from residential property taxes, as well.[59]

Moreover, available studies indicate that owners of tenant-occupied residential buildings usually shift the property tax to their tenants—the vast majority of whom are working people. And about 75 percent of property taxes on local industry and retail establishment is shifted to consumers.[60] Thus, it is not surprising that there is general agreement

58. The corporation income tax in the competitive sector is also borne by the consumer because profits are too meager to absorb the tax.

59. Mordecai S. Feinberg, "The Implications of the Core-City Decline for the Fiscal Structure of the Core-City," National Tax Journal 17, no. 3 (September 1964): 217. From 1950 to 1960, in the ten largest U.S. cities, revenues from property taxes actually rose. If assessed rates and prices had not changed, revenues would have fallen by 7 percent. If prices alone had not changed, revenues would have fallen in four of the ten cities.

60. Richard Musgrave's study of Michigan property taxes, cited in California Assem-

among economists that the property tax as a whole is regressive.[61]

All in all, however, property taxes are becoming a relatively insig-nificant source of revenue. In 1902 they raised over 80 percent of all state and local government revenues; today property taxes finance about one-half of the budgets of local governments, and only 5 percent of state government budgets (the largest cities are becoming increas-ingly dependent on intergovernment transfers, which are financed chiefly by income, sales, and excise taxes). In the past few years, tax-payer groups and politicians in dozens of states have been actively seeking to lower property taxes. And some kinds of property taxation (for example, taxes on personal property) are being eliminated al-together in many localities.

The only other wealth tax in the United States is the inheritance tax. Nominal rates of the federal tax range from 3 percent on $5,000–$10,000 to 77 percent on $10,000,000 or more, but the actual average rate is little more than 10 percent. The difference between the high nominal rates and the low actual rates is explained by exemptions for life estates and for gifts made more than three years before death.[62]

This brief survey warrants the conclusion that the owners of monopoly capital pay few taxes on their wealth,[63] and none on their corporate income. There is no general business tax in the United States, and unrealized capital gains go tax-free. To be sure, wealthy individuals who receive dividends and interest income are taxed at high marginal rates under the individual income tax, but top corporate controllers and managers receive most of their income in the form of tax-free interest from municipal bonds and realized capital gains, which are taxed at low rates. Capital thus protects not only its profits from taxation, but also personal wealth and income. This should not come as a surprise; profits are the key to the economic survival, and personal income and wealth are the key to the social and political survival of the ruling class.

bly, Interim Committee on Revenue and Taxation, *Taxation of Property in California,* December 1964, p. 30. Little or no shifting occurs if there exist rent controls, long-term leases, or competition between landlords.

61. Dick Netzer, *Economics of the Property Tax* (Washington, D.C., 1966), pp. 40–62. One economist has written: "The unevenness of its base, the wide variations in rates, and the imperfections in its administration probably make [the property tax's] impact such as to move the tax system as a whole away from, not toward, ability to pay" (Jesse Burkhead, *Public School Finance* [Syracuse, N.Y., 1964], p. 185).

62. Tax Foundation, *State Inheritance Tax Rates and Exemptions* (New York, 1966), p. 165.

63. The only period in which a capital levy was remotely possible was directly after World War I in Europe, when there was considerable popular discontent with war profiteering and the conscription of manpower. The best analysis of the political economy of wealth taxation is Manual Gottlieb, "The Capital Levy after World War I," *Public Finance* 7, no. 4 (1952): 356–385.

In addition to that portion of property and corporation income taxes that falls on the working class, tax exploitation takes the form of social security taxes, sales and excise taxes, and the individual income tax. The most important social security tax is the payroll tax used to finance old-age insurance. This is a regressive tax because a flat rate is applied to taxable earnings without regard to income levels; it is especially regressive for those who do not stay in the labor force long enough to accumulate sufficient credited employment to qualify for primary benefits.[64] Excise taxes are applied by both state and federal governments, and most state and many local governments have general sales taxes. These taxes are altogether regressive, and fall particularly hard on low-income workers.[65] Indicative of their importance is the fact that state governments raised nearly two-thirds of their tax revenues from sales and gross receipt taxes in 1967, while state individual income taxes accounted for only 16 percent of the tax revenues.[66]

The most oppressive instrument of tax exploitation is the federal individual income tax. First passed by Congress in 1894, on the heels of more than a decade of farmer and working-class agitation against big business, the income tax was originally conceived as a class tax. The tax rate was a flat 2 percent and provision was made for a $4,000 personal exemption, and thus the tax would have fallen on only a handful of wealthy individuals. The tax was declared unconstitutional.

The modern individual income tax did not win acceptance until 1913. The historical reasons for this delay were simple: First, the development of the income tax, and, in particular, the general application of the tax by the expedient of regularly lowering exemptions, was not possible until there existed a massive propertyless working class. Second, by the turn of the century, the United States economy was producing a wide range of substitutes for imported commodities and, as a result, workers were able to avoid tariff excises by reducing their consumption of imports.

Not only was an individual income tax historically possible, it was also ideally suited to the needs of corporate capital. On the one hand,

64. Ernest C. Harvey, "Social Security Taxes—Regressive or Progressive?" *National Tax Journal* 18, no. 4 (December 1965): 408.

65. Tax Foundation, *Retail Sales and Individual Income Taxes in State Tax Structures* (New York, 1962), pp. 29–30. Evidence of the class nature of these taxes is the federal excise tax reduction of 1965, which was expected to reduce excise tax revenues by almost $5 billion over a four-year period. But the tax law retained taxes on tobacco, gasoline, alcohol, and other wage goods, cutting taxes on a wide range of luxury and semiluxury commodities.

66. Bureau of the Census, *State Government Finances in 1967* (Washington, D.C., 1968), p. 7, table 1.

the income tax cannot be shifted to profits; on the other hand, the tax is regressive or proportional in content, although progressive in form. The myth of "tax equity" is preserved, and the reality of tax exploitation is concealed behind an elaborate progressive tax schedule, which in turn contains hundreds of loopholes deemed necessary for "economic growth," "economic stability," and "fiscal justice."

The income tax has increasingly encroached on wage and salary income since it was first introduced. The state has systematically reduced personal exemptions and credits for dependents from $4,000 (for a family of four) in 1913–1916 to $2,400 today. In 1913–1916 a single person was granted a $3,000 exemption; today, only $700. In terms of actual purchasing power, real exemptions have fallen even more. Further, popular consciousness of the tax burden has been reduced by the introduction of tax withholding—the highest form of tax exploitation. At present, 85 percent of income taxes are collected at the basic 20 percent rate, which applies to two-thirds of all returns.[67]

According to available studies, the average rate of taxation on the highest incomes is roughly 30 percent, chiefly because of the special treatment granted to capital gains income, deductions (mainly applicable to those who receive relatively high incomes), and income splitting and exemptions (which benefit high income families relatively more than low income groups).[68] In fact, no one apart from independent

67. In 1916 only 400,000 tax returns were actually taxable; taxable returns jumped to 2.5 million in 1925, 4 million by 1939, over 32 million in 1950, and more than 55 million today. In 1913 the initial rate of tax was 1 percent on the first $20,000 taxable income (after deducting personal exemptions). Today the figure is 20 percent on the first $20,000. In 1913 individual and corporation income taxes together yielded a little more than $35 million; today the individual income tax alone yields about $85 billion. Most advanced capitalist countries have experienced the same trends. In Japan, for example, the number of income taxpayers rose from 1 million to 19 million from 1935 to 1949; meanwhile the ratio of personal income tax revenues to national income jumped from less than 1 percent to 10.2 percent (Sei Fujita, "Political Ceiling on Income Taxation," *Public Finance* 16, no. 2 [1961]: 183–189).

68. Available studies also indicate that taxation *as a whole* is at best proportional and at worst regressive with respect to income, although some studies indicate a degree of progressivity in the higher income brackets. See, for example, Gerhard Colm and Helen Tarasov, *Who Pays the Taxes?* Temporary National Economic Commission Monograph no. 3 (Washington, D.C., 1941); Richard Musgrave et al., "Distribution of Tax Payments by Income Groups: A Case Study for 1948," *National Tax Journal* 4, no. 1 (March 1951); Richard Musgrave, "Incidence of the Tax Structure and Its Effects on Consumption," *Federal Tax Policy for Economic Growth and Stability,* papers submitted by panelists before the Joint Committee on the Economic Report, U.S. Congress, 1955; Richard Goode, *The Individual Income Tax* (Washington, D.C., 1964), p. 263; "Who Really Gets Hurt By Taxes?" *U.S. News and World Report,* 9 December 1968. Ross Abinati of San Jose State College has estimated that the average effective tax rate on the incomes of all strata of the working class and managers, officials, proprietors, and farmers is roughly 30–32.5 percent.

professionals and small and middle businessmen pays more than a 25 percent rate because of the ease of short-circuiting income into nontaxable forms (for example, expense accounts) and to tax evasion, which is most widespread among farmers and those who receive interest income and annuities. In recent years the state has failed even to pretend that the flat tax surcharge of 10 percent is progressive, and passed a tax cut in 1965 that benefited the rich far more than the poor—for the former the decrease is permanent, but for the latter (whose money income is rising) only temporary.[69]

7. THE TAX REVOLT

In the preceding sections, we have seen that the economic surplus is mobilized for the political-economic programs of corporate capital through the budget. Monopoly capital dominates the state budget and socializes various production costs and expenses, but resists the socialization of profits. Taxation is the only source of state revenue fully consistent with capitalist property relations: the burden of taxation necessarily falls on the working class.

The fiscal crisis consists of the gap between expenditures and revenues, which is one form of the general contradiction between social production and private ownership. The severity of the fiscal crisis depends upon the production and social relations between corporate capital, local and regional capital, state employees and dependents, and the taxpaying working class at large. In the absence of a serious challenge to the ideological hegemony of corporate capital, in particular in the absence of a unified movement organized around opposition to corporate liberal and imperialist budgetary priorities—a movement that seeks to unify the working class as a whole—the fiscal crisis will continue to divide state workers from state dependents (e.g., teachers from parents, social workers from welfare recipients) and state employees and dependents from workers in the private sector (e.g., teachers and students from taxpayers as a whole).

At present, growing taxpayer resistance to heavy, rising taxes both reflects and deepens the fiscal crisis. Although "taxpayers" as a group comprise the small business, professional, and working classes as a whole, tax resistance is not presently organized along class lines. In practice, tax issues are rarely seen as class issues, partly because of the

69. S. D. Hermamsen, "An Analysis of the Recent Tax Cut," *National Tax Journal* 18, no. 4 (December 1965): 425.

general absence of working-class unity in the United States, and partly because the fiscal system itself obscures the class character of the budget. As we have seen, although monopoly capital dominates the budget, the state mediates between labor and capital, and the working class benefits materially from state expenditures. In addition, monopoly capital has developed an elaborate ideological rationalization of the budget that is integral to capital's general view that material abundance, capital accumulation, and economic growth define social well-being. Finally, as we have seen, the aggregate, effective tax rate on the incomes of both lower- and higher-income families is roughly the same, indicating that tax exploitation is not confined to poor people, who have least to lose and most to gain from radical social change.

For these reasons, tax issues ordinarily are seen as interest group or community issues, and far from helping to unite the working class, the issues act to divide it. In particular, the growth of thousands of autonomous taxpaying units—the "1400 Governments" of the New York metropolitan area and the nearly five hundred separate tax-levying bodies in Illinois's Cook County, to cite two examples—and the proliferation elsewhere of autonomous trusteeships, municipalities, and school, water, sewer, and other special districts tend to set community against community, tax district against tax district, suburb against city. The fundamental class issues of state finance—the distribution of taxation and the division of expenditures between different social classes—emerge in a new form. The core cities are attempting to force the suburbs to pay their "fair share" of city expenditures, while the relatively well-to-do suburban populations not only are defending themselves against the programs of the core cities—tax redistribution, central city income taxes, commuter taxes, consolidation or merger of tax districts and entire metropolitan areas—but also are taking the offensive by offering inducements to private capital in order to establish an autonomous industrial and commercial base.

Apart from the cold war between city and suburb, the most militant form of tax resistance is that against the property tax. Decades ago, the function of the property tax was to finance public improvements for the benefit of property owners. Today there is little or no visible connection between property taxation and expenditures financed by it; rather, there is a tendency to use property tax revenues to finance social programs that many property owners oppose. In many cities, small homeowners are mounting tax referendum campaigns aimed at downtown business interests whose properties are undervalued for tax purposes. In the suburbs, there is widespread sentiment that the property tax should be replaced in whole or in part by other sources of revenue—

sentiment that right-wing state and local politicians are successfully exploiting for their own purposes.

Suburban resistance to increased taxation, agitation against the property tax, and the urban-suburban cold war, not to speak of tax avoidance and evasion and the general sentiment against "spendthrift" government, arise not only because of the rising level of taxation, but also because of government expenditure priorities.

The *priorities* of corporate liberalism are under attack, not only by the black movement and the organized left, but also by a significant part of the population at large. A study conducted in the early 1960s concluded that popular sentiment ran against space spending and support for agriculture, and in favor of domestic welfare and education programs. According to this study, no single government program inspired the majority of the population sampled to agree to expand the program through higher taxation.[70] A recent Harris poll stated that "the central motive for paying taxes has begun to disintegrate." Those polled opposed foreign aid, Vietnam War spending, space and defense, and federal welfare outlays (no doubt because of racism and the prevailing ideology that stresses the importance of "individual self-sufficiency"). Favored were aid to education, pollution control, help for the cities, and other domestic programs.

What is the significance of popular attitudes on taxation and spending for the left? The tax issue is complex, and cannot be separated from the questions of the level of state expenditures and spending priorities. In the past, the left has not been able to exploit the tax issue because it has been wedded to the modern liberal tradition that has sought an enlarged government role in the economy with little or no attention paid to the structure and burden of taxation. Chiefly for this reason, the right wing has enjoyed a near monopoly on the issue of taxation.

There are some signs that the left is breaking its self-imposed silence on taxation, and beginning to link up taxes and expenditures. Some unions—in particular, state employee unions such as the Transport Workers Union in New York and sections of the American Federation of Teachers—are incorporating demands that the tax burden be shifted to business into their programs for higher wages and better working conditions. This enlarged perspective on the state finances represents an advance, but it is clear that even a general critique of the relationship between expenditures and taxation is insufficient in and of itself. Of equal importance is a theoretical and practical demonstration of the relation between state expenditure priorities and the pattern and rhythm of *private* accumulation and spending. For example, tax referen-

70. George Katona, *The Mass Consumption Society* (New York, 1964), pp. 145–146.

dum campaigns organized around the issue of the relative burden of property taxation on residential versus commercial property should include a critique of the class character of education and urban renewal expenditures. Clearly, struggles against tax exploitation alone can have only a limited impact on either popular consciousness or the actual tax structure. Past struggles by populist, progressive, liberal, and left movements dramatically show that under conditions of monopolistic industry and administered prices it is impossible to influence greatly the distribution of the tax burden (and thus the distribution of wealth and income) without a simultaneous challenge to *both* state and private capital spending priorities.

Further, the left must begin to demonstrate the relationship between foreign and domestic spending, which, we have seen, public opinion radically separates. Struggles around regressive property and sales taxes, increases in fares for public services, and so on, should be informed by an understanding that domestic and international spending are integrally related; that is, that the maintenance of corporate liberalism at home depends upon the expansion and consolidation of imperialism abroad, and vice versa. Even on the left, it is sometimes not appreciated that foreign economic expansion and imperialism are required to maintain corporate liberalism by *expanding* national income and material wealth, thus muting domestic capital-labor struggles over the *distribution* of income and wealth. And the growth of social and welfare expenditures (and the establishment of class harmony) at home are preconditions for popular acquiesence in militarism and imperialism abroad. The "welfare-warfare state" is *one* phenomenon, and military and civilian expenditures cannot be reduced significantly at the expense of one another. An understanding of the relation between foreign and domestic programs requires comprehension of the *totality* of world capitalism—a difficult but necessary undertaking, precisely because there is presently a large constituency ready to support a massive expansion of corporate liberal domestic programs (except welfare) at the expense of military, space, and foreign aid expenditures.[71]

71. Nixon's new-federalism program makes it especially important to link up the issues of the tax burden, domestic and overseas expenditure, and private corporate priorities; that is, to develop a perspective of capitalism as a total system. Nixon's program envisages the redistribution of billions of dollars of federal tax monies to the states and cities in an attempt to alleviate the fiscal crisis at the local level. Redistribution will benefit local politicians—now caught between their need for the support of organized labor (and thus the need to keep taxes on residential properties low) and their dependence on downtown business (and thus the need to keep taxes on commercial property low). But the funds for redistribution will not be available in the absence of economic growth, which in turn is partly dependent on more foreign expansion.

8. MOVEMENTS OF STATE WORKERS AND DEPENDENTS

Partly a reflection of the tax revolt, and partly deepening the fiscal crisis that is producing the tax revolt, is the practical activity—union organizing, day-to-day agitation, strikes, demonstrations—of employees and dependents of the state. On the one hand, the developing awareness of state employees and dependents that they are subject to a gradual erosion of material standards is crucial to a general understanding of their socioeconomic condition and political future. On the other hand, employees, dependents, and clients of the state are also subject to profound *qualitative* changes in their relations with state administrators, politicians, and the corporate ruling class. In actual struggles against the state, quantitative and qualitative issues interpenetrate. The struggle for black studies programs is at once an attempt to win control over state expenditures and to produce fundamental changes in the nature of school curriculum and social relations. Teachers' unionism weaves the issues of control of the schools, curriculum development, programing of classroom time, and racism into the traditional themes of wages and hours.[72] In brief, the *social* meaning of the fiscal crisis goes well beyond immediate budgetary issues. For purposes of exposition, however, the two basic themes—the quantitative and qualitative—are analyzed separately, first in relation to state employees, and second in relation to state dependents and clients.

The most important response to the deterioration of wages and salaries of state workers is trade unionism, including strike activity, slowdowns, and other traditional weapons of organized labor. Labor union activity in both the state and private sectors of the economy aims to *protect* the standard of living and conditions of work; that is, unions function essentially as defensive organizations. Thus, for example, the American Federation of Teachers proposes collective bargaining as an answer to such problems as keeping salary schedules in line with those in private industry and ensuring that teachers maintain their "fair share" of control of the schools.

The uncritical acceptance by state employees of traditional modes of organization and struggle is easily understood; the themes of "economism" and corporate liberal reform have monopolized recent labor struggles, and state workers, no matter how militant or radical, have no alternative traditions. Yet traditional unionism is bound to fail the state

72. See, for example, *American Teacher* 54, no. 1 (September 1969).

employee, not only in the profound sense that the labor movement has failed workers in the private economy by binding the working population hand and foot to the corporate-dominated political consensus, but also in the immediate sense that state unionism increasingly will be unable to win wage advances and "deliver the goods."

The reason is that private workers and state workers occupy different places in the society. In the short run, the large corporations pass on wage increases won by private workers to consumers in the form of higher prices. State administrators do not have any equivalent indirect "taxing" mechanism. Instead, wage and salary increases must be absorbed by the taxpayer. In the long run, the corporations have responded to the militant economism of traditional unions by accelerating labor-saving technological change, lowering costs, and augmenting productivity. The corporations have protected profits directly by raising prices and indirectly by raising productivity, and hence over many years have contributed greatly to the absolute volume of goods and services available to the population. In other words, traditional labor struggles have forced the corporations to advance productivity, and, indirectly, real wages, in order to maintain and expand profits. State administrators are unable to increase productivity in the state sector. On the contrary, some are even under pressure to retard the application of modern technology to the state sector, and, in any case, they do not have any operative profitability criteria to guide decision making. In short, there is no way for wage struggles in the state sector to "pay for themselves."

Therefore, the state normally resists state unionism in general, and wage demands in specific, more adamantly than private corporations oppose private unions.[73] Labor struggles in the state sector are increasingly opposed by the taxpaying working class as a whole, and, as a result, the traditional conduct of these struggles tends to *worsen* the condition of state employees precisely because the struggles worsen the fiscal crisis itself. Finally, state unions ordinarily must stay on the defensive, insofar as economic demands are concerned. In the private sector, traditional unions regularly demand that workers get their "fair share" of increases in corporate income arising from productivity increases. Owing to the fact that the income of the state is dependent on the tax rate and tax base, state employee unions are unable to go on the offensive.

To the extent that state workers confine their activity to traditional

73. The resistance to unionization offered by some competitive and low-productivity industries and businesses operating on small profit margins in the private sector is an exception.

economism, they are fighting a losing struggle. As yet, there is no general understanding of the function of the state, and especially of the fact that state employees are employed not by the people but by capital as a whole. That is to say, there is no general understanding that the growing antagonism between state employees and state administration conceals an objective antagonism between wage labor and private capital.

At this point, we can tie together some of the themes already developed. Labor strikes are only effective when they stop the flow of profits and, hence, threaten the social existence of the ruling class. Strikes in the state sector cannot possibly be effective in this sense; state unionism thus cannot uncritically apply the experience of private unionism. Strikes in the state sector merely raise production costs for capital as a whole—leading to increases in prices and inflation—or lower the real wages of the taxpaying working class, or both. Strikes conducted by state unions always hold the potential of dividing the working class, and delaying the development of proletarian consciousness. Objectively, therefore, there is no successful reformist, economistic strategy available to state workers. The only way for state workers to win even substantial material gains is to radicalize themselves. And to radicalize themselves requires that they seek alliances with other workers, especially workers in other branches of the state economy. It is too early to predict the nature of these alliances, the form they take, the issues on which they will revolve, and their general political thrust. One or two conclusions, however, can be drawn from existing practice. It must be emphasized that traditional economic struggles mounted by state employees cannot be expected to win the support of the taxpaying working class; from a narrow economic point of view, the interests of private and state employees are opposed, precisely because the socialization of production costs and the expenses of maintaining the social order, including the evolving corporate liberal consensus, tend to worsen the material condition of state employees. Alliances are more likely to be forged over qualitative issues, even given the great difficulties involved.

There is no easy way for the state administration and ruling class to contain the struggles of state employees. In their frustration and disillusionment, the state workers may line up solidly behind the ruling class (as the police are doing now in many cities) and voluntarily adapt to the right-turning corporate liberal consensus. But this danger is minimal. It is impossible to train a person to perform an essentially *social* function, and arm him with the rudiments of critical thought, and subsequently expect him to be oblivious to the essentially *private* character of state power, particularly in a social milieu in which traditional labor organization and activity are largely irrelevant.

If state employees have the possibility of developing socialist consciousness, their potential is nothing beside that of state dependents: the mass of students, blacks, Third World groups, and the poor in general. Also difficult to contain are those in motion around the issue of environmental destruction, another movement that both reflects and deepens the fiscal crisis.

Needless to say, collective bargaining does not afford a solution to the problems of state dependents if only because of the impossibility of defining appropriate bargaining units. There is no traditional way to formalize, administer, and neutralize these struggles, in particular the struggles of those sections of the black and student movements that have already adopted an anti-imperialist, anticapitalist perspective. The corporate ruling class has begun to take the only available course of action. In the schools, it has mounted an attack on the traditional student-teacher relation, and has sought to substitute a systems approach to education in order to increase its control over the student population. In the black ghettos, it is circumventing both the local and federal bureaucracies and beginning to deal directly with the black militants, especially on the crucial issue of jobs. Politically, it is adopting a divide-and-conquer strategy; on the one side, it is trying with some success to co-opt sections of the black nationalist movement; on the other side, it is trying to smash the revolutionary socialists.

The movements of dependents and clients have many sources. This is not the place for a detailed investigation of them, but only for an analysis of the relation between these movements and the fiscal crisis. In the first place, these movements, insofar as they are responses to declining material conditions, obviously reflect the fiscal crisis. Insofar as they raise budgetary demands, they clearly deepen the crisis. And, insofar as they are redefining the meaning of material and social well-being, their activities may deepen the crisis (for example, demands for free clinics provided by the state) or leave it unaffected (for example, emphasis on self-help, new life styles).

In the narrow material sense the activities of state dependents and state employees, to the degree that the latter are struggling for more resources to serve the people, are in no sense antagonistic, but rather perfectly complementary. Alliances between teachers and students, welfare workers and clients, and public health workers and those who use public medical facilities are possible and likely. Unity among those who are directly or indirectly dependent on the state will sharpen the contradiction between taxation and expenditures and, thus, deepen the fiscal crisis.

The problem arises from the intermingling of quantitative and qualitative demands. Students in the fight against authoritarianism must confront their immediate "enemy"—the teacher. City planners, whose technical solutions to problems of renewal, relocation, zoning, housing, and so on, are frustrated by profit-seeking businessmen, confront those in the community who pose a third solution—planning by, for, and of those who reside in the community. Public health personnel trying to protect their "professional" status from the attacks by state administrators confront patients who demand not only technically competent medical services, but also *human* service. Professors struggling to maintain faculty "autonomy," "open campuses," and their traditional scholarly prerogatives confront black students and others who want to develop their own curricula and control their own faculties, and, indeed, redefine the meaning of traditional education.

Of all the service workers, probably the social and welfare workers, whose jobs put them constantly in touch with the lowest income groups, have learned most about dealing with their own authoritarianism. Yet, even welfare workers struggling to redefine their jobs and seek ways to help their clients, and not control them, confront masses of welfare clients with their *own* ideas about welfare and social work. And throughout the state economy, it is more difficult for employees to fight against their own racism because black people and other minorities are typically "clients to be looked after" rather than job peers, as in private production.

In short, state service workers are being proletarianized from above, and socialized from below. Under two general sets of pressures, one seeking to transform them into various kinds of "human capital," the other seeking to humanize them, service workers are subject to contradictory sets of conflicts. The only way for them to negate their proletarian condition is by helping to make a socialist revolution; the only way to participate in socialist revolution is to fight against their own professionalism, racism, and authoritarianism; and the only way to fight these evils is to relate organizationally to those "below" them— that is, relate as equals, not as professionals—clients, as they must in the context of the structure of the state bureaucracy.

Seen in this framework, it is no wonder that the response of state employees to pressures from above and below has been confused and irrational. It is no wonder that the development of class consciousness is uneven, irregular, and uncertain. It is no wonder that the exclusive repetition of themes of antiracism, antiimperialism, and antiauthoritarianism alone has not radicalized masses of service workers. And it is no wonder that in the absence of a specifically socialist perspective—which can help people comprehend all issues from the class nature of budgetary control, the determinants of state expenditures, and the nature of tax exploitation, to the process by which the uses of technology itself is decided by struggle—indeed, in the absence of a keen comprehension of the basic contradiction between social production and private ownership itself, unionists, organizers, and demonstrators necessarily function in a vacuum. In the absence of this kind of general historical consciousness, how is it possible for all those in motion to come to grips with even the immediate material, budgetary questions, not to speak of the questions of authority, control, professionalism, and service or, finally, the question of what will be the new material basis of social existence itself?

PART IV
ECONOMIC
IMPERIALISM

CHAPTER SEVEN
The Meaning of Economic Imperialism

There is still much controversy, and more confusion, about the meaning of economic imperialism. Monopolistic privileges and preferences, plunder of raw materials, seizure of territory, enslavement of local peoples, nationalism, racism, militarism—all of these phenomena have been closely identified with imperialism. Only on the association of imperialism with expansion—economic, political, cultural, and territorial—has there been any general agreement. But if imperialism means "the extension of political power by one state over another, then all through the sixty centuries of more or less recorded history,"[1] it has been a principal feature in human relations. Beneath the undergrowth of over half a century of historical, theoretical, and polemical writings, however, three general doctrines can be distinguished. Two of these reflect the period of European expansion which began during the 1880s and ended in 1914. The third is an interpretation of contemporary world capitalism, and, in particular, United States expansionism.

1. IMPERIALISM: A POLITICAL PHENOMENON

The first doctrine dissociates capitalism from imperialism. For Joseph Schumpeter, the leading exponent of this view, imperialism is "a heritage of the autocratic state . . . the outcome of precapitalist forces which the autocratic state has reorganized . . . [and] would never have been evolved by the inner logic of capitalism itself." The "inner logic"

---

1. Margery Perham, *The Colonial Reckoning* (London, 1963), p. 1.

of capitalism consists of nothing more or less than free trade and "where free trade prevails *no* class has an interest in forcible expansion as such . . . citizens and goods of every nation can move in foreign countries as freely as though those countries were politically their own."[2] Only the "export monopolist interests"—in particular, monopolies in the metropolitan countries which dump surplus commodities abroad behind high tariff walls—profit from imperialism. Schumpeter was confident that these interests would not survive capitalism's "inner logic." His confidence was, of course, misplaced; as we will see, the national and regional economic policies of the advanced capitalist countries today rightly merit Joan Robinson's label—the "new mercantilism." The reason is not hard to find: Schumpeter selected one characteristic of capitalism, "rationality," which he considered central, to the exclusion of other features.

The vast majority of bourgeois economists in the past and present adopt a position similar to Schumpeter's, even though few today would share his optimism in connection with the revival of free trade. The generally accepted "comparative advantage" theory of Ricardo and Mill holds that all parties in international commodity trade under competitive conditions benefit in accordance with the strength of the demand for their respective commodities. Nationalist economic policy and monopoly restricted free trade and inhibited the growth of income and economic well-being, but these barriers have been lowered by the breakup of the European empires. The trademark of this doctrine is that exploitive economic relations between the advanced and backward capitalist countries cannot survive in a world of politically independent countries. According to this line of thinking, the real problems of world capitalism today spring from the misplaced faith of the ex-colonies that nationalist economic policies which have created new and higher barriers to international investment and trade can put the backward countries on the path of self-sustained economic growth.

Schumpeter and other bourgeois writers uncritically dissociate capitalism from imperialism for three reasons: first, their criteria for distinguishing and identifying imperial and colonial relationships are ordinarily political and not economic (for example, Hans Kohn has developed the most sophisticated typology of imperialism, which he

2. Joseph Schumpeter, *Imperialism and Social Classes* (New York, 1951), pp. 98, 128. It should be stressed that my brief summary fails to capture the subtleties and complexities of Schumpeter's thesis, its primary aim being to provide a point of comparison with the other two doctrines.

understands in terms of the distribution of political power);[3] second, they do not consider capitalism as such to be an exploitive system; third, imperialism historically has contained certain features identified with the theme of expansionism which have not been uniquely associated with any given economic and social system. Thus bourgeois writers have concluded not only that imperialism predates capitalism but also that imperialism is essentially an anachronistic system. For this reason, there have been few investigations of the specific features of capitalist imperialism.

In connection with economic expansionism, precapitalist and capitalist societies differ in five general ways:

1. In precapitalist societies, economic expansion was irregular, unsystematic, not integral to normal economic activity. In capitalist societies, foreign trade and investment are rightly considered to be the "engines of growth." Expansion is necessary to maintain the rhythm of economic activity in the home or metropolitan economy, and has an orderly, methodical, permanent character.

2. In precapitalist societies, the economic gains from expansion were windfall gains, frequently taking the form of sporadic plunder. In capitalist societies, profits from overseas trade and investment are an integral part of national income, and considered in a matter-of-fact manner.

3. In precapitalist societies, plunder acquired in the course of expansion was often consumed in the field by the conquering armies, leaving the home economy relatively unaffected. In capitalist societies, exploited territories are fragmented and integrated into the structure of the metropolitan economy. Imperialism in effect potentially emancipated space-bound and time-bound man.

4. In precapitalist societies, debates within the ruling class ordinarily revolved around the issue whether or not to expand. In capitalist societies, ruling class debates normally turn on the question of what is the best way to expand.

5. In relation to colonialism, precapitalist and capitalist societies also differ in a fundamental way. In the former, colonialism (land

3. Hans Kohn, "Reflections on Colonialism" in Robert Strausz-Hupé and Harry W. Hazard, eds., *The Idea of Colonialism* (London, 1958). The different kinds of political control are as follows: (1) The metropolitan power can grant the subject people full autonomy, with the exception of foreign relations. (2) Subject peoples can be granted full citizenship, and assimilated into the foreign culture. (3) Indigenous peoples can be annihilated or expelled. (4) Subject peoples can be maintained in an inferior status. (5) The metropolitan power can tacitly claim the right to oust an unfriendly government.

seizure, colonist settlement, or both) was the only mode of control which the metropolitan power could effectively exercise over the satellite region. As we will see later in detail, capitalist societies have developed alternative, indirect, and more complex forms of control.

Not only do precapitalist and capitalist expansion depart from each other in significant ways, but also the character of expansion (especially the nature of trade and colonialism) in mercantile capitalist societies differs from that in industrial capitalist societies. To be sure, the definition of colonialism adopted by some writers—monopolistically regulated trade and investment at higher rates of profit than those obtaining in the home economy—applies with equal force to both the mercantilist and the industrial capitalist eras. In fact, the term "neo-mercantilism" has frequently been used to describe nineteenth-century imperialism, and, as we have mentioned, mid-twentieth-century nationalist economic policy has been labeled the "new mercantilism." In addition, throughout the history of capitalism, businessmen and traders have followed the same rule—extract capital from areas where the cost is lowest, invest where anticipated returns are highest.

The differences between mercantilism and nineteenth-century imperialism, however, outweigh the similarities.[4] First, the resemblance between monopolistic commercial organization in the two political-economic systems is only superficial. Mercantilist monopoly trading companies did not spring from the prevailing modes of production. They were formed to minimize physical and commercial risks along uncertain and distant trade routes. As "normal" patterns of trade were established, risk and uncertainty were reduced, and the great monopoly companies met increasing competition from other nationals and foreign companies. The East India Company, the last of the great monopolies, was dissolved early in the nineteenth century. From then until the last quarter of the nineteenth century, British manufacturers and merchants adopted free trade on principle because their control over advanced methods of production gave them a decisive competitive advantage. But Britain's foreign investments in Europe and the United States and the diffusion of industrial technology eliminated this advantage. And further advances in technology which were not consistent with small-scale enterprise led to the cartelization and monopolization of industry. Latter-day monopolies, unlike their forerunners, have proven not to be transitory.

A second important difference between mercantilism and imperial-

4. An excellent review of mercantile thought and practice is provided by Eric Roll, *A History of Economic Thought*, 3d ed. (Englewood Cliffs, N.J., 1957), chap. 2.

ism is related to the character of trade. Early mercantilism was commercial capitalism in its purest essence, middlemen exchanged goods for goods in a lively *entrepôt* trade, and mercantilist wars were mainly trade wars—the Anglo-Dutch wars of the seventeenth century were the purest commercial wars in history.[5] It is true that as early as the first decades of the seventeenth century the East India Company purchased raw materials in exchange for British manufactured goods. But this was not typical. It was only in the late mercantile and early industrial capitalist periods that Britain increasingly exported manufactured commodities for agricultural raw materials and minerals.[6] As late as 1800, for example, British ships took woolens and hardware to India and returned with cotton and silk products. Then, as the nineteenth century wore on, a new dimension was added to trade: capital goods financed by foreign loans and investments, as well as consumer manufacturers, were exchanged for foodstuffs and industrial raw materials.

Finally, there are superficial similarities between mercantilism and imperialism in the sphere of state economic policy. Both systems of political economy relied on active state participation in the direction, organization, and character of trade or investment. But the nature of state policy was fundamentally different. In England, after the prohibition on the export of bullion was abolished in 1663, the state employed commodity import and export controls with the aim of maintaining a favorable balance of trade, or export surplus, with *each* of Britain's trading partners, colonies and noncolonies alike. Gradually, a system of multilateral trade replaced the more primitive bilateral trade patterns. It was this system of multilateral trade which the imperialist states of the late nineteenth century inherited. Imperialist state policy revived the older technique of export promotion and import restriction (and invented new techniques, as well) with the aim of maintaining a favorable balance of trade *with the world as a whole,* not with any specific trading partner.

These contrasts between mercantilism and imperialism give rise to important differences with respect to colonization. In the first place, it is certainly true that the leading late mercantilist and imperialist powers discouraged both subsistence production and the manufacture of commodities in the colonies. But mercantilist industry was technologically primitive, small-scale, largely independent, and not vertically inte-

5. Charles Wilson, *Power and Profit: A Study of England and the Dutch Wars* (London, 1957).

6. This changeover set the stage for the ruin of Indian manufacturing industries, and can be roughly dated from the abolition of the East India Company's trade monopoly in 1813. The East India Company had provided an umbrella for India's weaving industry, which could not survive the massive importation of British cotton manufactures.

grated. Thus the exploitation of raw materials under mercantile impulses, and colonization itself, were of necessity *national* policies, and generated fierce national rivalries. From the late nineteenth century down to the present, however, national rivalries have increasingly given way to struggles between fully integrated corporations based in the metropolitan countries. These struggles have typically been resolved in compromise. The sharing of oil resources among the great oil monopolies in the Middle East is an excellent example of cooperation between integrated corporations (and, by extension, imperialist nations). To make the point slightly differently, in the mercantilist era it was impossible to conceive of an international ruling class; in the contemporary imperialist period, an international ruling class is an accomplished fact.[7]

Secondly, colonial conquest in the sixteenth and seventeenth centuries had as its chief purpose the mitigation of the hazards of trade and the preservation of monopoly control. The mercantilist powers established factories, trading bases, and forts where regional trade was already established.[8] By contrast, the seizure of territories in the late nineteenth century was motivated less to preserve commercial positions which had already been won by peaceful methods than to open up possibilities for trade and investment where none had existed before. Colonialism under mercantilism was therefore defensive in nature and required a passive state presence, while latter-day imperialism, by contrast, exhibited an aggressive character which stood in need of active state participation.

Mercantilism and imperialism departed from each other in still another important respect. The doctrine used to support rigid trade restrictions, and an important element of the theory on which the mercantile colonial system was based, was that the maximum inflow of bullion required a favorable balance of trade with each colony. This doctrine limited the scope of territorial conquest and seizure, as well as the development of commercial relations with other colonial powers. In the late mercantile era, however, the state gradually realized that an expansion of output was the key to maximum trade and therefore the

    7. This is not meant to imply that there are no important conflicts between international-minded capitalists and national-minded power elites.
    8. This of course does not exhaust the motives for colonial conquest. In the conquest of Mexico and Peru, the search for precious metals was of foremost importance. The east coast of Africa was at first seized for strategic reasons. But the characteristic sequence was followed in India and West Africa. In the latter region, Portugal had acquired a monopoly over trade based on coastal fortifications. Cloth, metal, and glass were exchanged on favorable terms for gold, ivory, and, above all, slaves. In the middle of the seventeenth century, Portugal's monopoly was broken by the Dutch, and then by the British and French.

nursing of home industry and the creation of employment became central goals of state policy. Thus were created the preconditions for the growth of complex, multilateral trade patterns, which in turn awakened the interests of the imperial powers in any and all underexploited regions.

In sum, industrial capitalist expansionism distinguished itself in the following important respects: it exhibited a more aggressive attitude toward the underexploited lands; it was less particular and more universal in character; it more fully integrated underexploited economic regions into the structure of the metropolitan country; it required the active participation of the state; and, finally, internecine warfare between the economic monopolies tended to be less acute. Imperialism thus contained the important contradiction which has afflicted the advanced capitalist countries down to the present day. On the one hand, the *national* power elites seek to advance the economic interests of their respective countries; on the other hand, the integrated, multinational corporations, or the *international* ruling class, extend their sway irrespective of the interests of the countries in which they are based. This contradiction is heightened by the aggressive, universal character of modern imperialist expansion.

(In our comparison of mercantilism and imperialism we have neither surveyed the differences between the early, middle, and late mercantilist era nor reviewed satisfactorily the relation of the free trade period to either mercantilism or imperialism. One school of thought sees a great deal of continuity between mercantilism and early industrial capitalism. M. Barratt-Brown, for example, argues that the decades after 1815 saw the expansion and consolidation of the British Empire based on the need to conquer and secure markets and keep trade routes open in the face of rivalries from developing European and United States capitalism and the first outbreaks of nationalism and anti-imperialism in the colonies. D. Fieldhouse, on the other hand, asserts that Britain's industrial supremacy after 1815 meant that the colonies and monopolistic privileges involved few benefits and large costs. He claims that the acquisition and defense of colonies were motivated chiefly for reasons of military security and administrative efficiency.)

2. IMPERIALISM: AN ASPECT OF MONOPOLY CAPITALISM

Against the view that dissociates capitalism and imperialism, Marxist economists have put forward many variations on fundamentally the same argument. The second doctrine of imperialism, also inspired by European expansionism in the late nineteenth and early twentieth centuries, holds that monopoly capitalism, imperialism, and colonialism are basically the same phenomena. Perhaps it is more accurate to call this view "neo-Marxist" because those who hold it have inherited few clear theoretical guidelines from Marx himself. In the three volumes of *Capital*, apart from the brief concluding chapter in volume 1, there are only two or three references to the economics of colonialism, the gist of which is that commodities produced under conditions of high labor productivity and sold in countries where labor productivity is low will command an abnormally high rate of profit.[9] Marx's relative silence on the economics of imperialism may have handicapped the development of Marxist theory, or it may have been a blessing in disguise. The absence of any theoretical precedent has forced (and continues to force) Marxists back on their own experiences and intellectual resources. Thus, older interpretations of imperialism as far apart as those of Lenin and Rosa Luxemburg, and modern theories as disparate as those of Paul Baran and Joseph Gillman, have arisen from basically the same critical tradition.

Nothing succeeds like success, however, and Lenin's ideas have dominated the field. Yet Lenin owed much to John A. Hobson's *Imperialism*, published in 1902, a book that is frequently (and legitimately) read as the precursor of Lenin's study. Hence, we will begin by sketching out the main ideas of Hobson and Lenin, later subjecting them to analysis on the basis of theoretical and historical studies published in recent years.

Hobson and Lenin wrote about imperialism during the heyday of colonialism (1885–1914), which naturally enough appeared to be *the* most significant economic-political phenomenon of the time. By making colonialism their focal point, however, both men equated imperialism with colonialism and thus failed to understand the significance of the "imperialism of free trade"—an expression coined to describe British economic expansion from the 1840s to the 1880s. Moreover, they barely acknowledged United States expansion and could not anticipate future modes of imperialist controls which have proved to be even more effective than formal colonial rule.

The distinctive feature of Hobson's theory is his conception of colonialism as the reflection of the unfulfilled promise of liberal democracy. As Hobson saw it, inequalities in the distribution of wealth and

9. *Capital*, Kerr, ed. (Chicago, 1909), vol. 3, pp. 278–279.

income in Britain dampened the consumption power of the British working classes, which in turn made it unprofitable for capitalists to utilize fully their industrial capacity. Unable to find profitable investment outlets at home, British capitalists subsequently sought them abroad in the economically underexploited continents. Britain therefore acquired colonies as a dumping ground for surplus capital. The end of imperialist conquest and decolonization would come about only when the British working classes acquired more economic and political power through trade unionism and parliamentary representation, which would set the stage for a thoroughgoing redistribution of income and hence the development of a home economy in which the volume of consumption corresponded more closely to the volume of production.

Hobson supported his thesis not only by his faith in the promise of liberal democracy, but also by reference to changes in Britain's trade and investments. He tried to show that the expansion of empire during the last two decades of the nineteenth century, when most of the world not already independent or under European rule was carved up among the European powers, resulted in a *decline* in British trade with her colonies in relation to trade with noncolonies.[10] He also underlined the obvious fact that the new colonies in Africa and Asia failed to attract British settlers in significant numbers. Through a process of elimination Hobson thus hit on what he considered to be the crucial element in British imperialism—foreign investments. He linked the vast outflow of capital from Britain during this period—British overseas investments rose from £785 million in 1871 to £3,500 million in 1911 and annual net foreign investments were frequently greater than gross domestic fixed investments—with the frantic struggle by the European powers for colonies, and inferred that the former caused the latter. The political struggles between the major European powers were thus dissolved into struggles for profitable investment outlets, and the explorers, missionaries, traders, and soldiers of the period were seen as the puppets of London's financial magnates.

Lenin agreed with Hobson that the prime cause of capital exports was the vast increase in the supply of capital in the metropolitan countries, especially Britain, and played down the role of the demand for capital in the underdeveloped regions. He also, like Hobson, causally

10. Cairncross has shown on the basis of more and better data than those available to Hobson that there was a relative increase in empire trade, most of it, however, with the older colonies such as India (J. Cairncross, *Home and Foreign Investments, 1870–1913* [Cambridge, 1953], p. 189). Cairncross's findings refine but do not contradict Hobson's argument.

linked foreign investments with the acquisition of colonies. The distinctive element in Lenin's theory related to the *cause* of the surplus of capital.

Lenin understood that imperialism is a *stage* of capitalist development, and not merely one possible set of foreign policy options among many. In particular, imperialism is the monopoly capitalist stage, and exhibits five basic features:

1. The concentration of production and capital, developed so highly that it creates monopolies which play a decisive role in economic life.

2. The fusion of banking capital with industrial capital and the creation, on the basis of this financial capital, of a financial oligarchy.

3. The export of capital, which has become extremely important, as distinguished from the export of commodities.

4. The formation of the international capitalist monopolies which divide up the world among themselves.

5. The territorial division of the whole earth completed by the great capitalist powers.[11]

The key element is the formation of local and international monopolies behind high tariff barriers in the metropolitan countries. Monopolistic organization develops "precisely out of free competition" in essentially four ways: First, the concentration (growth in absolute size) of capital leads to the centralization (growth in relative size) of capital. Second, monopoly capital extends and strengthens itself by the seizure of key raw materials. Third, financial capital, or the investment banks, "impose an infinite number of financial ties of dependence upon all the economic and political institutions of contemporary capitalist society," including nonfinancial capital. Fourth, as Lenin stated, "monopoly has grown out of colonial policy. To the numerous 'old' motives of colonial policy the capitalist financier has added the struggle for the sources of raw materials, for the exportation of capital, for 'spheres of influence,' that is, for spheres of good business, concessions, monopolist profits, and so on; in fine, for economic territory in general." In short, the new colonialism opposes itself to the older colonial policy of the "free grabbing" of territories.

11. V. I. Lenin, *Imperialism: The Highest Stage of Capitalism* (New York, 1926), pp. 71–76. By comparison, Rosa Luxemburg's *The Accumulation of Capital* bases its analysis of capitalist expansion abroad on Marx's models of expanded reproduction, which assume a *competitive* economy. Luxemburg saw imperialism as a necessary result of competition between capitalist enterprises that drove capitalism outward in search of new markets in areas that were not incorporated into the world capitalist system. Lenin, as we have noted, stressed the export of capital, not commodity exports. Moreover, Lenin viewed imperialist rivalries over areas already integrated into world capitalism as extensions of the struggles between the European powers over the underdeveloped continents.

The cause of the surplus of capital and capital exportation, and monopolistic industry, is the tendency of the rate of profit to fall.[12] Two underlying forces drive down the rate of profit in the metropolitan country: first, the rise of trade unions and social democracy, together with the exhaustion of opportunities to recruit labor power from the countryside at the going real wage, rules out possibilities for increasing significantly the rate of exploitation; second, labor-saving innovations increase the organic composition of capital. Monopoly is thus in part formed in order to protect profit margins. At the same time, economies of large-scale production (internal expansion) and mergers during periods of economic crises (external expansion) strengthen preexisting tendencies toward monopolistic organization.

Meanwhile, in the economically underexploited regions of the world, capital yields a substantially higher rate of return. For one thing, the composition of capital is lower; for another, labor power is plentiful in supply and cheap; and, finally, colonial rule establishes the preconditions for monopolistic privileges. Rich in minerals and raw materials required by the development of the metals, chemical, automotive, and other heavy industries in the metropolitan powers, the underexploited regions naturally attract large amounts of capital. Consequently, foreign investment counteracts the tendency for the rate of profit to fall in the metropolitan economy. On the one hand, high profit margins in the colonies pull up the average return on capital; on the other hand, the retardation of capital accumulation in the home economy re-creates the reserve army of the unemployed, raises the rate of exploitation, and, finally, increases the rate of profit.

Pushing this thesis one step forward, the precondition for a truly "favorable" investment climate is indirect or direct control of internal politics in the backward regions. Economic penetration therefore leads to the establishment of spheres of influence, protectorates, and annexation. Strachey suggests that the backward regions assumed a dependency status (the last step before outright control) in relation to the metropolitan powers chiefly because the former were in debt to the latter. What was significant about the shift from consumer goods to capital goods in world trade was that the colony-to-be needed long-term credits or loans to pay for the capital goods, and that, finally, the relationship between the backward country and the metropolitan country became one of debtor and creditor. And from this it was but a small step to dependence and domination.

12. In the following paragraph we will rely not only on Lenin's theory of the causes of imperialist expansion, but also on Maurice Dobb's and John Strachey's readings of Lenin (Maurice Dobb, "Imperialism," in *Political Economy and Capitalism* [London, 1937]; John Strachey, *The End of Empire* [New York, 1960]).

Whatever the exact sequence of events which led to colonialism, Lenin's economic definition of colonialism (and imperialism) is monopolistically regulated trade and/or investment abroad at higher rates of profit than those obtaining in the metropolitan country. "As soon as political control arrives as handmaid to investment," Dobb writes, "the opportunity for monopolistic and preferential practices exists." The essential ingredient of colonialism therefore is "privileged investment: namely, investment in projects which carry with them some differential advantage, preference, or actual monopoly, in the form of concession-rights or some grant of privileged status."[13]

The criticisms of Hobson's and Lenin's theories, and the alternative views that have been put forward, do not constitute a new theory so much as a catalog of historical facts which are not fully consistent with the older theories. These criticisms bear on three key aspects of Lenin's theory, two of which also figured importantly in Hobson's thought.

One line of criticism is that Lenin ignored the theme of continuity in European expansionism and was too eager to interpret the partition of Africa and the Pacific as a qualitatively different phenomenon. Alexander Kemp has shown that throughout the *entire* nineteenth century British net capital exports in relation to national income amounted to just over 1 percent during recession periods and about 6–7 percent during boom years.[14] Pointing to a similar conclusion is Richard Koebner's judgment that British "imperial responsibilities were enlarged step by step by a hesitant government."[15] Gallagher and Robinson also reject the idea that there were important qualitative differences between British expansionism in the first and in the second parts of the nineteenth century. In both periods the formula was "trade with informal control if possible; trade with rule if necessary."[16] In Egypt and South Africa, for example, they maintain that Britain was only responding to internal upheaval and that traditional controls could no longer be relied upon.

13. Dobb, "Imperialism," pp. 239, 234.
14. Alexander Kemp, "Long-term Capital Movements," *Scottish Journal of Political Economy* 3, no. 1 (February 1966): 137.
15. Richard Koebner, "The Concept of Economic Imperialism," *Economic History Review*, 2d ser., 2 (1949): 8.
16. Nevertheless, these historians believe that reasons must be found to explain the *pace* of colonial conquest from the 1880s on. Fieldhouse's explanation—that there was an overriding need for military security after 1870 because Europe had become an armed camp—they consider inadequate by itself. To the spillover from rivalries in Europe, they add the following reasons: the collapse of Western-oriented governments under the strain of previous European influences; the changing importance of Africa for British geopolitical strategy; and the need to relieve economic depression, especially relief from tariff increases by Germany in 1879 and France in 1892 (R. Robinson and J. Gallagher, *Africa and the Victorians* [New York, 1961], p. 18). As we have seen, the final "reason" itself was explained by Lenin.

Lenin was aware of the continuity in European expansionism but maintained that the development of monopoly capitalism led to a break in this continuity. In principle Lenin had solid earth under his feet because the generation of business savings and their absorption by new investments are governed by different laws in a competitive capitalist society than under monopoly capitalism. But in practice it is by no means certain that Lenin was right when he asserted that "at the beginning of the twentieth century, monopolies have acquired complete supremacy in the advanced countries."

In the most powerful imperialist country, Great Britain, there were few trusts or cartels of any consequence in 1900.[17] One highly qualified economic historian maintains that the British economy failed to enter the monopoly state until the early 1930s.[18] Lenin was aware that British capitalism was far from a model of monopoly domination, but slurred over the problem by referring to a "monopoly" of a few dozen companies and by interpreting Chamberlain's Imperial Preference System as Britain's reply to the European cartels. The German economy was not thoroughly trustified until after 1900, even though bank control of industry was established at a much earlier date. As for the United States economy, recent research has thrown doubt on the received idea that the great merger movement around the turn of the century resulted in the cartelization and trustification of heavy industry, and has substituted the thesis that the economy was more competitive in the first decade of the twentieth century than in the last decade of the nineteenth.[19]

The same line of criticism developed from a different perspective also casts doubt on Lenin's major thesis. The truth is that British capital exports to Africa were mobilized by small-scale speculators, not mainly by the big London banking houses. For the former, although not the latter, foreign lending was a precarious undertaking. One of the first of the African companies, The Royal Niger Company, "had to . . . enlist subscribers in order to make certain that the Company would be equal to its administrative undertaking."[20] Similarly, subscribers to the Imperial British East Africa Company and Cecil Rhodes' South African Company were mainly small-scale savers, such as pensioners and retired military officers. If monopoly capitalism is essentially a post-Lenin phe-

17. D. K. Fieldhouse, "Imperialism: A Historiographical Revision," *Economic History Review* 14 (1961), passim.
18. Richard Pares, unpublished book.
19. Gabriel Kolko, *The Triumph of Conservatism* (New York, 1963).
20. Koebner, "The Concept of Economic Imperialism," p. 12. The evidence brought to light by D. C. M. Platt suggests that with Latin American loans only the small lender, not the large financial interests, bore great financial risks ("British Bondholders in Nineteenth Century Latin America—Injury and Remedy," *InterAmerican Economic Affairs* 14, no. 3 [Winter 1960]: 3–45).

nomenon, it is readily understandable why the African companies were financed by small capital. The interesting point in this connection is that capital exports to the underdeveloped regions today conform closely to the Leninist vision. It is not the small investor attracted to an empire builder like Rhodes who provides the savings for foreign investment, but the giant multinational corporations such as Standard Oil, General Motors, and General Electric.

The second line of criticism challenges directly the thesis of Hobson and Lenin that the vast amounts of capital from Britain flowed into the new colonies. As Cairncross has shown in his definitive study, the great mass of British foreign investments penetrated India and what Ragnar Nurkse has termed the regions of recent settlement—the United States, Canada, Australia, Argentina, and South Africa.[21] These areas contained primary commodities, chiefly agricultural goods, which Britain required and which in turn needed a steady flow of foreign capital, mainly to finance railroad construction, to exploit. This analysis lays great stress on the increase in the demand for capital (and is sometimes called the capital-pull thesis) and plays down the significance of the capital surplus which Hobson and Lenin saw piling up in the metropolitan countries.

Maurice Dobb has countered this reasoning with the observation that Britain's need for foodstuffs and raw materials was specific to Britain and in no sense characteristic of the other imperial powers. Thus while the demand for British capital may have increased more rapidly than the supply, the same conclusions cannot be applied to France or Germany. What is more, repatriated interest and dividend payments on investments "pulled" from Britain in the early years of the colonial epoch may have been "pushed" out into both the old and new colonies during later decades. Fieldhouse has pointed out that there were not important differentials between home and foreign interest rates during the pre–World War I colonial era, concluding that capital could hardly have been attracted by colonial superprofits.[22] Taken at face value, this conclusion supports the Nurkse-Cairncross "capital pull" thesis. But the conclusion is fallacious because it was precisely the vast outflow of capital which depressed interest rates abroad and kept them firm at home.

The new colonies did fail to attract many investments during the period directly before and after their conquest. Egypt's indebtedness to Britain was a factor, to be sure, but it was the collapse of the Egyptian

21. Cairncross, *Home and Foreign Investments*, p. 185.
22. Fieldhouse, "Imperialism: A Historiographical Revision," p. 198.

government which led Britain to occupy that country in 1882 in order to protect Suez and the routes to the East.[23] As for the rest of Africa, British enterprise in the nineteenth century was restricted mainly to the palm oil trade on the west coast, and moderate investment activity in the Transvaal and Rhodesia. As Robinson and Gallagher have shown, Africa provided little trade, less revenue, and few local collaborators, and Britain supplied little capital and few settlers. Certainly, until the twentieth century, British ruling-class opinion held widely that there was no real economic reason for the partition of Africa.[24] In the Pacific, large-scale investments in Malayan tin and rubber were made considerably after the annexation of that country, and other late-nineteenth-century conquests in Asia and the Pacific failed to attract new investments in any significant quantity. This of course does not prove that these acquisitions were not economically motivated, but only that investors may have had overoptimistic expectations.

Lenin's description of the chief characteristics of the new colonial era—foreign investments, seizure of territories, monopolistic preferences—was therefore largely accurate. A single, or simple, theoretical pattern, however, cannot be imposed on the complex sequence of events which revolutionized the world capitalist system between the 1880s and World War I. More often than not, in Robinson and Gallagher's words, the "extension of territorial claims . . . required commercial expansion." Certainly the attitudes expressed by the German Colonial Congress in 1902 suggest that in point of time investment and trade followed the flag, rather than vice versa: "The Congress thinks that, in the interests of the fatherland, it is necessary to render it independent of the foreigner for the importation of raw materials and to create markets as safe as possible for manufactured German goods. The German colonies of the future must play this double role, even if the natives are forced to labor on public works and agricultural pursuits." Similar sentiments were expressed in one form or another by Joseph Chamberlain, Theodore Roosevelt, and a host of lesser leaders and ideologists of imperialism.

We have finally to discuss a criticism of Lenin's thesis which arises from the experiences of Britain in the period directly after World War II. Although domestic investment had been considerably in excess of foreign investment (thus reversing the pre-1914 ratio of home to foreign investment),[25] capital exports did not come to a complete halt with

23. Robinson and Gallagher, *Africa and the Victorians.*
24. Ibid., p. 15.
25. Kemp, "Long-term Capital Movements." In 1964, a year of high capital outflow, long-term capital exports amounted to only 9 percent of gross domestic investment.

the political independence of Britain's colonies. It has been inferred from this that formal colonial rule was really not necessary to provide profitable investment outlets. In defense of Lenin, the argument has been raised that British economic stagnation in the immediate postwar era can be attributed to the decline in repatriated earnings from foreign investments, and therefore a decrease in the rate of profit, in turn due to the removal of British economic interests from their monopoly over trade, banking, agriculture, and other branches of politically independent ex-colonies.[26] The empirical work published by Michael Barratt-Brown tends to confirm this line of reasoning: Barratt-Brown estimates that after deducting payments to foreign owners of property, net earnings from overseas investments in the postwar period amounted to only 1 percent of Britain's national income.[27]

These estimates, and the conclusion implicit in them, have been questioned by Hamza Alavi, who argues that informal economic control exercised by the advanced capitalist countries can be as effective, and as profitable, as formal political rule.[28] In our subsequent interpretation of contemporary imperialism we lay great stress on this idea and develop it in detail. Alavi challenges the estimates on three grounds. First, he maintains that the gross return, not the net return, on capital invested abroad is the relevant figure on the grounds that Britain incurred her liabilities independently. Second, he rightly stresses that profit remittances represent but a portion of the return flow on foreign investments. Although it proved impossible to arrive at any accurate estimates, income remitted in the form of monopolistic prices, "services" such as commission royalties, and head office charges should be included in the return flow. Lastly, Alavi states that income remissions in relation to the domestic economic surplus (and not relative to national income) is the relevant comparison for measuring the impact of foreign investments on the metropolitan economy. Alavi calculates that gross income from overseas investments in the postwar period (excluding the disguised income remissions listed above) amounted to 3.3–4.0 percent of the national income and 40–55 percent of domestic net investment. Clearly, if Britain financed perhaps one-half of her home investments from overseas profits, foreign asset holdings must have been a decisive element in the maintenance of the rate of profit at home.

26. Palme Dutt, *The Crisis of Britain in the British Empire* (London, 1953).
27. Michael Barratt-Brown, *After Imperialism* (London, 1963).
28. Hamza Alavi, "Imperialism Old and New," in Ralph Miliband and John Saville, eds., *The Socialist Register, 1964* (London, 1964), pp. 108–109.

3. NEO-IMPERIALISM: CONTROL WITHOUT COLONIALISM

A brief sketch cannot even begin to resolve the many theoretical and historical questions which run through the two major contending doctrines of nineteenth-century imperialism. It is clear, however, that two features of imperialism are not in dispute. The first concerns the general description of economic organization and economic policy. As we have seen, Dobb considers the essential ingredient of imperialism to be "privileged investment . . . investment in projects which carry with them some differential advantage." This feature must be placed in a wider frame of reference, as in Paul Sweezy's description of imperialism as "severe rivalry [between advanced capitalist countries] in the world market leading alternatively to cutthroat competition and international monopoly combines."[29] Schumpeter's view of imperialism is very similar. Cutthroat competition and international monopoly combines are seen as "protective tariffs, cartels, monopoly prices, forced exports (dumping), an aggressive economic policy, and aggressive foreign policy generally. . . ."[30] A second general area of agreement (generally implicit in the writings of both Marxists and non-Marxists) is that modern imperialism, whatever its causes, depends on colonial rule as the main form of economic and political control of the economically backward regions and that political independence would significantly reduce, or eliminate entirely, exploitive imperialist relations.

Opposed to these doctrines is what may be called the neo-Leninist or modern Marxist theory of imperialism. The economic domination exercised by the United States in the world capitalist economy and the failure of the ex-colonies to embark on sustained economic and social development have caused older Marxist economists to rework original doctrines and have given rise to a new theory of neocolonialism. Many of its outlines are still indistinct, but there is broad agreement that a sharp distinction should be made between colonialism and imperialism, while the original Leninist identity between monopoly capitalism and imperialism should be retained. In this view, which we adopt throughout this study, monopoly capitalism remains an aggressively expansionist political-economic system, but colonialism is seen as merely one *form* of imperialist domination, and frequently an ineffective one at that.

The phrase "neocolonialism" was first used in the early 1950s.

29. Paul Sweezy, *The Theory of Capitalist Development* (New York, 1942), p. 307.
30. Schumpeter, *Imperialism and Social Classes*, p. 110.

Anticolonial leaders in Asia and Africa focus on the element of control —in the words of Sukarno, "economic control, intellectual control, and actual physical control by a small but alien community, within a nation."[31] To cite a specific illustration of economic neo-colonialism, Nkrumah denounced as "neo-colonialism" the economic association of France's African colonies with the European Common Market. An example in which the political element was in the fore was France's claim to the right to suppress the revolt against the puppet ruler of Gabon in February 1964 in order to defend French economic interests in that country. A comprehensive summary of the chief manifestations of neocolonialism was made at the Third All-African People's Conference held in Cairo in 1961:

This Conference considers that Neo-Colonialism, which is the survival of the colonial system in spite of formal recognition of political independence in emerging countries, which become the victims of an indirect and subtle form of domination by political, economic, social, military or technical [forces], is the greatest threat to African countries that have newly won their independence or those approaching this status. . . .

This Conference denounces the following manifestations of Neo-Colonialism in Africa:

(a) Puppet governments represented by stooges, and based on some chiefs, reactionary elements, anti-popular politicians, big bourgeois *compradores* or corrupted civil or military functionaries.

(b) Regrouping of states, before or after independence, by an imperial power in federation or communities linked to that imperial power.

(c) Balkanization as a deliberate political fragmentation of states by creation of artificial entities, such as, for example, the case of Katanga, Mauritania, Buganda, etc.

(d) The economic entrenchment of the colonial power before independence and the continuity of economic dependence after formal recognition of national sovereignty.

(e) Integration into colonial economic blocs which maintain the underdeveloped character of African economy.

(f) Economic infiltration by a foreign power after independence, through capital investments, loans and monetary aids or technical experts, of unequal concessions, particularly those extending for long periods.

(g) Direct monetary dependence, as in those emergent independent states whose finances remain in the hands of and directly controlled by colonial powers.

(h) Military bases sometimes introduced as scientific research stations or training schools, introduced either before independence or as a condition for independence.[32]

31. As quoted in Kenneth J. Twitchett, "Colonialism: An Attempt at Understanding Imperial, Colonial, and Neo-Colonial Relationships," *Political Studies* 13, no. 3 (October 1965): 300–323.

32. "Neo-Colonialism," *Voice of Africa* 1, no. 4 (April 1961): 4.

This description supports two broad generalizations. First, modern imperialism requires the active participation of the state in international economic relationships; imperialist nations cannot singly or collectively implement a neocolonialist policy—via agencies such as the European Common Market, for example—without state capitalism. Second, neocolonialist policy is first and foremost designed to prevent the newly independent countries from consolidating their political independence and thus to keep them economically dependent and securely in the world capitalist system. In the pure case of neocolonialism, the allocation of economic resources, investment effort, legal and ideological structures, and other features of the old society remain unchanged—with the single exception of the substitution of "internal colonialism" for formal colonialism; that is, the transfer of power to the domestic ruling classes by their former colonial masters.[33] Independence has thus been achieved on conditions which are irrelevant to the basic needs of the society, and represents a part-denial of real sovereignty, and a part-continuation of disunity within the society. The most important branch of the theory of neocolonialism is therefore the theory of economic imperialism.

The definition of economic imperialism that we employ is the economic domination of one region or country over another—specifically, the formal or informal control over local economic resources in a manner advantageous to the metropolitan power, and at the expense of the local economy. Economic control assumes different forms and is exercised in a number of ways. The main form of economic domination has always been control by the advanced capitalist countries over the liquid and real economic resources of economically backward areas. The main liquid resources are foreign exchange and public and private savings, and real resources consist of agricultural, mineral, transportation, communication, manufacturing, and commercial facilities and other assets, including and especially labor power. The most characteristic modes of domination today can be illuminated by way of contrast with examples drawn from the colonial period.

Examples of control over foreign exchange assets are numerous. In the colonial era the metropolitan powers established currency boards to issue and redeem the local circulating medium against sterling and other metropolitan currencies. In its purest form, the currency board system required 100 percent backing of sterling for local currency. The East African Currency Board, for example, was established in 1919,

33. Pablo Gonzalez Casanova, "Internal Colonialism and National Development," *Studies in Comparative International Development* 1, no. 4 (Social Science Institute, Washington University, St. Louis, 1964).

staffed by British civil servants appointed by the Colonial Office, and at one time exercised financial domination over Ethiopia, British and Italian Somaliland, and Aden, as well as the East African countries.[34] The Board did not have the authority to expand or contract local credit, and therefore expenditures on local projects which required imported materials or machinery were limited to current export earnings, less outlays for essential consumer goods, debt service, and other fixed expenses. Measures to expand exports were thus necessary preconditions of local initiatives toward economic progress. In this way, British imperialism indirectly controlled the allocation of real resources.

This mode of control still survives in modified form in the Commonwealth Caribbean economies and elsewhere.[35] The Jamaican central bank, for example, has limited power to influence the domestic money supply, but sterling and local currency are automatically convertible in unlimited amounts at fixed rates of exchange. The local government is thus prohibited from financing investment projects by inflation, or forced savings, nor are exchange controls and related financial instruments of national economic policy permitted. The structure and organization of the commercial banking system aggravates the situation. Local banks are branches of foreign-owned banks whose headquarters are located in the overseas financial centers and are more responsive to economic and monetary changes abroad than in the local economy; specifically, local banks have contracted credit at times when foreign exchange assets have been accumulating. This combination of monetary and financial dependence has caused artificial shortages of funds and prevented the Jamaican government from allocating local financial resources in a rational manner.

A more characteristic form of control over foreign exchange today is private direct investment. In the nineteenth and early twentieth centuries, backward countries were often able to attract portfolio investments, and local governments and capitalists were thus able to

34. J. W. Kratz, "The East African Currency Board," International Monetary Fund Staff Papers 13, no. 2 (July 1966). In 1960 three new members were added to the Board, one from each of the three East African States. The Board was also granted the power to extend credit by fiduciary issues.
35. C. Y. Thomas, "The Balance of Payments and Money Supplies in a Colonial Monetary Economy," Social and Economic Studies 12, no. 1 (March 1963): 27, 35; William G. Demas, "The Economics of West Indian Customs Union," Social and Economic Studies 9, no. 1 (March 1960): 13–28. According to Thomas, the inability of the Caribbean economies to control their money supply is due not only to their monetary arrangements with Britain, but also to the dependent nature of their "open" economy. The prerevolutionary Cuban economy was also characterized by monetary dependence (Henry C. Wallich, Monetary Problems of an Export Economy: The Cuban Experience, 1914–47, [Cambridge, 1950], passim).

exercise some control over the use of foreign exchange made available by long-term foreign investment. Today direct investment constitutes the great mass of long-term capital exported on private account by the metropolitan countries. Foreign exchange receipts typically take the form of branch plants and other facilities of the multinational corporations—facilities which are difficult or impossible to integrate into the structure of the local economy. What is more, satellite countries which depend on direct investment ordinarily provide free currency convertibility and hence foreign-owned enterprises which produce for local markets have privileged access to foreign exchange earned in other sectors of the economy.

Another feature of economic domination is the control of local savings, which assumes two forms. First, economic rule means that local government revenues, or *public* savings, are mortgaged to loans received from the metropolitan powers. An extreme example is Liberia —a country with an open-door policy with regard to foreign capital— which in 1963 expended 94 percent of its annual revenues to repay foreign loans.[36] In the nineteenth century, persuasion, coercion, and outright conquest often insured that tariffs and other taxes were turned over to foreign bondholders. In the absence of direct colonial rule, however, foreign lending was frequently a precarious undertaking. Latin American countries, for example, had an uneven history of bond payments.[37] Foreign loans today are secured in more peaceful and more effective ways. The international capital market is highly centralized and dominated by the agencies of the main imperialist powers— the International Bank for Reconstruction and Development, the International Monetary Fund, and other financial institutions. No longer is it possible for borrowing countries to play one lending country off against another, or to default on their obligations or unilaterally scale down their debt without shutting the door on future loans. That no country has ever defaulted on a World Bank loan, or failed to amortize a loan on schedule, is eloquent testimony to the ability of the advanced capitalist countries to mortgage local tax receipts to foreign loans.

Second, *private* savings are mobilized by foreign corporations and governments in order to advance the interests of foreign capital. Foreign companies float local bond issues, raise equity capital, and generally attempt to monopolize available liquid resources in order to extend their field of operations and maximize profits. World Bank affiliates

36. K. Brutents, "Developing Countries and the Break-Up of the Colonial System," *International Affairs*, January 1966, p. 67.
37. Platt, "British Bondholders."

finance local Development Banks which scour the country for small- and medium-size savings to funnel into local and foreign enterprise. The United States government acquires a significant portion of the money supply of India and other countries through its policy of selling surplus foodstuffs for local currencies which it makes available to United States corporations. In these and other ways foreign interests today exercise control of local private savings.

A final feature of economic domination is the control of mineral, agricultural, manufacturing, and other facilities, and the labor power exploited therein and the organization and management of trade by foreign corporations. In Africa, for example, French bulk-buying companies in the ex-colonies monopolize the purchase and sale of coffee, peanuts, palm oil products, and other commodities produced by small and medium-size growers. In Mexico one foreign corporation organizes the great part of cotton production and exportation. Frequently control of commerce necessitates financial domination. The United States, for example, has penetrated Mexico's financial structure with the aim of restricting Mexican–Latin American trade in order to insure control of Latin American markets for itself.[38] Control of iron, copper, tin, oil, bauxite, and other mineral resources is in the hands of a handful of giant corporations. In some countries, foreign interests dominate the commanding heights of the economy—transportation, power, communication, and the leading manufacturing industries. These examples should suffice to show that foreign control of real, as well as of liquid, assets extends into all branches of local economies and penetrates every economically backward region in the world capitalist system.

The examples of specific kinds of economic domination illustrate most of the main features of contemporary imperialism, which can be summarized as follows:

First, the further concentration and centralization of capital, and the integration of the world capitalist economy into the structures of the giant United States-, European-, and Japanese-based multinational corporations, or integrated conglomerate monopolistic enterprises; and the acceleration of technological change under the auspices of these corporations.

38. James Schlesinger, "Strategic Leverage from Aid and Trade," in David M. Abshire and Richard V. Allen, eds., *National Security: Political, Military and Economic Strategy in the Decade Ahead* (New York, 1963), passim. In the past, the United States could discipline a satellite country by threatening to cut off supplies of needed commodities. Today, substitutes from other sources are ordinarily available. Thus the United States must threaten to damage other economies by curtailing access to markets that it controls.

Second, the abandonment of the "free" international market, and the substitution of administered prices in commodity trade and investment; and the determination of profit margins through adjustments in the internal accounting schemes of the multinational corporations.

Third, the active participation of state capital in international investment; subsidies and guarantees to private investment; and a global foreign policy which corresponds to the global interests and perspective of the multinational corporation.

Fourth, the consolidation of an international ruling class constituted on the basis of ownership and control of the multinational corporations, and the concomitant decline of national rivalries initiated by the national power elites in the advanced capitalist countries; and the internationalization of the world capital market by the World Bank and other agencies of the international ruling class.

Fifth, the intensification of all of these tendencies arising from the threat of nationalism and world socialism to the world capitalist system.

4. WHY IMPERIALISM?

The general features of contemporary imperialism are much better understood than the sources of economic expansion, the specific contradictions in the metropolitan economies which drive the multinational corporations to extend their scale of operations over the entire globe. As we have seen, Hobson explained nineteenth-century British imperialism by way of reference to inequalities in the distribution of income, while Lenin rested his case on the declining rate of profit in the home economy. Neither of these explanations is very useful today, at least in the form in which they have come down to us. In the first place, the advanced capitalist economies have become mass consumption societies; secondly, savings have become concentrated in the hands of the government, financial intermediaries, and trust funds, as well as a relatively few giant corporations; thirdly, the concept of "the" rate of profit is out-of-date. In the overcrowded competitive sector of the advanced capitalist economies the profit rate remains a datum, a given, but in the oligopolistic sector profit margins are themselves determined by corporate price, output, and investment policies.

Some contemporary Marxist economists have proposed an alternative approach to the problem of identifying the important economic contradictions in advanced capitalist societies. These approaches are based on the elementary concept of economic surplus, which Baran and

Sweezy define as the difference between total national product and socially necessary costs of production.[39] Total product is the aggregate value of all commodities and services produced in a given period of time, or, alternatively, total business, worker, and government expenditures. Nowhere in the literature is there a satisfactory discussion of the meaning of socially necessary costs. A working definition is the outlays which are required to maintain the labor force and society's productive capacity in their present state of productivity or efficiency.

Economic surplus consists of outlays which either augment productive capacity and increase labor skills and efficiency or are used for economically wasteful or destructive ends. Any specific expenditure item which can be reallocated from one use to another without affecting total production (e.g., military expenditures to foreign gifts) falls into the general category of economic surplus. An expenditure item which cannot be reallocated from one employment to another (e.g., wages of workers in basic food industries to military expenditures) without reducing total production can be defined as a necessary cost. Unlike total output, neither necessary costs nor surplus is easily quantifiable, particularly since many outlays, highway expenditures for example, comprise both costs and surplus. Hence it is not possible to calculate with any great precision the proportion of total product which is constituted by surplus, nor can the relation between total product and surplus over a span of time be known with absolute certainty. Nevertheless, there is powerful indirect evidence that the surplus in relation to total product in the advanced capitalist countries tends to increase historically.

Provisionally identifying surplus with corporate profits, sales expenditures, and taxes, Baran and Sweezy demonstrate easily that corporate price and cost policies result in an absolute and relative increase in the surplus. In a nutshell, the corporations stabilize prices around an upward secular trend, while constantly seeking to increase efficiency by reducing production costs. Cost reductions are not transmitted to consumers in the form of lower prices, but rather are channeled into new investment, sales expenditures, and taxes.

The questions thus arise: What are the various ways available to advanced capitalist countries of absorbing the increasing economic surplus, or raising the level of demand? and What are the limits on their absorptive capacity? These are obviously large and complex questions the answers to which we can do no more than suggest here.

Within the metropolitan economy the economic surplus is absorbed

39. Paul A. Baran and Paul M. Sweezy, *Monopoly Capital* (New York, 1966), passim. See also Shigeto Tsuru, *Has Capitalism Changed?* (Tokyo, 1961), passim.

in three distinctive ways.[40] Expenditures on productive investment in both physical and human capital are the first, and historically most important, mode of surplus utilization. Investment outlays are made on both private and government account. In the private sector of the economy, investment opportunities are available in two distinct spheres, oligopolistic industries, dominated by the giant conglomerate corporation, and competitive industries, characterized by relatively inefficient, small-scale enterprise. In the former, technological change, which was at one time the most important outlet for investment-seeking funds, no longer can be relied upon to absorb more than a tiny fraction of the surplus. In the first place, in the few older, stabilized industries where competition between firms for larger shares of the market is at a minimum, there is a tendency to suppress new technologies in order to preserve the value of the existing productive capacity. There is, in Dobb's words, "an increasing danger of the ossification of an existing industrial structure owing to the reluctance or inability of entrepreneurs to face the cost and the risks attendant upon such large-scale change."[41]

Secondly, Baran and Sweezy have shown that in industries in which firms struggle to increase their share of the market, and hence are under considerable pressure to lower costs, the rate of introduction of new technology is reduced, thus limiting the amount of investment-seeking funds that can be profitably absorbed during any given period. Lastly, as Gillman and others have demonstrated, there has been a historic rise in fixed capital stock per employed worker, and a decline in business-fixed investment and producer durable equipment expenditures in relation to total national product. Thus technological change—independent of the rate at which it is introduced into the production processes—tends increasingly to be capital-saving.[42] To put it another way, oligopolistic enterprises favor input-saving, rather than output-increasing, innovations when (and if) the industrial structure becomes relatively stabilized and a provisional market-sharing plan has been agreed upon. For their part, competitive industries are overcrowded, the turnover rate is high, profit margins are minimal, and they offer few incentives to corporations with investment-seeking funds.

Productive investment outlays are also made on government or state account, but most of these are merely special forms of private investment and hence are determined by the rhythm of capital accumu-

40. The scheme developed below is a greatly modified version of that of Tsuru, *Has Capitalism Changed?* pp. 197–198.
41. Quoted ibid., p. 143.
42. Joseph Gillman, *The Falling Rate of Profit* (London, 1957).

lation in the private sector. The costs of these complementary investments—water investments in agricultural districts, for example—are
borne by the taxpayer, while the benefits are appropriated by private
capitalists. The state also finances investments which aim to create
future profitable opportunities for private capital—examples are industrial development parks—but these discretionary investments are limited by the need on the part of the state bureaucracy to justify the extra
tax burden (due to the absence of long-term investment horizons generally shared by capitalist class and state officials), as well as by the lack
of new markets for final commodities.

Expenditures on private and social consumption over and above
economic needs, or in excess of outlays on necessary costs, constitute
the second mode of surplus utilization. These expenditures, like all
economically wasteful outlays, are limited to the degree that they can
be rationalized within the logic of capitalist economy—that is to say,
insofar as they lead to greater profits. The proportion of current earnings which the corporation can channel into advertising expenditures,
product differentiation, forced obsolescence, and other selling expenses, as well as other socially wasteful uses of the surplus, is limited
to the extent to which these outlays increase commodity demand, sales,
and profits. There are also limits on the absorption of the surplus via
borrowing private consumption demand from the future—that is, by
the expansion of consumer credit—which are determined by the relation of current consumer income to loan repayments. (In general, a
consumer will not be able to borrow in order to finance new consumption when economically necessary outlays [or costs], together with loan
repayments, equal current income.)

Consumption outlays are also made by local, state, and federal
government bodies. A greater or lesser portion of education, transportation, recreational, and cultural expenditures—in general, spending on social amenities—constitutes social consumption, a special form
of private consumption. Socially necessary costs make up a large part
of social consumption, while much of the remainder comprises economic waste. Again, government expenditures are limited by the ability
of the political authority to rationalize waste within the framework of
private profit making. In addition, there are political limits on the
expansion of spending destined for public housing, health, and other
socioeconomic activities which are inconsistent with the hierarchy of
rank and privileges in a capitalist society, or which compete with private
capital. The same conclusion can be drawn in connection with the
possibilities of redistributing income with the aim of raising the wage
and salary share of total product—and hence private consumption ex-

penditures—at the expense of private profits. The only major type of discretionary state expenditure consistent with private ownership of the means of production, social and economic inequality, and other central features of a capitalist society is military spending.

5. IMPERIALISM AS A USE OF SURPLUS

The preceding sketch in no sense substitutes for a full-dress analysis of the surplus absorption capacity of the advanced capitalist countries, in particular the United States, but rather provides a general background for the detailed exploration of the possibilities of utilizing the economic surplus in the backward capitalist countries and the other advanced capitalist societies. Our general conclusions are twofold. The first is that the multinational corporations are under unceasing pressure to extend their field of operations outside the United States. Economic prosperity in the United States during the decades since World War II has increasingly depended on military expenditures and overseas expansion. Between 1950 and 1964, United States commodity exports, including the sales of overseas facilities of United States corporations, rose nearly 270 percent, while commodity sales at home increased only 125 percent. Expectedly, earnings on foreign investments make up a rising portion of after-tax corporate profits—10 percent in 1950, and 22 percent in 1964. In the strategic capital goods sector of the United States economy, military and foreign purchases account for a surprisingly large share of total output—between 20 and 50 percent in twenty-one of twenty-five industries, and over 80 percent in two industries. Our second general conclusion is that overseas expansion since World War II has not weakened but intensified the antagonism between the generation and absorption of the economic surplus.[43]

Close examination of the two modes of surplus utilization overseas is required to substantiate these claims. Foreign commodity trade is the first, and, until the era of monopoly capitalism, the only important way of absorbing the surplus abroad. Contemporary state policies that seek to promote commodity trade encounter a number of crippling handicaps. For one thing, low-cost supplier credits and other forms of export subsidies provided by state agencies such as the Export-Import Bank merely export the surplus absorption problem abroad and hence meet with resistance from other advanced capitalist countries. A comprehen-

43. Harry Magdoff, "Economic Aspects of U.S. Imperialism," *Monthly Review* 18, no. 6 (November 1966): 17, table 1; 19; 25, table 4.

sive system of export subsidies is almost guaranteed to result in retaliation in kind. The widely adopted "most favored nation" clause in international trade agreements was an expression of the willingness to "give and take" on the part of the advanced capitalist countries in the immediate postwar period. Secondly, until recently United States commodity exports have run consistently ahead of imports, limiting the ability of the United States to wring tariff concessions from other countries without offering even greater reductions in return. Thirdly, United States penetration of Europe, regions in the sphere of influence of the European imperialist powers, and the semi-independent backward capitalist countries which employ tariffs, import quotas, and exchange controls to conserve foreign exchange by reducing imports is increasingly restricted by a revival of economic nationalism, as well as by the birth of a new economic regionalism—that is, by what Joan Robinson has termed the "new mercantilism."

Private foreign investments and state loans and grants constitute the second, and today far and away the most important, mode of surplus absorption. Capital exports may increase demand in one of two ways: by borrowing demand from the future and directly expanding the market for capital goods; and by raising production and income abroad and therefore indirectly increasing imports in the recipient country or in third countries.

In recent years there have been three new tendencies in capital exporting that support the conclusion that it will become increasingly difficult to find outlets abroad for the investment-seeking surplus generated by the multinational corporations. These tendencies are (1) increased collaboration between foreign and local capital; (2) the shift in the composition of foreign investments against primary commodity sectors and in favor of manufacturing and related activities; and (3) the shift in the composition of capital exports against private investment and in favor of state loans and grants. All three tendencies are related to the development of anticolonial and national independence movements in the backward capitalist countries. A brief review of the general implications of national independence for foreign investment opportunities is therefore in order.

Gillman and others have put forward two arguments that support the view that national independence reduces opportunities for the penetration of foreign capital. In the first place, it is asserted that public ownership of the means of production in the ex-colonies encroaches on the traditional territory of private capital and limits investment opportunities available to the international monopolies. This line of reasoning not only is at odds with the facts—in the backward capitalist countries joint state-private ventures are more characteristic than state enterprise—but also pushes aside the critical question of the control of capital. In a number of countries, including many European capitalist nations, the state is the nominal owner of many heavy industrial and infrastructure facilities, but control rests with an autonomous bureaucracy which is highly responsive to the needs of private capital. The vast majority of state and joint enterprises in the backward countries are market oriented, integrated into the structure of the private market. Far from discouraging foreign investors, one task of state enterprise in many countries is to attract new private investment.

Secondly, there is the argument that anticolonial sentiment and the urge for an independent field of economic action lead to exchange controls, restrictions on profit remittances, higher business taxes, more costly social legislation, and other policies which are repugnant to foreign capital. Against this view it should be stressed that the economic autonomy of politically independent countries is itself a question for analysis. Military coups in Brazil, Indonesia, and Ghana, to cite only three right-wing take-overs of the 1960s, provide dramatic evidence for the view that political autonomy must be insured by economic autonomy. Again, seven long-independent Latin American countries with such disparate attitudes toward foreign capital as Chile and Peru —historically the former has been less permissive than the latter— collectively signed the Treaty of Montevideo (1960) which favored foreign investment, and recognized the need for foreign capital in economic development.[44] On the other side, China, Cuba, and other countries which have abandoned the world capitalist system obviously hold little promise for foreign capital.

In reality, there are a number of reasons to believe that politically independent, economically underexploited countries will continue to welcome private foreign capital. First, and perhaps most important, local financiers and industrialists are eager to participate in profitable economic activities initiated by the multinational corporations based in the advanced countries. Joint ventures and other partnership arrangements are looked upon with great favor by local business interests.[45] Tariff policy is designed to encourage assembly, packaging, and other final manufacturing investments not only to promote the development of national industry but also to increase the flow of foreign capital and open up profit opportunities for the local bourgeoisie.

44. United Nations, Department of Economic and Social Affairs, Consultant Group Jointly Appointed by the ECLA and the OAS, *Foreign Private Investment in LAFTA* (New York, 1961), pp. 18–19.
45. Ibid.

Second, the Latin American countries, as well as the ex-colonies in Asia and Africa, are under great pressure from the masses to initiate and promote economic and social development. In these nonsocialist countries local sources of capital are dissipated in luxury consumption and other wasteful expenditures, or cannot be mobilized in the absence of fundamental agrarian and other economic reforms, and hence local governments increasingly depend on foreign capital, private as well as public. Most ex-colonial governments are desperately searching for ways to conserve foreign exchange and actively seek foreign investments and loans. Third, British and French foreign investments are welcome in backward countries which belong to one or the other of these metropoles' currency blocs, where exchange controls are minimal or entirely absent, because there are few if any ways to acquire private foreign capital from other advanced capitalist countries. British investments, for example, are more and more oriented to Sterling Area countries.[46] Fourth, backward countries which have no ambition beyond expanding exports of primary commodities require active foreign participation in the export sector because of the difficulties of independently acquiring and maintaining distribution channels and marketing outlets. After Bolivia nationalized the tin mines, for example, planning of production and sales was partly thwarted because the government "remained beholden to the same big companies for processing and sale."[47]

On the other side, there are at least two reasons for believing that political independence has discouraged some foreign investment, although it is difficult to even guess how much. In the first place, foreign corporations hesitate to invest in the absence of political controls which prevent local firms from using unpatented production processes to invade third-country markets or to pass on to competitors.[48] Secondly, the ex-colonies have eliminated or reduced in many spheres of the economy the special privileges and exclusive rights which corporations based in the colonial power once took for granted. The increased risk and uncertainty that face foreign capital has discouraged investments by small-scale enterprises that are unable to finance multiplant, multicountry operations.[49]

Anticolonialism, political independence, and the elimination of the

46. Kemp, "Long-term Capital Movements," p. 145.
47. Allen Young, "Bolivia," *New Left Review,* no. 39 (September–October 1966), p. 66.
48. Raymond Vernon, "The American Corporation in Underdeveloped Areas," in Edward S. Mason, ed., *The Corporation in Modern Society* (New York, 1966), p. 254.
49. J. Behrman, "Promotion of Private Investment Overseas," in Raymond Mikesell, ed., *U.S. Private and Government Investment Abroad* (Eugene, Ore., 1962), pp. 174–175.

colonial powers from many formal economic command posts have contributed to three new tendencies in foreign investment that reduce the surplus absorption capacity of the backward capitalist countries. There is overwhelming evidence of the first tendency, the growing mobilization of local savings and capital by foreign corporations which diminishes the need for capital exports from the advanced countries. In Latin America, local capital is the most important source of financing for wholly owned subsidiaries of United States corporations.[50] One-half of American and Foreign Power Company's $400 million postwar expansion program in eleven countries was financed from local savings, the other half from retained earnings.[51] A $72 million investment in Argentina by five oil companies illustrates the character of modern overseas finance; the corporations' investment amounted to only $18 million; debentures raised $30 million in Argentina; and the United States government and local investment corporations supplied the remainder.[52] In the capitalist world as a whole, roughly one-third of total U.S. corporate financing overseas in 1964 comprised foreign borrowing or equity financing, and foreign supplies of capital made up two-thirds of the increase in financing over 1963 levels.[53]

The multinational corporations mobilize local savings and capital in a variety of ways: bonds and equities are sold in local capital markets; joint ventures and mixed enterprises mobilize private and state capital, respectively; local development and investment banks acquire local savings directly, and indirectly via local governments;[54] foreign and domestic banks, insurance companies, and other financial intermediaries have access to pools of local savings. To cite one example, Morgan Guaranty Trust Company's sixteen correspondent banks in Venezuela hold 55 percent of privately owned commercial bank resources, and help foreign firms raise local funds. Morgan is also part owner of a large Spanish investment bank which in a two-year period raised $40 million for local and foreign companies.[55] The World Bank pioneered in the

50. J. Behrman, "Foreign Associates and Their Financing," in Mikesell, ed., *Investment Abroad,* p. 103.

51. H. W. Balgooyen, "Problems of U.S. Investments in Latin America," in M. Bernstein, ed., *Foreign Investment in Latin America* (New York, 1966), p. 225.

52. John McLean, "Financing Overseas Expansion," *Harvard Business Review* 41 (March–April 1963): 64.

53. Samuel Pizer and Frederick Cutler, "Financing and Sales of Foreign Affiliates of U.S. Firms," *Survey of Current Business* 45, no. 11 (November 1965): 26.

54. William Diamond, "The Role of Private Institutions in Development Finance: Service Oriented Profit Making," *International Development Review* 7, no. 1 (March 1965): 10.

55. *Wall Street Journal,* 23 February 1966, advertisement. Morgan Guaranty has eighteen correspondent banks in Spain with resources equal to 85 percent of privately owned commercial bank resources.

organization and contributes to the financing of local development banks, develops and integrates capital markets in countries where monetary institutions are weak, and acts as a wedge for private foreign capital into established capital markets.[56]

The growing demand by the international monopolies for local capital is prompted by both political and economic factors. First, and probably most important, both the multinational corporations and the local bourgeoisies are eager to form partnership arrangements, the former to exercise indirect control over, and politically neutralize, the latter; the latter in order to share in the profits of the former.[57] In Nigeria, for example, "foreign investors are beginning to realize that their presence constitutes a political problem and that it is in their interest to encourage Nigerian participation in the structure of their firms to enhance acceptability."[58] Joint ventures and partnerships are up-to-date versions of the colonial policy of creating a dependent, passive local bourgeoisie; British capital, to cite perhaps the most important instance, allied itself with the largest and best-organized Indian monopolies, such as those dominated by the Tatas and Birlas, as a hedge against possible discriminatory action by the Indian government.[59]

Second, the alliance between foreign and local capital inhibits potential economic competition and paves the way for the diversification of the foreign operations of the international monopolies, and extends their control over related product fields in the local economy.[60] Even in countries such as Mexico, where the government refuses to extend its cooperation to foreign corporations which compete with local business or displace local capital, foreigners often have "decisive influence" over company policy because domestic equity ownership is dispersed and minority stock ownership is concentrated in the hands of one or

56. Industrial finance institutions in East Africa are typical. "National Development Corporations" were established before political independence to promote and direct new ventures and to participate in existing enterprises by subscribing to equity capital issues. "Development and Finance Corporations," in which British and German capital is deeply involved, were established more recently; they specialize in loans and grants, and promote partnerships between African and European capital (Economic Commission for Africa, Conference on the Harmonization of Industrial Development Programmes in East Africa, "Industrial Financing in East Africa," Lusaka [October 26–November 6, 1965], E/CN. 14/INR/103).

57. There is some evidence that monopolistic corporations are more interested than competitive firms in acquiring local partners (Wolfgang Friedmann and George Kalmanoff, *Joint International Business Ventures* [New York, 1961], pp. 81–82).

58. Douglas Gustafson, "The Development of Nigeria's Stock Exchange," in Tom Farer, ed., *Financing African Development* (Cambridge, Mass., 1965).

59. Nural Islam, *Foreign Capital and Economic Development: Japan, India and Canada* (Rutland, Vt., 1960), p. 175.

60. McLean, "Financing Overseas Expansion."

two United States corporations.[61] Extending the sphere of corporate operations opens up opportunities for increased profits in the form of royalties and fees for technical services, patents, and brand names. What is more, the use of local capital reduces the risk of conducting operations in foreign countries; local capital is smaller and less diversified than foreign capital and therefore is more vulnerable and assumes a disproportionate risk. In addition, local businessmen are valuable for their knowledge of domestic product and labor markets, government contacts, and other information which insures secure and profitable operations overseas. Finally, the international monopolies profit by spreading their capital thin in branches of production characterized by economies of large-scale operation.

The growth of private foreign investment in manufacturing industries, with the relative decline of agricultural and mining investments, is the second new tendency in capital exporting. The development of synthetic fibers, the rise in agricultural productivity in the advanced countries, the inelastic demand for foodstuffs, the reduction in the mineral component in production (e.g., nonferrous metals), and tariff walls erected by the advanced capitalist countries against imports of primary commodities have reduced the demand for investment funds abroad in mining and agriculture. Tariffs, quotas, and other measures to protect manufacturing industries in the backward countries and regional marketing arrangments in Europe and elsewhere have compelled the large corporations in the United States to construct or purchase manufacturing facilities abroad to retain traditional markets. In turn, the expansive impulses of the multinational corporation have affected worldwide capital flows and the production and distribution of commodities.

Between 1940 and 1964 United States direct manufacturing investments in Latin America (which absorbs about 60 percent of U.S. manufacturing investments in all backward regions) increased from $210 million to $2,340 million, or from 10 percent to 25 percent of total Latin American holdings. In the same period, agricultural investments remained unchanged, mining investments doubled, and the value of petroleum holdings rose from $572 million to $3,142 million. A similar trend is visible in connection with British investments in India. In 1911 about three-quarters of all direct private investments were in extractive industries, utilities and transportation accounted for roughly one-fifth, and the remainder was divided between commerce and

61. Mario Ramon Beteta, "Government Policy Toward Foreign Investors," *The Statist* (London), 8 January 1965.

manufacturing. In 1956 manufacturing investments made up over one-third of the total, commerce another one-fourth, and plantation investments only one-fifth. As Hamza Alavi has written, "this is a complete contrast from the old pattern" of investment holdings.[62] Of all British direct foreign investments (excluding oil) in 1965, Kemp has estimated that manufacturing investments constituted about one-half, the great part located in other advanced capitalist countries.[63]

Most United States manufacturing investments in backward countries are concentrated in consumer goods fabrication, assembly and packaging, and light chemicals. The pattern is roughly the same in the advanced capitalist economies, with the single exception that investments in industrial equipment facilities are more common. During 1958–1959, of 164 U.S. investments in new or expanded manufacturing enterprises in Latin America, 106 were located in the chemical and consumer good sectors; in other backward regions, the number of facilities were 34 and 24, respectively.[64]

In connection with opportunities for capital exporting, and the significance of capital exports for absorbing the economic surplus, nineteenth-century and mid-twentieth-century imperialism differ in a number of profound respects. In the earlier period, foreign investments were concentrated in raw material and mineral production, and the economic satellites were no more than extensions of the metropolitan economies. Overseas capital expenditures opened up cheap sources of productive inputs, and lowered the costs of production in manufacturing industries in the metropoles. In turn, home and foreign demand for manufactured goods increased, prompting an expansion of output and fresh rounds of foreign investment. To the degree that capital exports were channeled into railroad and other transportation facilities, there were favorable indirect effects on the availability of raw materials, and hence manufacturing costs in the metropoles. For nineteenth-century Great Britain, this cumulative, expansive system worked to perfection. Income generated in the satellites by the inflow of capital was expended on British manufactured exports. During periods of rising foreign investment, British exports rose faster than imports, and a consistently favorable balance of payments was maintained.[65]

To be sure, contemporary imperialist powers continue to import many raw materials, and petroleum needs expand at a rapid pace. The

62. Alavi, "Imperialism Old and New," p. 118.
63. Kemp, "Long-term Capital Movements," p. 148.
64. Behrman, "Promotion of Private Investment Overseas," in Mikesell, ed., *Investment Abroad,* Table 7–1, pp. 168–169.
65. Kemp, "Long-term Capital Movements," p. 139.

economic relationships between the metropolitan economies and their satellites, however, differ in important respects. Petroleum production is concentrated in the hands of a few oligopolists who maintain rigid price structures and fail to pass on reductions in exploration, drilling, and production costs to consumers, although organized labor benefits from greater efficiency in the form of higher money wages. The same conclusion can be drawn with regard to other raw materials (iron and copper, for example) for which the ratio of imports to U.S. production is higher than in the prewar era. Moreover, in comparison with other regions, imports have increased more rapidly from Latin American countries, which have met the expansion of demand for copper, tin, manganese, cocoa, and other commodities largely by diverting sales from other markets, rather than by expanding supplies. The basic reason is that Latin American raw material production is today highly monopolized, and, in addition, operates under conditions of decreasing returns to large-scale production. Thus neither new capital outlays nor modernization investments have significantly reduced the costs of production of primary commodities, and, unlike investments in the earlier period, are not self-perpetuating. What is more, international commodity agreements and regional marketing arrangements reduce competition between raw material producing countries, and tend to maintain prices at relatively high levels.

Manufacturing investments in backward countries fall into one of two categories. "Runaway shops" in search of cheap labor abroad are limited by the opposition of organized labor in the metropolitan countries. Tariff-hopping investments, quantitatively most significant, are defensive moves which enable the international corporations to retain established export markets, and merely change the locale of investment from the metropole to the satellite. These outlays fail to expand commodity demand, and hence do not provide growing outlets for the economic surplus. Opportunities for other manufacturing investments in backward countries are also generally limited to import-substitute activities because domestic markets are typically oriented toward middle- and upper-class consumption patterns which are imitative of those in the advanced countries. Export markets for satellite manufactured goods are weak because national and regional monopolies operate behind high tariff walls, and, in addition, monopoly controls which the multinational corporations exercise over international distribution systems and marketing outlets place insurmountable barriers to large-scale satellite manufacturing exports. For these reasons, the United States has shown a growing interest in new regional marketing groupings such as the Latin American Free Trade Area and the Central American Common Market. One of the chief objectives of the Common Market during its formative period (1958–1962) was to attract fresh supplies of foreign capital. There are two important barriers, however, to flourishing regional marketing arrangements in economically backward areas. First, less productive, entrenched local monopolies put up a tenacious struggle to retain their privileged market positions—by contrast with the giant, integrated European cartels and monopolies which promoted the European Common Market. Second, the new preferential trading areas in backward regions are too small to compete effectively with Britain's Sterling Area or the European Economic Community. In sharp contrast to the upsurge of United States investment in Canada after the expansion of the Imperial Preference System in 1932, to cite one example, dollar flows of fresh investment to the new trading areas will be limited.[66]

We have finally to consider opportunities for manufacturing investments in other advanced economies. As we have seen, in recent years the great mass of United States manufacturing investments has been in Europe and Canada. Most of these investments have been tariff-hopping operations, or have been channeled into the purchase of existing facilities. Moreover, United States corporations have increasingly been compelled to penetrate lines of production which are competitive with United States exports. Similar to the effect of British reconstruction investments in Europe following World War I, United States capital flows to other advanced capitalist countries tend to be self-defeating in the long run. An excellent illustration is provided by one study of the impact of 112 British subsidiary companies in Europe on British exports; only 5.6 percent of the subsidiaries' capital outlays was expended on British capital goods.[67] Only investments in distribution facilities, specifically motivated to expand foreign sales, can be expected to significantly increase commodity exports.

These lines of analysis suggest that the surplus absorption capacity of both the advanced and backward countries—in both traditional and newer branches of the economy—will in the future be limited to replacement demand, together with the modest flow of new investments necessary to keep pace with expanding incomes abroad. Reflecting the marginal impact of foreign investments on United States commodity exports is the continuing, although muted, crisis in the United States balance of payments.

Roughly the same conclusion can be drawn in connection with

66. Vernon, "American Corporation," p. 244.
67. Kemp, "Long-term Capital Movements," p. 153.

public and international loans. The third, and perhaps most striking, tendency in capital exporting is the substitution of state loans for private capital outflows. About two-thirds of all capital exports are on state or international (public) account. Nearly three-quarters of all loans and investments destined for backward capitalist countries originate in the public or international sector. In 1964 the net outflow of resources to satellite countries and multinational agencies (which in turn loans funds to the satellites) amounted to nearly $8 billion, of which less than $2 billion was private.

The relationship between private and public capital flows is highly complex, and a brief analysis inevitably runs the risk of oversimplification. Reduced to essentials, however, state loans serve two main purposes. First, public funds which build up the infrastructure of backward countries frequently complement private capital flows and represent merely a special form of private investment, the costs of which are borne by taxpayers in the lending country. With regard to surplus absorption capacity within the infrastructure sectors of backward countries, the same conclusion reached in our discussion of private investment can be applied *a fortiori*.

Second, the character of United States "aid" programs underlines their growing importance as projected points of entry for private capital. Many Export-Import Bank loans are made to encourage the flow of private investment; since 1960 the Bank has offered long-term loans of up to five years.[68] Provisions of Public Law 480, the Food for Peace program, are "designed almost entirely for the purpose of stimulating the flow of U.S. private investment to the less-developed countries."[69] Under this program, the United States government loans local currencies acquired from the sale of surplus agricultural commodities to American corporations in order to finance the local costs of investment projects. The greatest portion of both the interest and the principal is reloaned to either private investors or local governments. "How useful to our own foreign aid and foreign development programs could it be," the president of one multinational corporation has written, "if these funds, in local currencies, were to be loaned on an increasing scale to competitive private borrowers—either Americans or others—for local investment. . . ."[70] Finally, the United States Agency for International

68. Raymond Mikesell, *Public International Lending for Development* (New York, 1966), p. 30.
69. Ibid.
70. Harvey Williams, "New Dimensions for American Foreign Operations," in International Management Association, *Increasing Profits from Foreign Operations* (New York, 1957).

Development grants survey loans to American corporations, paying one-half of the cost of feasibility studies in the event it is decided not to proceed with the investment.

The international agencies, in particular the World Bank, are also beacon lights for private investment. Originally regarded by the leading imperialist nations as a way to restore private international capital movements by guaranteeing private loans, the World Bank has been compelled to centralize and rationalize the world capital market. The Bank has eliminated many of the anarchic features of international capital movements, supervises vast amounts of capital which penetrate the backward countries, and acts as a funnel for private capital in search of safe, profitable returns—banks and investment houses participate in World Bank loans, and the Bank frequently floats bond issues in United States and European money markets. In part dependent on private money market conditions, most Bank activities are financed by subscribed or borrowed government funds. The Bank is thus relatively autonomous, and allocates vast amounts of capital for large-scale infrastructure projects in order to clear the way for private investment flows.

6. MODERN IMPERIALISM'S FOREIGN POLICY

Whether or not private capital responds to the incentives held out by national governments and international agencies depends on a host of factors, chief among which are the investment "climate" in the satellite economies and the character of other state political-economic policies. Suffice it for now to note some of the major differences between imperialist foreign policy in the nineteenth and that in the mid-twentieth centuries.

First, and most obvious, modern imperialism attempts to substitute informal for formal modes of political control of countries in the backwash of world capitalism. The methods of establishing political control are varied. The use of old economic and political ties is practiced whenever possible; these include the relationships formed within the British Commonwealth and the French Community, closed currency zones, preferential trading systems, military alliances, and political-military pacts. Economic, political, and cultural missions, labor union delegations, joint military training programs, military grants, bribes to local ruling classes in the form of economic "aid," substitute for direct colonial rule. Only when indirect policies fail are the older instruments of coercion and force brought into play, and the principle of continuity in change applies. An excellent example is the United States–instigated and –supported counterrevolution in Guatemala in 1954, the accomplishments of which the State Department listed under four headings:

1. The conclusion of an agreement with a United Fruit Company subsidiary providing for the return of property expropriated by the Arbenz Government.

2. The repeal of the law affecting remittances and taxation of earnings from foreign capital.

3. The signing of an Investment Guarantee Agreement with the United States.

4. The promulgation of a new and more favorable petroleum law.[71]

Within Guatemala, the Armas regime in the post-1954 period was maintained in office via contracts with United Fruit, Bond and Share, and other monopolies.[72]

Second, contemporary imperialist states enjoy relatively more financial, and hence political, autonomy. In the nineteenth century, imperialist countries regarded themselves as dependent on the private capital market for raising funds for discretionary state expenditures and were compelled to pursue economic and fiscal policies designed to make it possible for their colonies to meet their private debt service. The dominant state capitalist countries today are financially independent and can follow a more flexible policy toward their satellites. The reason is that both the potential and the actual economic surplus are comparatively large. The potential surplus is large because the normal tendency of monopoly capitalist economies is stagnation and unemployment of labor and capital, attributable to a deficiency of aggregate demand. State expenditures—including military expenditures and foreign loans and grants—normally increase not only aggregate demand but also real income and output, and hence the tax base. A rise in expenditures thus increases revenues, even if tax rates remain unchanged. State expenditures are partly self-financing and virtually costless in terms of the real resources utilized. The actual economic surplus constitutes a relatively large portion of national product because of technological and productivity advances. For these reasons, taxes (and state expenditures) can make up a large share of national product with few serious adverse effects on economic incentives, and thus on total production itself.

The significance of the financial independence of the contemporary

71. Department of State *Bulletin,* 1 April 1967.
72. Alfonso Bauer Paiz, *Cómo opera el capital Yanqui en Centroamérica: El caso de Guatemala* (Mexico D.F., 1956).

imperialist state for foreign policy lies in its ability to export capital—
or absorb the surplus overseas—without a *quid pro quo*. The Marshall
Plan, the extensive program of military aid and grants, and the low-cost
loans extended to backward countries by AID are the main examples
of this mode of surplus absorption. The surplus absorption capacity of
satellite countries which are closely tied to the United States political-
military bloc is for practical purposes unlimited. Two factors, however,
circumscribe state grants without a *quid pro quo*. First, low-cost state
loans and grants-in-aid, or capital exports which are not extended on
normal commercial principles, compete "unfairly" with private loans
and are resisted by private capitalist interests in the metropolitan
economy. Second, metropolitan governments are unable to discipline
their satellites effectively unless there are economic strings attached to
international loans. Moreover, state bilateral and multilateral loans
financed in private capital markets in the advanced countries must earn
a return sufficient to cover the cost of borrowing and administration.
Opportunities for capital exports extended on commercial principles
are limited by the availability of profitable investment projects.

Nineteenth-century and mid-twentieth-century imperialism depart
from each other in a third important respect. In the nineteenth century
there were few important antagonisms between Great Britain's role as
the leading national capitalist power, on the one hand, and her role as
the dominant imperialist power, on the other. Policies designed to
expand Britain's home economy extended capitalist modes of production and organization to the three underexploited continents, directly
and indirectly strengthening the growing British imperial system.[73] For
this reason, foreign policy ordinarily served private foreign investors
and other private interests oriented to overseas activity. Only occasion-
ally—as in the case of Disraeli's decision to purchase Suez Canal shares
in 1875[74]—was foreign investment employed as a "weapon" of British
foreign policy. Even less frequently did Britain promote private foreign
investments with the purpose of aiding global foreign policy objectives.
(It has been suggested by one expert, however, that private investments
were made to serve specific foreign policy objectives more frequently
than it is ordinarily believed.)[75]

73. The argument that Britain's home economy suffered because it was deprived of
capital that was absorbed abroad is fallacious. On the one hand, given the prevailing
distribution of income and industrial organization, there were few profitable opportunities to absorb the surplus at home; on the other hand, the return flow on foreign
investments more than offset the original capital exports.

74. Leland Jenks, *The Migration of British Capital* (New York, 1963), p. 325.

75. Herbert Feis, *Foreign Aid and Foreign Policy* (New York, 1963), pp. 33–40.

By way of contrast, the national and international ambitions of the United States in the mid-twentieth century are continually in conflict. In the context of the limited absorption capacity of the backward capitalist world and international competition from other advanced capitalist economies and the socialist countries, the United States is compelled to employ a wide range of policies to expand trade and investment. To further national ends, a "partnership" between "public lending institutions" and "private lenders"—with the former "leading the way" for the latter—has been formed.[76] Underlining the role of the state in the service of the multinational corporations, in 1962 Secretary of State Rusk described the newer government policies that extend beyond state loan programs—investment guarantee programs in forty-six backward capitalist countries that cover currency inconvertibility, expropriation, war, revolution, and insurrection; instructions to local embassies to support business interests by making "necessary representations to the host governments . . ."; the creation of a new Special Assistant for International Business in the State Department in order to insure that private business interests receive "prompt representation" in the government.[77] Especially when public loans are disguised or special forms of private loans (see above), the commitment of the United States government to national capitalist interests inhibits state policies which seek to strengthen the industrial bourgeoisie and ruling classes in other advanced countries and the national bourgeoisie in the backward nations. Perhaps this is the most important limit on capital exports on public account.

As the leading international power, the United States is under constant and growing pressure to strengthen world capitalism as a system, including each of its specific parts. Policies that aim to recruit new members for local comprador groups, stimulate the development of capitalist agriculture and the middle farmers, reinforce the dominance of local financial and commercial classes, and reinvigorate local manufacturing activities—these general policies pose a potential or real threat to the interests of United States national capital. Alliance for Progress funds destined for the middle sectors of Latin American agriculture, Export-Import bank loans to foreign commercialists, loans and grants to foreign governments dominated by the urban bourgeoisie, loans and subsidies to the Indian iron and steel industry, Mexican industry and agriculture, and other branches of production in countries

76. Mikesell, ed., *Investment Abroad*, p. 7.
77. Dean Rusk, "Trade, Investment, and U.S. Foreign Policy," Department of State *Bulletin*, 5 November 1962.

which are slowly industrializing—these and other stopgap and long-range measures help to keep the backward countries in the imperialist camp in the short run, but directly or indirectly create local capitalist interests which may demand their independence from United States capital in the long run.

United States private capital increasingly requires the aid of the state, and the state enlists more and more private and public capital in its crusade to maintain world capitalism intact. Specific and general capitalist interests serve each other, finally merging into one phenomenon. This must have, finally, its institutional reflection. The multinational corporation has become the instrument for the creation and consolidation of an international ruling class, the only hope for reconciling the antagonism between national and international interests.

7. SURPLUS ABSORPTION·OR SURPLUS CREATION?

The preceding analysis supports the conclusion that the surplus absorption capacity of the backward countries—and, probably to a lesser degree, the other advanced economies—and hence opportunities for utilizing investment-seeking funds overseas, are circumscribed in a variety of ways. Opportunities for "enterprise," or profit making, however, show few signs of weakening. We have touched on some of the reasons: First, the multinational corporations increasingly mobilize and utilize local and state savings and capital, undertake more ambitious investment projects, and profit from economies of large-scale production and more efficient intracorporate planning. Second, a larger share of the retained earnings of corporation branch plants and subsidiaries is absorbed by modernization investments, which reduce costs and raise profits. Third, the multinational corporations monopolize patents, brand names, and production processes in the greatest demand, and are able to establish control over national and international markets via licensing and similar agreements which require relatively small capital outlays. Fourth, the giant international corporations are more and more integrated and diversified, and production and sales are subject to less risk and uncertainty. Lastly, the international monopolies can count on the active participation and aid of the state.

For these reasons, the multinational corporations command growing profit margins on their overseas operations. Small amounts of capital are sufficient to penetrate, control, and dominate the weaker, less productive national economies. The price of disposing of a given amount of economic surplus this year is the creation of even more surplus next year—hardly a high price for the individual corporation to pay, but from the standpoint of the metropolitan economy as a whole, the problem of surplus absorption tends to become increasingly severe.

The United States government, the European powers, and the United States–dominated international agencies are thus under growing pressure by the international monopolies to formulate and implement political-economic policies which will create an "attractive" investment climate abroad, in particular in the underexploited countries. Looked at from another angle, the imperialist powers are increasingly compelled to "promote economic development" overseas or, to put it differently, to integrate the backward areas even more closely into the structure of world capitalism. In effect, the advanced countries are desperately seeking to expand outlets for the economic surplus. To be sure, the imperialist powers view the problem as one of surplus creation (or profit realization), rather than of surplus absorption—their line of vision generally corresponds in this respect to the perspective of the corporations themselves. These are merely different sides to the same coin: by promoting profitable opportunities abroad for private capital, the state lays the basis for the absorption of a portion of this year's surplus, and, simultaneously, for the creation of additional surplus next year.

For United States economic, political, and foreign policy this line of analysis has a number of important consequences. In the first place, national economic development programs in the backward countries which seek the participation of the socialist countries and other advanced capitalist countries have been and will continue to be opposed by the United States. Secondly, investments in lines of industry which are noncompetitive with United States products, especially those which increase demand for United States products, have been and will continue to be encouraged.

Thirdly, the United States will continue to initiate antisocialist, anticommunist military and political pacts and alliances with both backward and advanced capitalist countries—for the international monopolies the basic importance of state loans and aid lies in the long-run impact on the demand for arms, capital equipment, and consumer goods in those satellites which have developed intimate political and military bonds with the United States.

More generally, because the expansion of commodity exports, as well as capital exports, generates even more surplus in the future—

because the process of surplus creation and absorption is a cumulative one—the United States is increasingly compelled to follow the policies of a militant, expansive imperialist power, all in the name of economic development for the underdeveloped countries. The task facing the United States in relation to the backward countries is truly Herculean.

At one and the same time, the United States must convince the backward countries that the growing penetration of United States capital and the growing control of the multinational companies over local economies are useful and necessary for their economic growth and development, at a time when politically oppressive policies which aim to create more favorable conditions for private investment are followed. Thus economic development is oriented by the multinational companies, and where there are national development plans which on paper assign a certain limited role to private investment, in fact private investment assigns a role to the plan. The underdeveloped world becomes bound up even more closely in a new imperialist system in which investments in consumer goods industries replace investments in raw materials and minerals; in which the backward countries are compelled to deal with a unified private capital–state capital axis; in which political control by the World Bank and the other international agencies, together with the political arm of the official labor movement, the giant foundations, and other quasi-private political agencies, replace colonial rule; and in which the national middle classes in the underdeveloped countries are slowly but surely transformed into a new class of clients and compradors, in every important respect equivalent to the old class of traders, bankers, and landlords which for centuries bowed and scraped before their imperial rulers in China, India, Latin America, and elsewhere. A new era of imperialism is just beginning, an era which holds out contradictory promises to the imperial powers and their clusters of satellites. Whether or not the advanced capitalist countries can deal with this crisis of their own making depends on two basic factors: the power of peoples in the underexploited continents to resist, and the flexibility of the structure of the imperialist system.

CHAPTER EIGHT

International Corporations and Economic Underdevelopment

1. INTRODUCTION

United States, European, and Japanese international corporations presently own or control between 20 and 30 percent of the monetized resources in the underdeveloped countries (including Canada). Indirect control of local capital in Asia, Latin America, and Africa is pervasive: the mobilization of local capital,[1] control of subcontractors and other suppliers, "management contracts" which afford foreign capital day-to-day control of joint ventures,[2] and licensing agreements which restrict the use of technology by prohibiting "fundamental investigation and research"[3] extend the sway of foreign capital still further, and multiply the quantitative impact of the international corporations on the misutilization of resources abroad.

The general reasons for the expansion of foreign capital during the 1950s and 1960s, especially capital organized by the giant United States international corporations, are well known. In the first place, the United States economy tends to generate more economic surplus than large-scale business can profitably absorb at home. Foreign investments absorb some of the surplus in the short run, but generate even greater amounts of surplus in the long run. The large corporations are thus

Personal thanks are due my friends Lloyd Best and Norm Girvan, West Indian economists whose pathbreaking studies of the international corporations and economic underdevelopment provide the frame of reference for the present article. Thanks are also due Paul Sweezy, whose criticisms of this article have been very helpful.

1. As of 1964, 95 percent of U.S. investments in Canada were raised from Canadian sources, 17 percent from Canadian financial institutions, and 78 percent in the form of retained earnings (Kari Levitt, "Canada: Economic Dependence and Political Disintegration," *New World Quarterly* 4, no. 2 [1968]: 74). As of 1957, 74 percent of U.S. investments in Brazil were raised in Brazil, 36 percent from Brazilian financial institutions and other sources, and 38 percent from depreciation and retained earnings (Claude McMillan, *International Enterprises in a Developing Economy: A Study of United States Business in Brazil* [East Lansing, Mich., 1964], p. 205).

2. "Management Contracts Abroad," monograph published by *Business International* (New York 1963).

3. Hamza Alavi, "Indian Capitalism and Foreign Imperialism," *New Left Review*, no. 37 (May–June 1967), p. 83.

compelled to become even more expansion minded and seek fresh investment opportunities.[4] As shown below, branch plant investments of U.S. corporations absorb surplus generated in the United States by providing major export markets for parent corporations.

In the second place, modern technology requires oil and special raw materials, mainly metals, many of which are found only in under-developed countries. In addition, short supplies of raw materials in the North American continent have compelled U.S. corporations to exploit new sources in the underdeveloped world. Moreover, U.S. corporations are under constant pressure to develop fresh raw material sources, as a hedge against competitors and as a way to reduce business risk by diversifying supplies.[5]

It is also well known that U.S. corporations have been operating in an especially favorable economic and political environment since the end of World War II. There have been few important political barriers preventing American capital from insinuating itself into the defeated empires of Germany and overseas Japan, and the decayed empires of Britain, France, and Holland in Asia and Africa. In Latin America the failure of national-oriented import-substitution industrialization poli-cies to promote ongoing economic development has accelerated the conquest of Latin American capital by U.S. corporations.

Another familiar story concerns the general political-economic effects of U.S. control of an increasing part of the capitalist world's economic resources. Canada's independent economic foreign policies are confined to the agricultural sphere, still under the control of Canadian capital. India's domestic economic policies have been in-fluenced at every turn by the United States, owing to her dependence on U.S. "aid," U.S. government control of a large share of India's money supply, and the growing penetration of U.S. private capital. Fiscal and monetary policies in Brazil, Argentina, and many smaller countries are often dictated by the U.S.-dominated International Mone-tary Fund. Everywhere in the underdeveloped world the World Bank influences or controls development plans, because of the Bank's monopoly position in the international market for long-term capital funds. In Latin America only Cuba has escaped the bondage of U.S. imperialism, although in Guatemala, Colombia, Bolivia, and elsewhere revolutionary forces are fighting to free these countries as well.

4. Paul A. Baran and Paul M. Sweezy, *Monopoly Capital* (New York, 1966), pp. 104–108. A more detailed analysis of the process of surplus absorption and creation abroad is provided in Chapter Seven above.

5. Far and away the best account of the importance of raw materials for modern capitalism is in Harry Magdoff, *The Age of Imperialism* (New York, 1969).

Less familiar is the story of how U.S. corporations actually cause economic underdevelopment, or prevent ongoing development in the underdeveloped countries. Thanks to the work of André Gunder Frank, Clifford Geertz, Gunnar Myrdal, and others, but above all to Paul Baran's pathbreaking book, *The Political Economy of Growth,* the general historical mechanisms of the process of development-under-development are understood. Almost invariably, when precapitalist societies were integrated or reintegrated into the world capitalist system the result was underdevelopment in the economically more backward poles and development in the advanced poles. Economic development and underdevelopment did not merely go hand in hand historically; the one *caused* the other. Only in a handful of regions, such as West Africa, where the existence of unused land and underemployed labor opened the possibility of expanding subsistence and export production simultaneously, did specialization in raw material production for export fail to undermine subsistence agriculture, small-scale local manufacturing, and, in general, any local base for autonomous development. Although not the typical case, Britain's relations with her economic and political colonies highlight the development-underdevelopment process. Britain developed a balanced industrial economy which was able to "capture" economies of large-scale production and external economies of scale *because* most of her colonies (including her Latin American economic colonies in the last half of the nineteenth century) were *underdeveloped*—that is, because they became unbalanced, nonindustrial economies specializing in the production of raw materials for export.

We do not have a comparable comprehensive account of how the development of international corporations, based mainly in the United States, prevents the development of Asia, Latin America, and Africa, or causes the underdevelopment of these regions. It goes without saying that this is a question worth studying. Fortunately, there are enough partial studies now available to attempt a beginning, general analysis of the subject. This is the purpose of the present essay.

2. TYPES OF FOREIGN INVESTMENT

As a beginning, it is well to list the main types of U.S. foreign investments, in rough order of their historic priority. First, of course, are investments in raw materials production, including the necessary infrastructure investments (e.g., Anaconda's copper mines in Chile and

Reynolds' bauxite mines in Jamaica and Guyana). Second are investments in raw material processing, such as the nickel-processing facilities in prerevolutionary Cuba. Third are investments in manufacturing facilities, chiefly final assembly operations taking the form of branch plants of parent U.S. corporations. These are the so-called tariff-hopping investments, which import many raw materials, intermediate goods, parts, and sometimes even fuel from the parent corporation or elsewhere in the developed countries, and sell final products in the local market. Branch-plant investments have become increasingly popular since World War II, and, in fact, constitute the only way that many underdeveloped countries are able to acquire foreign private capital. The many automobile assembly plants in Latin America are a good example. Fourth, there are the true "multinational" investments, plants that purchase inputs from one branch of a corporation located in the same or a different country and sell outputs to another branch of the same corporation located elsewhere—that is, investments characterized by "product-by-plant" specialization. Multinational investments are mainly confined to petrochemicals and computers, although electronic and other assembly plants in cheap labor havens such as northern Mexico, Puerto Rico, Taiwan, and South Korea often produce for reexport to the parent company.

Most international corporations confine their foreign investments to only one or two of the above types, although a handful—International Telephone and Telegraph and Standard Oil of New Jersey are two examples—are represented in all four categories. For expository purposes, and because each type of investment works somewhat different effects in the underdeveloped regions, our analysis will focus on the specific effects of the various forms foreign investment takes.

Next, what is required is a general description of the world capitalist system from the standpoint of the international corporations. These companies provide the institutional framework—or the accounting framework for resource utilization—for many underdeveloped countries, especially the smaller, more vulnerable economies. Integrating more and more resources into their own structures, the international corporations are able to mobilize, transform, and dispose of capital on a regional or even worldwide scale—in effect, constituting themselves as extraterritorial bodies.

Production goals and techniques, investment policies, labor relations, prices, profit allocation, purchasing, distribution, and marketing policies are all decided from the standpoint of the profit goals of the international corporation *whether or not these goals are consistent with local economic development*. The corporations are the channels for the diffusion of technology and consumption patterns; again, profits come first, local needs second. Even big business ideologists are coming close to admitting what has long been a truism for Marxists; one of them concedes the possibility that the "utilization of resources to maximize profits" may not be "compatible" with the interests of the "host country."[6]

In what specific ways are the goals and policies of the international companies detrimental to local economic development? We will consider in turn the effects of corporate *investment, production,* and *purchasing and sales policies* on the local economy, subsequently discussing the effects of the international corporations on *technological change* and on the *balance of payments* in the underdeveloped countries.

The effects of foreign investments in raw material production and processing are too well known to require more than brief mention.[7] In a nutshell, raw material investments tend to make underdeveloped countries mere appendages of developed countries, depriving them of any opportunity for autonomous, ongoing economic development, and thwarting the development of industry and an industrial bourgeoisie.

Foreign investments in manufacturing in the form of branch plants and wholly or partially owned subsidiaries have less familiar effects. The basic purpose of these investments is to control markets by affording the large corporation the opportunity to retain and expand export markets in the face of high tariffs, that is, to control the market for parts, components, and raw materials. In India, for example, Pavlov has shown that Indian tariff policy largely determines the industrial and sectoral composition of joint ventures and wholly owned subsidiaries of foreign corporations.[8] Surveying the key international corporations, the National Industrial Conference Board concluded that "marketing strategy was clearly the dominant element in investment decisions." A study made by the U.S. Department of Commerce in 1963 disclosed that over one-third of the corporations sampled invested abroad mainly to expand exports. More evidence is provided by data on U.S. exports to Latin America: in 1964, of total U.S. exports to manufacturing affiliates of U.S. firms in Latin America, 57 percent consisted of parent

6. Gilbert Clee, "Guidelines for Global Business," *Columbia Journal of World Business* 1, no. 1 (Winter 1966): 97–104.

7. Baran and Sweezy, *Monopoly Capital;* André Gunder Frank, *Capitalism and Underdevelopment in Latin America: Historical Studies of Chile and Brazil* (New York, 1967); C. Rollins, "Mineral Development and Economic Growth," *Social Research* 23, no. 3 (Autumn 1956); Alvin Wolfe, "The African Mineral Industry," *Social Problems* 11, no. 2 (Fall 1963); Dudley Seers, "Big Companies in Small Countries," *Kyklos* 16, no. 4 (1963): 599–609; James O'Connor, *The Origins of Socialism in Cuba* (Ithaca, N.Y., 1970).

8. V. I. Pavlov, *India: Economic Freedom Versus Imperialism* (New Delhi, 1963), p. 92 n.

exports of capital equipment and materials for processing and assembly to affiliates.[9] Profit figures provide more evidence of the importance of export markets for foreign investments; some parent corporations make most of their money abroad by exporting materials and equipment to their branch plants; next in importance are revenues from royalties and fees; dividend revenue for these corporations is marginal.[10]

Put briefly, the significance of this for the underdeveloped countries is that investment decisions are not made on the basis of local priorities, or the ranking of alternative yields, but rather on the basis of promoting exports. Thus, in an economy receiving private foreign capital in the form of branch plants there is a tendency toward overinvestment, high costs, and excess capacity—that is to say, there are too many production units, all of them too small for efficient operations.[11]

In addition, in the branch-plant economies there is a tendency for existing local industry to be eroded away as a result of the effects of overcrowding on the rate of profit, particularly since local industry, unlike the affiliates, cannot charge losses back to a parent corporation. Foreign capital, in the words of David Felix, outcompetes local capital partly because of its ability "to self-insure against risk and to inflate the capital base of subsidiaries by transferring to them already depreciated equipment and designs from their more advanced home plants." Local capital thus tends to be either co-opted by foreign capital or confined to especially risky undertakings. Further, branch-plant industrialization fragments the local capital market; branch-plant savings are not ordinarily available to other sectors of the local economy, being reinvested, used to purchase facilities from local capital, or repatriated. All in all, branch-plant investments promote the misutilization of capital, and generate severe immobilities in the local capital market.

9. Norman Girvan and Owen Jefferson, "Corporate vs. Caribbean Integration," *New World Quarterly* 4, no. 2 (1968): 53.

10. This analysis is consistent with the thesis that within the giant corporation "production literally 'takes care of itself' " and that financing is no longer a problem, thus that "the corporate decision-maker may be left with one main function—merchandising" (James O'Connor, "Finance Capital or Corporate Capital?" *Monthly Review* 20, no. 7 [December 1968]: 34–35). In general, however, branch profits and dividends far exceed royalties, licenses, and rentals, probably because of the heavy concentration of manufacturing investments in advanced capitalist economies.

11. Besides being unable to seize advantages from economies of large-scale production, branch-plant industry fails to benefit from locational specialization and from complementaries of inputs in the use of natural and technical resources (William G. Demas, *The Economics of Development in Small Countries with Special Reference to the Caribbean* [Montreal, 1965], pp. 8–10).

The third type of foreign undertakings are the pure "multinational" investments. Again, investments are not made on the basis of local priorities, or with an eye to the local resource base and local needs. Rather the motive is to minimize costs of production to the corporation. Thus, once a sizable market for a standardized commodity has been established in the advanced countries, the corporations are free to make long-term commitments to build production facilities in the under-developed countries where labor costs are low.[12] The facility imports the bulk of its inputs, exports nearly all of its output, and hence remains unintegrated into the local economy.

3. THE EFFECT OF CORPORATE PRODUCTION POLICY

Next we will consider the impact of corporate production policy on the development of underdeveloped countries. So far as raw materials are concerned, Baran has shown that production is optimum only from the standpoint of the corporation's total profit picture, or from the standpoint of the needs of the developed countries. In Chile, for example, the two international corporations which monopolize copper production have acquired more profits by expanding output in competing areas, which also enables the monopolies to pressure the Chilean government for more favorable treatment locally. Examples could be multiplied no end; two more are drawn from the Caribbean: in recent years, rivalries between metropolitan-based international corporations which dominate Caribbean banana production have helped to ruin small-scale peasant producers by promoting an unlimited expansion of production. Again in recent years, Bookers Sugar Estates Ltd. and the Demerara Co., which control nearly all of Guyana's sugar production, have established sugar plantations in Nigeria from profits made in, and in competition with, Guyana.[13]

The effects of corporate production policy in the industrial sphere present somewhat different problems. Three key features stand out. First, it is clear that the international corporations have every motive to defend their export markets, and hence order their branch plants to discriminate against local supplies in favor of imports from the parent

12. See the model developed in Raymond Vernon, "International Investment and International Trade in the Product Cycle," *Quarterly Journal of Economics* 80, no. 2 (May 1966): 190–208.

13. George Beckford, "Issues in the Windward-Jamaica Banana War," *New World Quarterly* 2, no. 1 (1965); Horace B. Davis, "The Decolonization of Sugar in Guyana," *Caribbean Studies* 7, no. 3 (1967): 37.

company. There is no evidence that the governments of the smaller underdeveloped countries have been able to compel the corporations to produce with local supplies, although some of the larger countries, such as Brazil, have partially succeeded in doing this.

Second, it is also clear that the international corporations—excepting the true multinational companies—have little or no interest in producing for *export,* especially when export production competes with other branches of the same corporation in the international market. The significance of this is that an economy which is undergoing "branch-plant industrialization" is developing little or no export capacity, a process which was crucial to the growth of the developed countries of Europe, as well as Japan and the United States.

Third, in the underdeveloped countries the demand for commodities is increasingly based on the diffusion of "tastes" from the developed countries, together with the prevailing social structure and distribution of income. As Levitt has pointed out, the international companies seek to homogenize world demand in order to spread fixed costs and capture economies of scale in research, product design, and technology. ". . . The profitability of the parent corporation," she writes, "is assisted by every influence which eliminates cultural resistance to the consumption patterns of the metropolis. The corporation thus has a vested interest in the destruction of cultural differences and homogenization of the [U.S.] way of life, the world over." In addition, as Stavenhagen points out, "the diffusion of manufactured articles is directly related to the overall level of technology as well as to effective demand [in the underdeveloped country]."[14] We must return to the basic Marxist theory of consumption to assess the significance of this for economic development. Marx demonstrated that production creates not only the objects that satisfy economic needs, but also the economic needs satisfied by the objects; in short, production determines consumption. Today consumption in the underdeveloped countries tends to be determined by production in the developed countries, and hence economic needs in the former are satisfied poorly or imperfectly. In specific, branch-plant production of a wide variety of heavily advertised differentiated products is very wasteful in poor countries with small markets.[15]

14. Rodolfo Stavenhagen, "Seven Fallacies About Latin America," in James Petras and Maurice Zeitlin, eds., *Latin America: Reform or Revolution?* (New York, 1968), p. 25.
15. Mention of the "production" of bank credit by branches of metropolitan banks is in order. In the smaller underdeveloped countries which are still dominated by foreign banks, branch banks tend to be more responsive to liquidity conditions in the metropoli-

4. THE EFFECT OF CORPORATE PURCHASING POLICIES

Let us turn next to the effect of corporate purchasing and sales policies on economic development. As expected, these policies reinforce the negative effects of corporate investment and production decisions. Borrowing from the work of John Kenneth Galbraith, who argues that the large corporation subjects decisions previously made in the market to administrative control, Girvan and Jefferson have developed a framework for an analysis of this problem.[16] In this model, the international corporation seeks the fullest possible utilization of capacity in all its vertically and horizontally integrated activities. The basic motive is to spread overhead costs and avoid paying profits to other corporations. Thus, the international company places a large "premium on intra-company product and factor flows" which creates "rigidity in the product and factor flows between companies producing similar sets of commodities, whether these companies are producing in the same region or in the same country, or not." The result is regional economic fragmentation; for example, some of Reynolds' Guyana bauxite production reaches the aluminum smelting industry of Venezuela via Reynolds alumina plants in the United States. Another result is national economic fragmentation; according to Girvan and Jefferson, "Reynolds bauxite output in Guyana and Jamaica has not so far been available to the existing processing capacity in both countries because the capacity is owned by a different company."[17] Still another result is that intracorporation purchases tend to be insensitive to changes in foreign exchange rates; for example, the 1962 Canadian devaluation was accompanied by a 17 percent *increase* in imports.

Economic fragmentation means that many of the resources of the Caribbean and Latin America reach other countries in the area in a more finished form via processing plants in the U.S. On the one side, the bulk of U.S. imports of raw materials take the form of imports from

---

tan countries than in the local economy. In the Caribbean, for example, branch banks have *contracted* credit during export booms—that is, when the local economy has relatively high foreign exchange reserves and thus a real base for expanding credit locally.

16. John Kenneth Galbraith, *The New Industrial State* (Boston, 1967); Girvan and Jefferson, "Corporate vs. Caribbean Integration," pp. 52–54.

17. A recent study concludes that national or regional integration in aluminum is highly unlikely because the prospects for the development of smelters and processing capacity in the underdeveloped countries are small (Sterling Brubaker, *Trends in the World Aluminum Industry* [Baltimore, 1967]). It should be noted that in the oil industry there is a widespread practice of exchanging crudes and oil products between companies.

subsidiaries and branches to the U.S.-based parent corporation; leading examples are Caribbean bauxite; Mexican iron ore, manganese, flourspar, lead, zinc, and asbestos; Chilean copper, lead, and zinc; and Brazilian manganese. On the other side, in the Caribbean alone, over one-third of the imports of *metal* manufactures, machinery, and transportation equipment by the four largest Commonwealth territories is supplied by the United States.

From this line of analysis, Girvan and Jefferson rightly conclude that the existing *competitiveness* of underdeveloped countries is a poor guide to potential economic *complementarity*. Moreover, the present built-in bias toward importation of supplies from parent corporations inhibits import-substitute industrialization programs. The Caribbean offers the extreme case—local governments have actively promoted industrialization for years; one result has been a growth of per capita income, but there has been no simultaneous change in the structure of imports. At best, import-substitute industrialization under the auspices of the international corporation merely changes the composition of imports, leaving the dynamic of expansion with the traditional export sector.

A general understanding of the impact of purchasing and sales policies on underdeveloped countries requires a brief review of corporate price policies. In general, the international corporation is an effective instrument for maximizing the appropriation of surplus from satellite economies by metropolitan economies. On the one hand, the parent corporation charges its branch plants (in both the raw materials and manufacturing sectors) the highest price possible, in order to maximize profits on exports, and as a hedge against local government restrictions on profit remittances. (The exception are corporations that intend to reinvest abroad and thus desire to maximize foreign profits and minimize profits reported at home, in order to escape U.S. taxes.) Meanwhile, the parent corporation's interests are best served by keeping final product prices in the underdeveloped country as high as possible, consistent with the role of the branch plant as the parent's export market.

On the other hand, the parent corporation buys raw materials from its branches and subsidiaries at the lowest possible price. Bauxite, iron ore, and copper—among other minerals—all tend to be undervalued.[18] The reasons are plain: first, the large corporations seek to purchase the outputs of small independent producers at depressed prices; second, low prices discourage the development of new independent producers,

18. Girvan and Jefferson, "Corporate vs. Caribbean Integration"; Seers, "Big Companies in Small Countries"; Frank, *Capitalism and Underdevelopment*.

and hence potential competition; third, depressed prices reduce foreign exchange risks when local governments attempt to reduce profit remittances; and, last, low buying prices mean that the corporations pay fewer taxes and lower royalies and wages.

5. INTERNATIONAL CORPORATIONS AND TECHNOLOGICAL CHANGE

We have finally to discuss the impact of the international corporation on technological change in underdeveloped countries, as well as on the satellite economies' balance of payments. As we have seen, the international corporations seek to keep control over technology themselves. In Alavi's words, "typically, strict control is sought over the use to which the techniques imported are put. . . . The supplier of the new technique is often fully protected from imparting a complete technology by clauses which specially exclude 'fundamental investigation and development.' . . . the Indian concern is often effectively prevented from adapting products or processes to local conditions and materials, or from encouraging local ancillary industries and so becomes even more dependent on imported supplies."[19] In effect, control of technology (foreign capital tends to be more technologically integrated than local capital, and foreign production more specialized) means control of markets.

Besides licensing agreements restricting local control of technology, the international corporations often discourage their branches from applying technological resources to *local* technological bottlenecks. Thus U.S.-owned sugar firms in prerevolutionary Cuba conducted little research into the problems of raising cane yields, increasing the sucrose content of cane, or mechanizing the harvest. Again, U.S. aluminum companies in Jamaica spend nothing on iron separation techniques, even though Jamaican bauxite has a high iron content; on the other side, the same companies finance intensive research into the problem of recovering aluminum from high-alumina clays in the United States.

In the underdeveloped countries undergoing some degree of branch-plant industrialization, the impact of the international corporations is equally negative. Assembly plants and other facilities oriented to higher stages of manufacturing are relatively small-scale, fail to capture economies of large-scale production, and frequently embody out-

19. Alavi, "Indian Capitalism and Foreign Imperialism."

of-date techniques. Saddled with small-scale production units and obsolete equipment, the branch-plant economies are characterized by "perpetual and certain backwardness in research and technology."[20]

The international diffusion of technology is thus under the control of the international corporations. Perhaps the most significant consequence for the underdeveloped countries is that the large corporations make technological decisions with an eye to the resource base (or "relative factor supplies") of the United States or world capitalism as a whole, and not to the resource supplies of the underdeveloped country or region. In Felix's words, "Despite their involvement in activities in which sustained profits are supposed to depend on a continual replenishment of technological advantages, neither domestic nor foreign-owned firms [in Latin America] have tried to modify imported technology or products through local research and development." This has led to the use of techniques which generate little additional employment of labor in the underdeveloped world. Branch-plant industrialization thus not only assures technological backwardness and prevents the development of production processes and products more suitable to local conditions, but also inhibits the growth of manufacturing employment. In Latin America as a whole, for example, industrial production compared with total production rose by 16.5 percent from 1950 to 1960; meanwhile, industrial employment in relation to total employment *fell* by 10 percent.[21]

At this point, we can turn our attention to the impact of the international corporations on the balance of payments of the underdeveloped countries. Taken together, the specific effects of the corporations discussed above cause a heavy and increasing burden on the local balance of payments. For one thing, the lack of integration of foreign investments into the local economy, especially branch plants which exist only to provide a market for the parent corporation, places heavy pressures on foreign exchange reserves. As Furtado has shown, the shift away from traditional raw material exports to import-substitute industries producing final commodities compels the underdeveloped countries to

20. Levitt, "Canada: Economic Dependence," p. 81.
21. The "industrialization" of Trinidad and Tobago offers the extreme example of the negative effects of branch-plant investments on employment (Edwin Carrington, "Industrialization by Invitation in Trinidad and Tobago since 1950," *New World Quarterly* 4, no. 2 [1968]). As Baran has shown, imported technology creates little employment even in the traditional raw materials sectors. In Chile the copper industry employs only 5 percent of the labor force; in Venezuela petroleum production provides jobs for only 3 percent of the labor force.

accelerate imports of capital goods, and hence suffer severe balance of payments problems.[22] Second, repatriated profits, whether in an open or disguised form, place a greater drain on scarce foreign exchange and constitute a kind of permanent debt service. So do technological monopolies, which mean costly royalties, management fees, and salaries of foreign technicians. In addition, local consumption patterns based more on demand in the developed countries than on local needs lead to needless imports of both consumer and capital goods. And, finally, the lack of *regional* integration prevents trade and investment between the underdeveloped countries and unnecessarily uses up even more scarce hard currencies. Although there seems to be no simple way to estimate the quantitative impact of these factors on the balance of payments of the underdeveloped world, the burden is bound to be very great indeed. Taking the case of Latin America during the period 1961–1963, profit remittances, debt service, royalties, and other invisible financial services alone accounted for nearly 40 percent of the region's foreign exchange earnings.

6. CONCLUSION

Although the critical study of the role of international corporations in underdeveloped countries (especially in manufacturing industries) remains in its infancy, it may not be premature to offer some general observations about the relationship between economic development and underdevelopment in the present era. The evidence at our disposal strongly suggests that the development of the large international corporation at home and abroad, and hence the development of the advanced capitalist countries, *causes* the underdevelopment of the economically backward countries and regions. The relationship between the developed and underdeveloped poles in the world capitalist system thus has not been fundamentally changed, even though many of the forms of exploitation have been altered.

Certainly this conclusion can be applied to the small under-

22. Celso Furtado, *Development and Underdevelopment* (Berkeley, Calif., 1967), chap. 5. In this essay, I have confined our analysis to the impact of private international corporations, and have ignored the role of the U.S. government and the international lending agencies. Needless to say, public policies tend to reinforce the existing pattern of resource misutilization. For example, Furtado exposes the reactionary role of the International Monetary Fund, which continues to push "monetary" solutions to structural economic problems, in turn generating monetary symptoms.

developed countries, as it has been by Lloyd Best in his summary description of the Caribbean economy. The international companies, Best writes,

> form parts of wider international systems of resource allocation. This is true of the mining corporations, the sugar companies, the hotel chains, the banking, hire purchase and insurance houses, the advertising companies, the newspapers and the television and radio stations. . . . Insofar as there is harmonization among these concerns, it is for the most part achieved within the context of the metropolitan economies where they are based, and not in the peripheral economies of the countries where the companies actually operate. Moreover, the policies of the corporations are determined by their parent companies operating somewhere in the northern hemisphere and not by local need to integrate industries and to increase interdependence between different sectors of the economy. The economy is therefore hardly more than a locus of production made up of a number of fragments held tenuously together by Government controls—themselves often borrowed from elsewhere. In other words . . . it seems to be inherent in the structure of the international corporations which operate in the region that the Caribbean economies remain fragmented and unintegrated. . . .[23]

The political significance of economic "balkanization" should be obvious. In the case of Bolivia, after the nationalization of the tin mines, the U.S. government enjoyed a great deal of leverage in its maneuvers to push the Bolivian government to the right, partly because the country "remained beholden to the same big companies for processing and sale."[24] In Canada, Levitt describes the process of the "balkanization of the political structure whereby the growing economic powers of the corporations and the provincial governments threaten to destroy the [Canadian] nation state."[25] And of course Cuba has maintained her political independence from the United States only at a very high economic cost. Economic and political fragmentation thus lie at the very heart of the nature of neo-colonialism, as indicated by the report of the Third All-African People's Conference, held in Cairo in 1961. Among the "manifestations of Neo-Colonialism in Africa" were "regrouping of states, before or after independence, by an imperial power in federations or communities linked to that imperial power. . . . Balkanization as a deliberate political fragmentation of states by creation of artificial entities, such as, for example, the case of Katanga, Mauritania, Buganda, etc. . . . The economic entrenchment of the colonial power before independence and the continuity of economic depend-

23. Lloyd Best, "Size and Survival," *New World Quarterly,* Guyana Independence Issue, 1966, p. 61.
24. Allen Young, "Bolivia," *New Left Review,* no. 39 (September–October 1966), p. 66.
25. Levitt, "Canada: Economic Dependence," p. 81.

ence after formal recognition of national sovereignty. . . . Integration into colonial economic blocs which maintain the underdeveloped character of African economy."[26] In the extreme cases—some Caribbean countries, South Korea, and Thailand are examples—the international corporations are in a position to play off one against another, just as domestically they play off one state against another in an attempt to obtain low business taxes, cheap unskilled labor, a reserve of skilled technical labor, and other concessions.

This line of analysis leads into the question of economic reform and, in particular, the efficacy of economic integration within the underdeveloped regions and countries. The general subject of economic reform is large and complex, and we cannot even begin to give it adequate treatment here, except insofar as it relates to economic integration.

Certainly in Brazil, Mexico, and India, governments have had a certain degree of success in "legislating" *national* economic integration by compelling the international corporations to purchase more and more of their supplies locally. Meanwhile, however, foreign capital, especially in Brazil, has taken over a larger share of the local economy. Further, even though from a strictly economic standpoint there is considerable scope in these countries for the development of a great number of capital goods industries, every country in the underdeveloped world remains largely dependent on imported machinery and other capital equipment. The truth is that nowhere has there been, nor can there be save by socialist revolution, the structural changes in agriculture, state policy (especially tax policy), wealth and income distribution, and so on necessary for ongoing, self-generated development. Only Mexico has had a significant "agrarian reform"—that is, the displacement of the *ejido* sector by the capitalist sector dominated by large corporate farming. But income distribution in Mexico is far too unequal to sustain a domestic market for any length of time, and, as a consequence, Mexico is looking hungrily at Central America, long dominated by the United States. Tax reform in most of the underdeveloped world is a joke; the Chilean government, for example, has not used taxes and royalties to integrate the copper mining industry into the local economy (nor did Chile use nitrate royalties to this end in the nineteenth century), but rather to increase imports of consumer goods and to finance the government payroll. And of all the underdeveloped countries, only Cuba has promoted a deep-going redistribution of wealth and income.

Proposals for *regional* economic integration in the form of free trade

26. "Neo-Colonialism," *Voice of Africa* 1, no. 4 (April 1961): 4.

areas and common markets—especially in the Caribbean, Central America, Latin America, and Africa—should also be viewed skeptically given the prevailing pattern of integration imposed by the international corporations. As of 1966, the Central American Common Market's Economic Integration Program (EIP) had developed only two "integrated industries"—one in tire and tube, another in caustic soda and insecticide production. The Program has not gotten off the ground because the international corporations do not want Central America to develop its own basic capital goods industries, and because there are few business interests in Central America which are willing and able to develop local markets for themselves. The corporations do not want to be controlled by EIP, which insists on regulating prices to prevent monopoly abuses, determining the pattern of industrial location, and sharing in other basic economic decisions. Thus, the large corporations have confined their investments to individual Central American countries, where development is not guided by EIP and where there is little or no resistance to more branch plants and subsidiaries producing and assembling consumer goods.

In Latin America the most significant development in economic integration has been the Latin America Free Trade Area (LAFTA). Largely the brainchild of the Economic Commission for Latin America (ECLA), and for a long time opposed by the United States government, economic integration is now seen in reform circles as the "solution" to Latin American development. Needless to say, much of Latin America is *already* integrated by the international corporations. Reductions of tariffs, elimination of import quotas, and removal of controls over foreign exchange can only strengthen the position of the corporations.[27] As *Fortune* magazine puts it, "for U.S. private enterprise, the common market spells enticing new opportunity. . . . U.S. businessmen are beginning to see in the Latin American the advantages that they seized upon in the European Common Market: the chance to move to the broader, more competitive, and potentially more profitable task of supplying a market big enough to be economic on its own terms. . . . In many a boardroom, the common market is becoming a serious element in planning for the future."[28]

Certainly here we have the reason why the U.S. government now favors economic integration, and why, finally, there has developed a "harmony of interests" between the United States and the ECLA re-

27. Miguel Teubal, "The Failure of Latin America's Economic Integration," in Petras and Zeitlin, eds., *Latin America*, pp. 138–144.
28. Quoted in Edie Black, "Whose Common Market Is It?" *NACLA Newsletter*, August 1967.

formers. Apart from revolutionary forces in the underdeveloped world, there are few if any remaining economic and political interests which cannot be contained within or reconciled with the international corporations. Such is the nature of modern imperialism, a worldwide system of social production in which the giant, conglomerate international corporation stands as the highest (and final) form of social integration consistent with private ownership of the means of production.

Aarnovich, Sam, 55
Abinati, Ross, 141 n
Abrams, Charles, 125 n
Advertising, 47–49, 75
Affluent Society, The (Galbraith), 97
Agency for International Development, 132, 133, 189–190, 192
Agriculture, U.S. Department of, 112
Alavi, Hamza, 168, 186, 197 n, 207 n
Aluminum Company of America (Alcoa), 74, 75
All-African People's Conference, Third, 170
Alliance for Progress, 193
American and Foreign Power Company, 183
American Federation of State, County and Municipal Employees, 107
American Federation of Teachers, 107, 144, 146
Anaconda Copper, 75, 199
Anderson, Martin, 125 n
Anheuser-Busch, 48
Anticolonialism, 182
Anton, Thomas J., 118 n
Appalachia, 132
Argentina, 183
Associations, industry, 109
Automobile industry, 131

"Back to earth" movement, 3
Baldwin, William, 133 n
Balgooyen, H. W., 183 n
Banks and banking, 55–59, 62–65, 72–74
Baran, Paul A., x, xiii, xiv, 44–54, 55, 56, 59 n, 66 n, 75, 79, 99 n, 160, 175, 176, 177, 198 n, 199, 201 n, 203, 208 n
  general theory of capitalism of, x
Barber, Richard, 56 n, 63 n
Barratt-Brown, Michael, 159, 168
Basso, Lelio, 111

Bator, Francis M., 84 n
Bauer Paiz, Alfonso, 191 n
Baumol, William J., 85, 101
Bazelon, David T., 100 n
Beckford, George, 203 n
Behrman, J., 182 n, 183 n, 186 n
Bergmann, 105 n
Best, Lloyd, 197, 210
Beteta, Mario Ramon, 185 n
Bethlehem Steel Corp., 78
Birnbaum, Norman, 105 n
Black, Edie, 212 n
Black studies programs, struggle for, 146
Bolivia, 198, 210
Brandeis, Louis D., 74
Brazil, 181, 204, 206, 211
British Commonwealth, 190
Broude, Henry W., 126 n
Brubaker, Sterling, 205 n
Brutents, K., 173 n
Buchanan, James B., 102–103
Budget, Bureau of the, 111, 115, 117–118
Budget and Accounting Act (1920), 115
Budgetary analysis, political framework for, 108–112
Budgetary planning, 96–97
Budgetary policy, economic growth and, 94–95
Budgetary principles and control, state capitalist, 113–119
Budgets
  financing of, 134–142
  line-time, 116
  national income, 117
  program, 116
Burkhead, Jesse, 116
Business Advisory Council, 111

Cairncross, J., 161 n, 166
Canada, 188, 197, 202, 205, 210

Capital
  bank, 58
  centralization of, 43
  concentration of, 43
  finance, Fitch and Oppemheimer's the-
      ory of, 55–78
  knowledge as, 128
  private accumulation of, 100
Capital goods, overproduction of, 33
"Capital pull" thesis, 166
Capitalism, 1–42
  Baran's and Frank's general theory of, x
  characteristics of, 5, 18–21
  concept of, 16–21
  entrepreneurial, 11
  essence of, 21
  imperialism dissociated from, 153–155
  labor and, 17–26, 34
  monopoly, 43–54
    imperialism as aspect of, 159–168
    microeconomics and, 72–78
  social needs and, 8–10
  social production and, 4–8
Capitalism and Underdevelopment in Latin
      America (Frank), 201 n, 206 n
  general theory of capitalism in, x
Capitalists
  concept of, 60
  monopoly, goals of, 63–71
Carnegie, Andrew, 66, 66 n
Carrington, Edwin, 208 n
Casanova, Pablo Gonzalez, 171 n
Central American Common Market, 187–
      188, 212
Chamberlain, Joseph, 167
Chamberlain's Imperial Preference
      System, 165
Chile, 181, 199, 203, 206, 211
China, 181, 196
Chrysler Corporation, 70–71, 75
Chubb, Basil, 115 n
Class conflict, 112
Class consciousness, 110, 111, 115
Class struggle, 104–105, 127
Clayton Act, 72
Clee, Gilbert, 201 n
Cold war, 100
Collective bargaining, 146, 149
Colm, Gerhard, 87 n, 141 n
Colombia, 198
Colonialism, 155–156, 158, 160, 164
  control without, 169–175

Commerce, U. S. Department of, 112
Committee for Economic Development,
      92, 111
Commodities, 5, 6, 9, 18
  planned obsolescence of, 48
Communes, 3, 8, 18
"Comparative advantage" theory, 154
Competition, 43
Conglomerates, 11, 76–78
Consumer goods, underconsumption of,
      33
Cooperation, 4
Corporations, 11, 43–78
  conglomerate, 11, 76–78
  control of, 57–63
  multinationalism 194
    economic underdevelopment and,
        197–213
    technological change and, 207–209
  vertically integrated, 11
Cotton textile industry, 3
Council of Economic Advisers, 111, 118
Credit, 43
Cuba, 181, 198, 200, 207, 210, 211
Cutler, Frederick, 183 n

Davis, Horace B., 203 n
DDT, 131
Decision making, 12, 56, 57, 65
Defense, U. S. Department of, 83, 109,
      111, 116, 117, 120
Demas, William G., 172 n, 202 n
Democracy, liberal, 160–161
Dependents, movements of, 146–151
Diamond, William, 183 n
Disraeli, Benjamin, 192
Distribution, 4, 7
  income, 87–89
  material, 16
  of public goods, 101
Dividends, 64
Dobb, Maurice, xiii, 56, 128, 163 n, 164,
      166, 169
Domar, Evesy, 95
Domhoff, G. William, 110
Due, John F., 102 n
Du Pont, de Nemours, E. I., &
      Company, 72, 73, 74
Dutt, Palme, 168 n

Eakins, David, 110
Earley, James, 44

East African Currency Board, 171–172
East India Company, 156, 157, 157 n
Eckstein, Otto, 87
Economic Commission for Latin America, 212
Economic development, 195
    effect of corporate purchasing policies on, 205–206
Economic growth, 87
    budgetary policy and, 94–95
Economic integration, 10–11, 12
Economic Integration Program (EIP), 212
Economic Opportunity, Office of, 132
Economic stabilization, 87, 96
Economic surplus, 50
Economics, official, main purpose of, xii
Economics of Welfare (Pigou), 81
Economists, distorted view of human nature of, xii
Education, 82, 98, 127 n, 129–130, 133
Egalitarianism, 21
Eisenstein, Louis, 136, 137 n
Electrical power industry, 12
Employees, public, strikes and, 107, 148
Employment, public, 105–106
Engler, Robert, 109
European Common Market, 170, 171, 188
European Economic Community, 11, 188
Exchange relations, 6, 7, 10, 18
Exchange value, 19, 22–24
    of the product of labor, 22–24
Excise taxes, 140
Executive branch of government, 113–115
Expansionism, economic, 155–156, 159
Expenditures
    government, 49, 79–80, 95
    military, 132
    social capital, 119–130
Exploitation, 17, 21–22, 163
Export-Import Bank, 179, 189, 193
Externalities in production, 82

Fabricant, Solomon, 136 n
Factory industry, 5
Featherbedding, 38
Federal Aid to Highways Act (1944), 121
Federal Mediation and Conciliation Service, 112
Federal Reserve System, 13, 109
Feinberg, Mordecai S., 138 n

Feis, Herbert, 192 n
Felix, David, 202, 208
Feudalism, 11, 21
Fieldhouse, D. K., 159, 164 n, 165 n, 166
Finance, public, 79–151
Fiscal policy, 79–80
Fishing industry, 82, 133
Fitch, Robert, 57–78
Food for Peace program, 189
Ford, Henry, 36
Ford Motor Company, 75
Foreign aid, 105, 133, 189
Foreign policy, 100
Foreign Policy Association, 111
Frank, André Gunder, x, 199, 201 n, 206 n
    general theory of capitalism of, x
Freedom, 20–21
French Community, 190
Friedmann, Wolfgang, 184 n
Fujita, Sei, 141 n
Furtado, Celso, 208, 209 n

Gabon, 170
Galbraith, John Kenneth, 12 n, 97–102, 126 n, 127 n, 205
Gallagher, J., 164, 167
Geertz, Clifford, 199
General Electric Company, 48, 75, 166
General Mills, 11
General Motors Corporation, 52, 53, 72, 73, 166
Ghana, 181
GI Bill, 129
Gillman, Joseph, 160, 177 n, 180
Gintis, Herbert, 127 n
Girvan, Norman, 197, 202 n, 205, 206
Goldscheid, Rudolf, 136 n
Goldsmith, Raymond W., 136 n
Goode, Richard, 141 n
Goodrich-Gulf combine, 11
Gottlieb, Manual, 139 n
Government, 12–13, 79–151
Government expenditures, 49, 79–80, 95
Government policy, scientific and ideological elements in, economic theory of, 79–103
Grants-in-aid, 133
Gross national product, 7, 49
Guatemala, 191, 198

Gustafson, Douglas, 184 n
Guyana, 200, 203, 205

Hamilton, Walton, 109, 110
Hartz, Louis, 126 n
Harvey, Ernest C., 140 n
Hayek, F. A., 98, 99
Health, Education and Welfare, U. S. Department of, 112
Heller, Walter, 102 n
Hermansen, S. D., 142 n
Highways, 101
  expenditures for, 120, 121–123
Hippies, 20
Hobson, John A., 160–161, 164, 166, 175
Hoover Commission, 135
Housing Act (1949), 125 n
Hughes, Howard, 73–74
Hughes Tool Company, 73

Ideal output, concept of, 81
Imperial British East Africa Company, 165
Imperialism, 43, 44, 153–213
  as a political phenomenon, 153–159
  as a use of surplus, 179–190
  as an aspect of monopoly capitalism, 159–168
  capitalism dissociated from, 153–155
  economic, meaning of, 153
  foreign investments and, 153–212
  Lenin on, 160–168, 175
  mercantilism compared with, 156–159
  modern, 169–175
    foreign policy of, 190–194
  neo-, 169–175
  new era of, 196
  reasons for, 175–179
Income, distribution of, 87–89
Income effect of a price decline, 31 n
Income tax, 140–142
Income theory, 92–94
India, 184, 185, 196, 201, 207, 211
Individuality, 10
Indonesia, 181
Inflation, 39, 94
Influence, spheres of, 163
Inheritance tax, 139
Institute for Government Research, 115
Interest groups, 55, 109–110
International Bank for Reconstruction and Development, 133, 173, 183, 198

International Monetary Fund, 133, 173, 198
International Telephone and Telegraph Corp., 200
Interstate Commerce Commission, 69, 109
Investments, 14
  complementary, 120–121
  in economic infrastructure, 130
  discretionary, 120, 121
  endogenous, 46–47
  foreign, 44, 46, 153–213
    types of, 199–203
  imperialism and, 153–212
  theories concerning, 90
Islam, Nural, 184 n

Jackson, R., 137 n
Jacomet, Robert, 119 n
Jamaica, 172, 200, 205, 207
Jefferson, Owen, 202 n, 205, 206
Jenks, Leland, 192 n
Johnson, Lyndon, 119, 122

Kalmanoff, George, 184 n
Kamershen, David, 76 n
Katona, George, 144 n
Kemp, Alexander, 164, 167 n, 182 n, 186 n, 188 n
Keynes, John Maynard, 91, 92, 102 n
Knowledge
  as capital, 128
  technical, 11–12, 13
Koebner, Richard, 164, 165 n
Kohn, Hans, 154, 155 n
Kolko, Gabriel, 65, 109, 110, 165 n
Kratz, J. W., 172 n
Kuh, Edwin, 56 n

Labor
  capitalism and, 17–26, 34
  division of, 4, 5, 7, 10, 11, 23, 28, 32, 98
  forced, 19–20
  organized, 112
  productivity of, 22
Labor, U. S. Department of, 112
Labor unions, 32, 37, 112
  public employees and, 107, 146–148
Lange, Oscar, 4
Latin American Free Trade Area, 187, 212

Lehmann-Haupt, Christopher, 16
Lenin, V. I., 56, 104, 105 n
  on imperialism, 160–168, 175
Levitt, Kari, 197 n, 208 n, 210 n
Liberia, 173
Lighthouses, 83
Lintner, John, 55
Little, I. M. D., 85 n
Lockouts, 23
Logrolling, 110
Lukács, Georg, 104, 105 n
Luxemburg, Rosa, 160, 162 n

Macroeconomic theory, 89–91
  critique of, 91–94
Magdoff, Harry, 179 n, 198 n
"Make-work" practices, 38
Man, modern, 9
Mandel, Ernest, xiii, 4
Manorial system, 11
Manufacturers Hanover Trust Co., 70
Marginal private costs, 82
Marginal social costs, 82
Marshall, Alfred, 82
Marshall Plan, 192
Marx, Karl, 1, 2 n, 22, 27, 35 n, 43, 47,
    51, 60, 94, 104, 111, 128 n, 160,
    162 n, 204
McConnell, Grant, 109
McLean, John, 183 n, 184 n
McMillan, Claude, 197 n
Medicare, 132
Medicine, relationship between other
    sciences and, 93
Medina, Harold R., Judge, 75 n
Mendès-France, Pierre, 119 n
Menshikov, 58 n, 62, 64 n
Mercantilism, 156
  imperialism compared with, 156–159
Mesthene, Emmanuel G., 13
Mexico, 174, 184, 200, 206, 211
Microeconomics, monopoly capitalism
    and, 72–78
Mikesell, Raymond, 189 n, 193 n
Military expenditures, 132
Mill, John Stuart, 82 n, 154
Milliken family, 64 n
Money, 6, 13, 17, 22
Monopoly, 43–47, 82, 162–163
Monopoly Capital (Baran and Sweezy), xi,
    xiii, 43–54, 55, 59 n, 66 n, 75

Monotheism, 9
Montevideo, Treaty of, 181
Moody, John, 62
Morgan Guaranty Trust Company, 183
Mosquito control, 84
Movements of state workers and depend-
    ents, 146–151
Musgrave, Richard, 96–97, 138 n, 141 n
Myrdal, Gunnar, 79, 199

National Industrial Conference Board,
    201
National Labor Relations Board, 112, 132
National Mediation Board, 112
Natural resources, 2
Navy, U. S. Department of, 116
Needs
  production of, 1–3
  social, capitalism and, 8–10
Neighborhood effects, 84
Neocolonialism, 169–171
Neo-imperialism, 169–175
Neo-mercantilism, 156
Netzer, Dick, 139 n
New York Stock Exchange, 55–56
Nigeria, 184, 203
Nishikawa, Kiyoharu, 119 n
Nixon, Richard M., 145 n
Nkrumah, Kwame, 170
Novick, David, 116 n
Nurkse, Ragnar, 166

Obsolescence, planned, 48
O'Connor, James, 57 n, 78 n, 201 n,
    202 n
Oppenheimer, Mary, 57–78
Organization, social, 10–15
  private property and, 13–15
Ott, Attiat F., 115 n, 117 n
Ott, David S., 115 n, 117 n
Output, ideal, 81

Pares, Richard, 165 n
Pavlov, V. I., 201
Peacock, Alan T., 79, 95
Penn Central Transportation Company
    (railroad), 68–69
Perham, Margery, 153 n
Perlo, Victor, 55
Peru, 181
Petrochemical industry, 3

Phillips Petroleum Co., 11
Pigou, A. C., 81
Pizer, Samuel, 183 n
Planning, budgetary, 96–97
Platt, D. C. M., 165 n, 173 n
Political Economy of Growth, The, (Baran),
   xiv, 199
  general theory of capitalism in, x
Pollution, 12, 131
Porter, Sylvia, 137 n
Price, 22, 23
  monopoly, 45
Pricing, 45
Production, 17
  capitalist, 17
  externalities in, 82
  material, 16
  military, 133
  need for, 1–3
  relations of, 104, 111
  relationship between technology and,
   127–129
  responsibility for, 25
  social nature of, 4, 104
  social expenses of, 130–134
  surplus value, modes of, 26–39
Profits, 22, 45
Property, private, social organization and,
  13–15
Property tax, 138–139, 143–144
Protectorates, 163
Provesta Corporation, 11
Public goods, 83, 97–98
  distribution of, 101
Puerto Rico, 200

Quality control, 7
Quarantine laws, 84

Radio programs, 83
Railroad industry, 38, 68–70
Revisionists, corporate, 97–103
Revolution, 20, 24, 25
Rhodes, Cecil, 165, 166
Ricardo, David, 154
Robbins, Lionel, 102 n
Robinson, Joan, 154, 180
Robinson, R., 164, 167
Rogin, Leo, 39 n
Roosevelt, Theodore, 167
Rossant, M. J., 135 n

Rostow, W. W., 97 n
Royal Niger Company, 165
Rusk, Dean, 193

Sales effort, 47, 48, 75
Sales taxes, 140
Salvatori, Henry, 64 n
Samuelson, Paul, 88, 94
Say, Jean-Baptiste, 82 n
Scarcity, 2
Schlesinger, James R., 116 n, 117 n, 118,
  174 n
Schumpeter, Joseph, 153–154, 169
Seers, Dudley, 201 n
Selling, expenses of, 130
Serfs, 21–22
Shonfield, Andrew, 119 n, 126 n
Sherman, Roger, 122 n
Slavery, 21, 26
Smith, Adam, 9, 28, 82 n
Smithies, Arthur, 116
Social capital expenditures, 119–130
Social insurance, 132
Social integration, 11, 12, 13, 104, 128
Social organization, 10–15
  private property and, 13–15
Social Security Administration, 112
Social security tax, 140
Socialism, 15, 17–18, 20, 80
Solow, Robert, 94
South African Company, 165
Specialization, 4, 5, 7, 10, 11, 23, 28, 32
Speculation, stock, 67
Speedup, 28
Spending, government. *See* Expenditures,
  government
Spheres of influence, 163
Spillovers, 84
Standard Oil, 166
State, the, 79–151
  fiscal crisis of, 104–151
State spending. *See* Expenditures, govern-
  ment
State workers, movements of, 146–151
Stavenhagen, Rodolfo, 204
Steel industry, 66, 66 n, 71
Stocks, corporate, 55–56
Strachey, John, 163
Stretch-out, 28
Strikes, 23, 24
  economic consequences of, 24

effectiveness of, 148
public employees and, 107, 148
"Structural functionalism," Talcott Parsons' theory of, xii
Subsidies, 11, 82, 83, 97, 122, 126, 130–131, 132, 134
Substitution effect of a price decline, 31 n
Suburbs, 13, 14, 131
Sukarno, 170
Surplus
  economic, 50
  imperialism as a use of, 179–190
Surplus value, 21–42, 60–63
  absolute, 27–28, 32, 60–61, 66
  appropriation of, 29, 30
  direct, 32
  disposition of, 29
  indirect, 39–42
  production of, 26–39
  realization of, 30
  relative, 27, 28, 34–37, 60, 61, 66, 67
Sweezy, Paul M., xiii, 44–54, 55, 56, 59 n, 66 n, 75, 169, 176, 177, 197, 198 n, 201 n

Taft Commission on Economy and Efficiency, 116
Taiwan, 200
Tarasov, Helen, 141 n
Tax Foundation, 137 n, 139 n, 140 n
Taxation, 79, 80, 83, 84, 88, 113, 134–142
  high, revolt against, 107–108, 142–147
Taylor, Payntz, 121 n
Technical knowledge, 11–12, 13
Technology, 2–3, 5, 6, 7, 8, 14, 47, 113, 126
  relationship between production and, 127–129
Television programs, 83
Tennessee Valley Authority, 116
Teubal, Miguel, 212 n
Third World, 132, 133
Thomas, C. Y., 172 n
Tobin, James, 91 n
Traffic problems, 12
Transport Workers Union of America, 144
Transportation, 82, 121–124
Transportation Act (1958), 69

Treasury, U. S. Department of, 13
Treaty of Montevideo (1960), 181
Tsuru, Shigeto, 72, 177 n
Tullock, Gordon, 103 n
Turvey, Ralph, 85 n
Trans World Airlines (TWA), 73–74
Twitchett, Kenneth J., 170 n

Underdevelopment, economic, international corporations and, 197–213
Unemployment, 46, 94, 105, 132
Unions, 32, 37, 112
  public employees and, 107, 146–148
  teachers, 146
Uniroyal, 75
United Fruit Company, 191
United States Tariff Commission, 109
Universities, 13, 129
Urban renewal, 124–125, 133
Urbanization, 98
U.S. Rubber, 72, 74
United States Steel Corporation (U.S. Steel), 74, 75
Use value, 19

Value
  exchange. See Exchange value
  surplus. See Surplus value
  use, 19
Venezuela, 205
Vernon, Raymond, 182 n, 188 n, 203 n
Violence, 24

Wages, 6, 18, 22, 23, 31, 33
Wall Street, 70
Wallich, Henry, 98, 172 n
Walras, Léon, 82 n
War Industry Board, 111
War Mobilization, Office of, 111
War on Poverty, 119
Waste, economic, 97, 99
Webb, Lee, 136 n
Weinstein, James, 110
Welfare economics, 80, 81–89
  Marxian critique of, 86–87
  traditional criticisms of, 85–86
Wesolowski, W., 110 n
Whole Earth Catalog, 8
Wicksell, Knut, 82 n, 103
Wiedenbaum, Murray, 133 n
Williams, Harvey, 189 n

222   INDEX

Williams, William Appleman, 110
Wilmerding, Lucius, Jr., 114 n, 115 n
Wilson, Charles, 157 n
Wiseman, Jack, 79, 95
Wolfe, Alvin, 201 n
Work, 18–21
  alienated, 19

forced, 19–20
World Bank. *See* International Bank for
    Reconstruction and Development
"World proletariat," 9

Young, Allen, 182 n, 210 n